NARRATIVE NETWORKS

NARRATIVE NETWORKS

Storied Approaches in a Digital Age

 BRIAN ALLEYNE

Los Angeles | London | New Delhi
Singapore | Washington DC

Los Angeles | London | New Delhi
Singapore | Washington DC

SAGE Publications Ltd
1 Oliver's Yard
55 City Road
London EC1Y 1SP

SAGE Publications Inc.
2455 Teller Road
Thousand Oaks, California 91320

SAGE Publications India Pvt Ltd
B 1/I 1 Mohan Cooperative Industrial Area
Mathura Road
New Delhi 110 044

SAGE Publications Asia-Pacific Pte Ltd
3 Church Street
#10-04 Samsung Hub
Singapore 049483

Editor: Chris Rojek
Assistant editor: Gemma Shields
Production editor: Libby Larson
Copyeditor: Audrey Scriven
Proofreader: Martin Noble
Marketing manager: Michael Ainsley
Cover design: Shaun Mercier
Typeset by: C&M Digitals (P) Ltd, Chennai, India
Printed in Great Britain by Ashford Colour Press
Ltd, Gosport, Hampshire

Library of Congress Control Number: 2014940526

British Library Cataloguing in Publication data

A catalogue record for this book is available from the British Library

ISBN 9780857027832
ISBN 9780857027849 (pbk)

MIX
Paper from
responsible sources
FSC
www.fsc.org   FSC® C011748

At SAGE we take sustainability seriously. Most of our products are printed in the UK using FSC papers and boards. When we print overseas we ensure sustainable papers are used as measured by the Egmont grading system. We undertake an annual audit to monitor our sustainability.

For Cristina

CONTENTS

LIST OF FIGURES
AND TABLES

Figures

Tables

LIST OF BOXES

ABOUT THE AUTHOR

Brian Alleyne teaches sociology at Goldsmiths, University of London. He worked as a photographer and then a computer programmer before studying sociology and development studies at the University of the West Indies. After a period in New York, where he studied sociology at the CUNY Graduate Center and worked as a research assistant at the CLR James Institute, he moved to the UK. He gained a PhD in social anthropology from the University of Cambridge in 1999 and began teaching sociology at Goldsmiths in that same year. For many years he was a volunteer at the George Padmore Institute, made up of a collective of activists, writers and activists about whose work Brian wrote a book, *Radicals Against Race* (Berg, 2002), which was awarded the British Sociological Association's Philip Abrams Memorial Prize 2002. Brian keeps up his interest in new technologies by hacking code in his spare time. He is working on hacker representations and migrant/cosmopolitan stories, using narrative methods.

ACKNOWLEDGEMENTS

In working on this book, I benefitted greatly from the input of many people. I got useful advice and feedback from David Oswell and Sari Wastell. My sociology colleagues at Goldsmiths remain a fantastic group with which to interact. Colleagues and students at the Anthropology Department's seminar in late 2013 asked many searching questions that helped me to improve the work. I have presented some of the ideas here in my undergraduate lectures and I gained a great deal from the questions asked by my students. Brett St Louis, Kirsten Campbell, and Tom Henri were and remain very supportive as colleagues and as friends. The three anonymous reviewers offered comments that improved the text; though I followed most of their suggestions, the final text remains my own responsibility. Chris Rojek and Jai Seaman first encouraged me to tackle this project, Gemma Shields took the work through the final stages with professionalism and enthusiasm, and Lynda Porter advised me on how to cope. Finally, I must acknowledge the encouragement, feedback and emotional support of my partner, Cristina Chimisso. This one is for her.

INTRODUCTION

I will present myself, whenever the last trumpet shall sound, before the Sovereign Judge with this book in my hand, and loudly proclaim, 'Thus have I acted; these were my thoughts; such was I. With equal freedom and veracity have I related what was laudable or wicked, I have concealed no crimes, added no virtues; and if I have sometimes introduced superfluous ornament, it was merely to occupy a void occasioned by defect of memory: I may have supposed that certain, which I only knew to be probable, but have never asserted as truth, a conscious falsehood. Such as I was, I have declared myself; sometimes vile and despicable, at others, virtuous, generous, and sublime; even as Thou hast read my inmost soul: Power Eternal! assemble round Thy throne an innumerable throng of my fellow-mortals, let them listen to my confessions, let them blush at my depravity, let them tremble at my sufferings; let each in his turn expose with equal sincerity the failings, the wanderings of his heart, and if he dare, aver, I was better than that man.'

J.J. Rousseau, *Confessions*

The Storytelling Animal

Narrative is ubiquitous to the human. It makes humans as well as being made by humans. The human is a storytelling creature. The passage of time shapes and is shaped by narrative, but how time is conceived varies socially and culturally. The creation and retelling of stories is found across societies and cultures. These are some of the premises of this book.

Narrative research in the social sciences is concerned both with treating narrative as the 'raw material' for research, and with the process of narrating as one of the fundamental means of producing and reporting social research findings. These two dimensions are termed 'analysis of narrative' and 'narrative analysis' by Donald Polkinghorne (1988). This book addresses both dimensions of narrative research from the standpoint of social researchers in sociology and anthropology mainly. I pay special attention to narrative approaches to social networking and to digital media more generally. Indeed, a unique feature of the book is that it sets its discussion of narrative approaches against the backdrop of network society – the contemporary and emergent scenario of the majority of global humanity being interconnected through the World Wide Web, and of lives increasingly affected by information technologies.

What does it mean to say that the human being is a storytelling animal? It should be fairly uncontentious to state that humans are a uniquely intelligent species of ape. Part of what makes us unique in the world of animals, which includes our closest relatives the apes, is that we have an elaborate system of communication and representation called language. One of the many uses of language is the creation, communication and reception of stories.

My starting definition is that a narrative is a presentation of a story. As to story itself, let us take it to mean a sequence of events. The terms 'events' and 'sequence' are important: events because stories are about what happened to something or to somebody; and sequence is important because a story is about a series of events, where we take earlier events to be the causes of, or at least to have influenced, later events. Narratives include stories but are not just stories: narratives are also about the way these stories are presented. Time passes within the narrative itself, or more properly on the definition I am using here, within the story, and of course there is time involved in present-ing the narrative. Story time and narrative time are not the same. It is also common in defining narrative to further distinguish between the 'story', which as we see, is what the narrative is about – the actual people and sequence of events – and the 'narrative discourse', which concerns itself with how the story is told. It may seem rather confusing that narrative is defined in terms of story and narrative discourse (the term 'narrative' being repeated in the definition). We will unpack this definition further in a later chapter, but take it as a starting point for now. It follows from the way narrative is presented here that a given story can be told in a number of different ways, or to put it another way, a given story can be rendered through different narrative discourses. This becomes clear when we consider that we can change the way we tell a story by changing the point of view, from first person to third person for example, or we can use different media or even different genres. We do all of these while holding constant the sequence of connected events, i.e. the story. We can even change the order of events to some extent and still keep the story intact: we can, for example, present the closing events first and then use flashbacks to fill out the story.

So, what is narrative? Narrative, in its simplest sense, consists of a sequence of connected events, and a particular way in which these events are told. The first element is the story, and the second element is the narra-tive discourse. A narrator (the person telling the story) is real or implied in most cases. Narrative is used in many different ways in different disciplines by different authors. The term is sometimes used to refer in a very general sense to any non-quantitative data. This use of narrative is useful in making a distinction in terms of the kind of data being considered, and though it is sometimes too vague to be useful to a narrative researcher, it is nonetheless still worth keeping in mind as it is a usage frequently encountered in social research literature. For many social scientists who work mainly with quantitative approaches, as well as for those who employ 'mixed methods' (Teddlie & Tashakkori, 2008), narrative data are simply textual data – i.e. any data not originally in, or later summarised into, numerical form.

In literary theory it is common to conceptualise narrative as encompassing a story and a discourse or narrative discourse. Abbott (2008) writes that a story is a chronological sequence of events involving entities (people, animals or inanimate things). The story is conveyed through a narrative discourse (sometimes termed a 'plot' as Abbott notes, but he prefers the use of 'story', as do many theorists in this field), which is the 'story as narrated' (told or showed). It follows from this that a story can be rendered through different narrative discourses. With respect to plot, we can think of this as a particular arrangement of the basic events of the story, which compares intriguingly with the plot as in a graph, which is a particular arrangement for presentation of data. So plot in narrative, as with plot in data visualisation, is about organising basic data for presentation in order to entertain or persuade the audience.

There are two main uses of the term 'narrative', according to Abbott (2008: 14): the first is 'compact and definable' despite some disagreement over definitions; the second is 'loose and generally recognizable' in 'longer structures that we call narratives even though they may contain much non-narrative material'. These longer structures appear in familiar genres such as comedy or tragedy, in fiction and non-fiction works, in drama, film and poetry, among others. Abbott notes that it is hard to determine on what grounds a long text is or is not narrative, but the establishment of what he terms 'narrative coherence' would make a long text a good candidate for inclusion as a narrative.

For Genette (1983), in a widely read work on narrative, there are two usages of narrative in literary theory. The first, broader usage sees narrative as 'the narrative statement, the oral or written discourse that undertakes to tell of an event or series of events'; the second, more restricted to theorists, has narrative 'refer to the succession of events, real or fictitious, that are the subjects of this discourse and to their several relations of linking, opposition, repetition, etc.' (1983: 25). Genette uses 'the word story for the signified or narrative content (even if this content turns out, in a given case, to be low in dramatic intensity or fullness of incident), to use the word *narrative* for the signifier, statement, discourse or narrative text itself, and to use the word *narrating* for the producing narrative action and, by extension the whole of the real or fictional situation in which the action takes place' (1983: 27). Genette's usage of narrative to refer to the text itself is most useful for the kinds of social scientific analysis that form the main concerns of this book. In a later work Genette writes that 'story' refers to the events taken together and 'narrative' is the written or oral discourse that narrates them.

For Coffey and Atkinson (1996: see Chapter 3) the many formal distinctions between narrative and story are of questionable value to working social scientists. They propose the use of narrative as an inclusive category and restricting the term 'story' to 'those genres that recount protagonists, events, complications, and consequences' (1996: 54). There is no escaping the many and overlapping usages of 'narrative', which can refer to 'the process of making a story, to the cognitive scheme of the story, or to the result of the process – also called "stories," "tales," or "histories"' (Polkinghorne, 1988: 13). In the same passage, Polkinghorne sets out a usage that I will generally follow in this book: 'I will be using "narrative" and its cognates to refer to both the process and the results; the context should clarify which meaning is intended.'

For Roland Barthes (1915–1980) narrative encompassed spoken and written forms, still and moving images, and various kinds of genre (Barthes, 1993). For him the narrative was everywhere, in myriad forms, found in every age and every society and culture. Narrative is a human universal. Given this, he asks, what *is* the significance of narrative? If narrative is everywhere then is it anywhere in any significant manifestation? His answer is couched in terms of one of the defining ideas of the structuralism of which he was himself a key figure. Just as structuralist linguistics asserted that in order for specific languages to exist there had to be a general universally present capacity for language, for Barthes narrative was a deeply embedded and universally existing structure which set the background or terrain from which specific narratives would emerge in specific historical, social and cultural contexts. Narrative then is a systemic capacity and a system from which various elements can be combined to fashion a virtually limitless set of actual narratives – spoken, written, audio-visual.

For Barthes the act of narrating is universal, and as is the case with speech, the person narrating draws upon a pre-existing system which provides the 'grammar' and other elements from which to craft a narrative. So just as we speak in particular languages in particular social and cultural contexts, so too do we narrate, for Barthes, in particular social and cultural contexts. He developed a system for the structural analysis of narratives which we will look at in greater detail in a later chapter.

Let us put some of these initial ideas to work on a story about a vampire.

On Dracula

Bram Stoker's (1847–1912) *Dracula* is one of my favourite novels. I am not alone in my liking of the book: since its initial publication in 1897, millions of copies in dozens of languages have been sold, and numerous film and television adaptations made. *Dracula* is told through a series of diaries and letters, in what is termed epistolary form, which – though it strictly speaking applies to a fictional text told mainly through letters – could be expanded to encompass diaries and journals as well. In any event, Stoker used letters *and* diaries in his novel.

The novel opens with London lawyer Jonathan Harker's journey to Count Dracula's castle in Transylvania, and ends with the destruction of Dracula (though being the 'living dead' can a vampire be 'killed'?) in the vicinity of Dracula's castle. In the novel we can clearly see the difference between story time – the time elapsed in the story itself, including events narrated in the diaries and letters of the various characters, and in passages where characters relate events that are not part of the main plot of the story – and narrative discourse time, which is the time taken to read the novel. This distinction highlights one of the most salient characteristics of narrative: the differentiation of story (a series of events in a strict sequence) from the way in which the story is told, which is the discourse or narrative discourse. For now let us use 'story' to refer to the sequence of events, and 'discourse' to refer to the way(s) in which the story is told/written. Later chapters will go more deeply into these concepts, but on these initial working definitions, the account of the discovery of the vampire, the consequences of his move to London, and the quest of the small group who set out to destroy his evil, among other events that Stoker presents, together comprise the story of the novel ('novel' here is understood as a kind of fictional narrative). We can plot the events in different ways. What would happen if we were to rearrange the events of the original story and then 'glue' them together in a different way? What if we opened our reworking of *Dracula* with Mina Murrary/Harker or with any character other than Jonathan Harker? When we turn to consider the discourse (or narrative discourse) of *Dracula* we find that there are many points from which we can enter the text. What if we used *only* letters, or if we projected email back to the 1890s and told the story through 'Victorian email' (or telegraphic text message) exchanges? We *could* do all of these and still stick to the story as written by Stoker. But a story of Dracula told by opening with Mina's journal or letters and using 'Victorian email' would be a different discourse and therefore a different narrative, though still a story that was close to Stoker's original text.

In fact, we have over the past decades seen the story of Count Dracula told in many different ways in different genres, settings, languages and media. In terms of fictional genre Stoker's novel has come to be a defining work of Gothic horror. In addition to the novel there have been quite a few widely seen cinematic adaptations. Within the cinematic adaptations, if we compare *Nosferatu* (1922), the first film version adaptation of the novel, to the Francis Ford Coppola film *Bram Stoker's Dracula* (1992), we can enter into a very detailed discussion of the differences in acting, direction, camera technique, characterisation and such. The point is that the story of *Dracula* can be, and has been, told in many different ways. There are many Dracula stories and many Dracula narratives. This is so even if we stick to the strict set of events which Stoker set out in his novel.

The Francis Ford Coppola film adaptation of *Dracula* is a different narrative discourse for a number of reasons: for one, the medium of film has its own set of storytelling techniques and conventions; for another, the film departs from the Stoker novel in that Coppola's Dracula is based partly on the historical figure of Vlad the Impaler (1431–1476). This move in fact serves to almost humanise the vampire, which is quite ironic given Vlad's horrible reputation. Moreover, Coppola's Dracula/Vlad is a man who, when he was alive in the fifteenth century as Prince Vlad, was married to Elisbetta (a character not present in Stoker's novel), who was tricked by Vlad's enemies into believing that her husband had been killed in a major battle. Overcome by grief, Elisabetta took her own life. And so the story of Dracula is changed for the film, from Stoker's story. Moreover, the discourse is also changed. The basic form remains epistolary (with a few images of handwritten diary entries for effect), but the film has flashbacks to the life of Dracula as Vlad, and Mina Murray (later Mina Harker) also has vague memories that seem to connect her to Elisabetta, the fifteenth-century wife of Vlad. Coppola's film lies in a general trend of humanising and even 'sexing up' the vampire, with the culmination of that trend seen in the hugely popular *Twilight* series of novels and films.

The Coppola film has elements of the classic love story genre, with tragic lovers in the persons of Dracula/Vlad and Mina/Elisabetta. Dracula's quest that takes him from Transylvania to late 1890s' London is not only about expanding his power through breeding more vampires in what was then the world's greatest city, but is also a quest to find his long dead lover whom he believes has been reincarnated in the figure of Mina Harker. Coppola's tragic vampire seeks to regain his lost humanity. We are given glimpses of that lost humanity through one of the various bodily forms Dracula takes on. In his encounters with Mina, he shape-shifts between a wolf, a half wolf, a half human monster, and an elegant middle-aged man. His normal state seems to be an old man, ranging from the very old to the horribly decayed. The form of Dracula as an elegant middle-aged man is the one that Mina sees – or is it the one that she chooses to see? In scenes involving both Mina and Dracula, you can't really be sure that what she sees is what you see. Mina in the film is a character who is split between the Mina of Victorian England, and the Elisabetta of fifteenth-century Transylvania. And Mina Harker is herself split: a Victorian woman torn between her love for her fiancé (and later husband) Jonathan, and her seemingly mysterious attraction to the elegant foreign nobleman (Count Dracula).

This human interest love story may well have broadened the appeal of the film – the reviews were both in favour and against – and it certainly appealed to contemporary dramatic and romantic tastes, which are at some remove from those of Stoker's time. The representation of female sexuality in the Stoker novel is cloying and saturated with Victorian Christian piety; in contrast, the Coppola film represents women in terms more familiar to contemporary mainstream Euro-American views on sexuality. Sex-lust-blood-death in the Stoker novel is re-figured in the Coppola film rendering: possessed-by-evil women such as Lucy Westenra and the three female vampires trapped in Dracula's castle are all attractive in terms of norms in contemporary Euro-American popular film, arguably inspiring more desire than disgust on the part of the contemporary viewer.

Coppola's film is innovative in its narrative. While many of the elements of the story told in the Stoker novel are present in the Coppola film, the film grafts on elements from two other stories, that of the historical figure of Vlad the Impaler, and a fictional story of the historical Vlad and his fictional wife Elisabetta, and connects two of the main characters, Dracula and Mina Harker, to these two 'historical' figures. And of course, being a film, the medium is clearly different from that of a novel. The film and the novel differ in their narrative discourse because even though the film borrows much of its story from the novel, it tells a *different* story partly because the imagined new historical connection creates a new story.

But back to Bram Stoker's original novel. This opens with Jonathan Harker travelling east from London to Transylvania by train to meet a client of his legal firm. He knows little of this client except that he is a Romanian nobleman who lives in a remote castle. Jonathan Harker's opening accounts in his diary display many of the qualities of works produced by Victorian explorers, and of the works written by nineteenth-century Christian missionaries in far-flung parts of the British Empire. Harker is a rational man who has prepared for his journey by doing research in the library of the British Museum; he has studied maps and read what was available on the country to which he is bound. As a late nineteenth-century, middle-class Englishman, Harker has a quite clear sense of the difference between his modern English world, in which the trains run on time, and a world in which, the further he goes east, trains become ever more unreliable, at the same time that the people he carefully observes and documents become ever more exotic.

In the opening pages of *Dracula,* through Harker's journal, we see a number of narrative conventions at work that are similar to those which shape the pioneering ethnographic works of the mid to late nineteenth-century imperial explorers and the middle-class social explorers who stayed at home but went into deprived urban areas to document the exotic close at hand. Like the pioneering ethnographers Harker is a careful empiricist: he creates a sequence of dated entries, descriptive accounts of his observations, and he contextualises these by also recording his own thoughts and reflections on what he observes. He is fascinated by the differences he sees, but in his writing he is more curious than condescending. And like a good Victorian he wants to capture some of the exotic Other and take it home in the form of recipes for Mina, his betrothed. In Harker's early journal entries his movement through space as he leaves Western Europe is also a movement back in time as the places and people he sees become ever more removed from the standard of modernity that shaped his world in late nineteenth-century England. This tale of displacement is one of the characteristic narrative discourses – that is to say, ways of telling a story – of nineteenth-century travellers' accounts and early ethnographic descriptions of other people and places. Textual construction of the faraway and exotic as the past of the explorer's own society is a common textual move in nineteenth-century European or North American traveller's tales of

primitive Africa, or urban explorers' accounts of the European urban poor, as
we shall see in the chapter that follows this Introduction.

Approach of the Book

Why a book on narrative?

This book is a response to the ever-growing production and consumption of
stories about real people and places of all kinds in popular and academic cultures. No observer of contemporary culture can fail to notice how stories have
grown with the expansion of digital media and the Web. We might be tempted
to dismiss the inexorable rise of the reality TV show, and the continued growth
of biography – especially celebrity biographies and autobiographies – to take
just a few examples, as a narcissistic degeneration of the public sphere. That
would be too hasty a judgment however, and in any event I would argue that
social researchers should document first and judge later. Never before have so
many captured their lives in text and images: more than a billion people are
regularly recording and sharing life events both great and small on social networking sites like Facebook, and using social media such as Twitter. Much of
this activity can be interpreted in story form, which in turn suggests that
we need to think anew about the place of narrative in our collective self-
understanding as a globally networked species. With this book I hope to
contribute to broader considerations of how ubiquitous information
technology offers new possibilities for writing and reading narratives.

What is special about the book?

I focus on narrative both as data and as method, mainly in the disciplines of sociology and social/cultural anthropology (which I will hereafter refer to as
'anthropology' throughout the book). This is for the very practical reason that
sociology and anthropology are the fields most familiar to me. But I hope that the
book would be of interest to persons working in those disciplines where there is
a tradition of interdisciplinary work with sociologists and anthropologists: educational studies, social work, cultural studies, some areas of social policy, and
development studies. Narrative use in the fields of psychotherapy, psychology and
psychiatry is a highly specialised area, and due to the specific character of practice
in these areas, is beyond the scope of this text; nonetheless, persons in these areas
might still find something of interest here. The same holds true for historical
research: narrative in historiography is a vast and specialised area, and is also
beyond the scope of the current text. Even though I draw on ideas from literary
criticism and linguistics, I do so only insofar as those ideas help to advance my
project of showing how and why narrative is important for social science research.
Social scientists are always advised to tread cautiously with regard to literary

criticism. After three decades of steadily growing interest in narrative among social scientists, the days are long gone when any one text could survey the whole field of narrative research approaches. I do not address two recent areas of interest among narrative researchers: performativity and visual narrative.

To help guide you when reading this book, please visit the accompanying website: www.narrativenetworks.net. Some key features of the website include:

- Narrative research project designs and report templates.
- Templates to assist in carrying out various kinds of narrative analysis.
- Video demonstrations of software tools to assist the narrative researcher.

On Information Technology

Information technology (i.e. computing devices, software, and the Web that ties them all together) features in this book in several ways. First, some of my case study material is drawn from the worlds of computer enthusiasts and hacking that I have been involved with since the 1980s, and which remain an area for ongoing research. Second, I examine how people use digital technology to engage in reading, writing and sharing narratives of various kinds. Third, I look at how narrative researchers can employ digital technology to support their research. I take the view that digital technologies are deeply intertwined with narrative, and this book has as one of its aims an exploration of those interconnections. One positive consequence of drawing on textual cases from the digital sphere is that the full texts are readily available on the Web, so that the reader may explore them in full with minimal effort. This book's website is: www.narrativenetworks.net.

Plan of the Book

Chapter 1: In the beginning there was the social explorer

In the opening chapter of the book I provide an overview of historical developments in the fields in which narrative approaches have had significant impact. I pay special attention here to the emergence of what I call the 'narrative of reform' in the nineteenth century, drawing upon work on social realist fiction, social reform, and the institutionalisation of academic sociology and anthropology. At the same time as both of these latter disciples were gaining acceptance in the university, their practitioners were innovating in writing form. I discuss the emergence of early ethnographic texts in the wider context of social realist writing, and then contextualise these by looking at wider institutional developments in the history of sociology and social anthropology.

Chapter 2: Narrative ways of knowing

In the second chapter I discuss the underlying epistemology and methodology of narrative approaches. I focus on work by Polkinghorne (1988) who distinguished between analysis of narrative – where we collect and examine many kinds of narrative in terms of categories – and narrative analysis – where we use the narrative form to inscribe social scientific knowledge. In analysis of narrative, the narrative is the object to be analysed: the social scientist begins with the narrative, reading it in order to draw out generalisations, and looking for themes and issues that can be explored in other narratives. I show how this can be termed a 'categorising' approach because we are seeking to organise a multitude of narrative texts into distinct categories. By contrast, in narrative analysis, the researcher's data consist of actions, recorded conversations, observations and other artefacts and they then write these up as stories: the narrative is thus constructed from the research encounter. Another way to think of this second approach is in terms of making connections among elements in order to construct a narrative.

From this I address methodological issues and their epistemological underpinnings as these impact on narrative in social research and go on to consider the researcher engaging with the theoretical and philosophical implications of making narrative part of a research programme. I examine the classic methodological problems of reliability and validity with regard to narrative, discussing how the problem of moving between the particular and the general has been tackled. When dealing with narrative as method, we must consider method in terms of implications of methodological issues for how we employ narrative both as a research tool and a data source. On the one hand methodological issues may be held constant in a more or less pragmatic project of narrative research, while on the other a researcher may seek out affinities between a methodological position or standpoint and a particular method or set of methods. Actual methods of narrative research are only introduced here, as these will be treated more fully and exemplified in later chapters.

Chapter 3: Analysing narrative

When we begin with material in narrative form, how might we analyse such material? What can we say about narrative in terms of structure, content and use in social interaction? In presenting answers to these questions, in this chapter I address different approaches to analysing narrative as a research object. I discuss classical structuralist models of narrative, showing how these constitute a conceptual framework against which the narrative is read. I then show how a researcher may bring thematic questions to the narrative being analysed in order to focus on the content of that narrative. I also introduce some key concepts in discourse analysis that are relevant across a range of techniques for narrative analysis.

Chapter 4: Narrative at work in the world

This chapter shifts the focus to scenarios in which people use narrative to advance aims that are not necessarily concerned with narrative itself. I look at people making and sharing narrative, the tellers/writers/readers and the relations between them, and the media employed in the making of the narratives. I examine stories of the self that are created in journaling and blogging culture and in CVs. I move next to narrative in the world of Facebook, the most widely used social networking site. I follow that with a discussion of work that uses narrative approaches to study videogames. I close the chapter with a discussion of stories that are told about hackers and that hackers tell about themselves. For all of these cases I examine the structural and thematic aspects of narratives.

Chapter 5: Constructing narrative

In this chapter I explore scenarios in which a social researcher assembles their analyses and findings in the form of a narrative, or more specifically, a narrative research report. I begin by considering the different types of personal narratives, and how these are constituted from many different sources: diaries, journals, letters, photographs, official records, and oral testimony. I discuss the special case of autoethnography and look at techniques for using narrative as a way of presenting findings, drawing on work in creative nonfiction and the new journalism.

Chapter 6: Techniques and tools for the narrative researcher

Here I discuss tools and techniques that are of use to the narrative researcher, paying special attention to issues of research design and making effective use of software tools. I offer practical advice on planning a research project. In order to work effectively today a researcher must know how to use the vast range of software available to the social scientist. Much narrative work involves recording, scanning, transcribing, tagging, indexing, and coding, and all of these can be more effectively and accurately done if the appropriate software is employed. But making effective use of software depends on having a suitable research strategy and a proper understanding of the methodological implications of computer-assisted data analysis, so I make explicit links back to discussions in earlier chapters in order to integrate theory, method and technology.

Coda: I end the book with some reflections on narrative research.

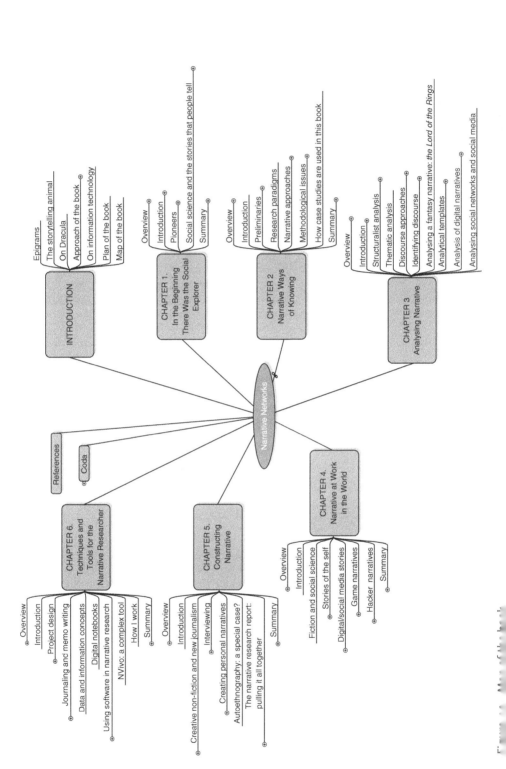

Figure 1.1 Map of the book

1

IN THE BEGINNING
THERE WAS THE SOCIAL
EXPLORER

OVERVIEW

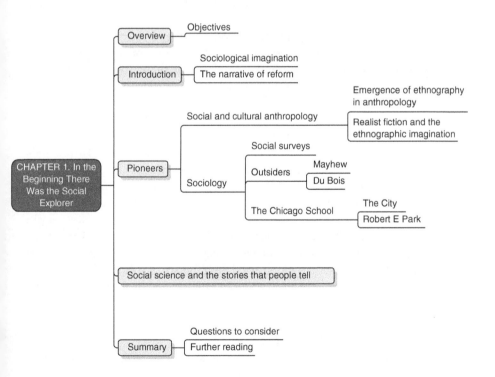

Figure 1.1   Chapter map

Introduction

In this first chapter I discuss some of the pioneers of narrative use in the social sciences. Modern sociology and anthropology can be said to have begun as forms of writing. The discoveries, by Europeans it must be stressed, of exotic places and peoples abroad, and of exotic people 'at home', were discoveries on paper (Thornton, 1983), by which I mean that these were made as much as they were reported in the texts of the nineteenth-century social surveys and ethnographies that were at the heart of early sociology and social/cultural anthropology. Growing quantities of travel writing and missionary reports met together with the growth of the reading public among the newly expanding middle class in England. The scene was thus set for the emergence of a readership for ethnographic writing. Pioneering ethnographers drew upon existing conventions of realist writing in shaping their accounts of others – other places, other people and other cultures. As with their colleagues in what became social anthropology, the British pioneer social surveyors drew upon realist conventions in shaping their accounts of the lives of the urban underclass. That urban underclass was textually constructed as offering a kind of 'close to home' contemporary parallel to the exotic others in colonial spaces. The audiences were again the educated middle classes whose often liberal and reformist worldviews and expectations formed the normative basis on which social surveys were written. Liberal reformers saw a need to generate accounts of the lives of the working class in order to have some empirical basis for social reform.

Sociological imagination

For C. Wright Mills (1916–1962) , the mark of good social science writing was that it sought to understand how the individual biography was related to social and historical forces (Mills, 1959). Of the three elements, two (biography and history) are defining forms of narrative. In order to understand the social, the sociologist must find a way to blend research findings about people, institutions and social change with narratives about individual lives and historical processes. Mills's programme is in a sense humanist in its concern with the individual biography, but it avoids the voluntarism of some forms of humanism by taking into account the way that history and social structures enable *and* constrain people to different degrees. Mills was broadly on the Left, combining a wide ranging radical standpoint with a suspicion of orthodox Marxism. He was a public intellectual who believed that scholarly work must advance critical understanding of society in order to improve people's lives. The vision of sociology that Mills developed in the course of a relatively short but exceptionally productive career was one which was interdisciplinary long before that term became fashionable in the academy, and well before the cultural turn in the social sciences that emerged in the wake of the cultural revolutions of 1968 (Aronowitz, 2012).

Writing the kind of social study that Mills advocated required social scientists to be mindful of both the technical requirements of communicating their work − *The Sociological Imagination* is rich with advice on the craft of writing − and the importance of sociologists reflecting on their own biographies, goals, development and place in society. That for Mills sociology was in large measure a textual practice is further seen in his advice that the scholar should keep a journal (see the appendix to Mills, 1959), which is standard in social/cultural anthropology but not in sociology. That journal, as an ever-growing account of the sociologist's intellectual development, was for Mills an essential tool for the craft of research, whatever the methodological perspective of the researcher. Indeed, for Mills the choice of this or that methodological prescription was far less important than the cultivation of the skill of writing because it was the writing that mattered. Writing well, which for Mills was largely a matter of writing clearly, was one of the main means whereby the public service role of the intellectual could be fulfilled. That his work is still popular today is largely explained by his ability to craft work that was theoretically sophisticated, empirically rich, and above all accessible. I believe it was his emphasis on taking seriously the narrative texture of social life that gave his work its analytical and communicative power.

The narrative of reform

Let us now consider literary realism in the nineteenth century. This development in letters was linked in complex ways to the coming to prominence of the bourgeoisie in western societies (Morris, 2003; Walder, 1996). I have in mind here principally Britain, the United States, and France: three places where literary realism is seen to have emerged and taken hold most significantly in the nineteenth century. This is not to say that I believe realism was not a characteristic of literature elsewhere in the western or for that matter non-western world at this time, but my focus here is mainly on Britain, and to a lesser extent the USA. Economic growth and the expansion of the middle class led to an expanded reading public, which in turn provided a market that spurred the growth of print culture both in Britain and the United States (Claybaugh, 2007). A virtuous cycle was then set in train in which a steadily expanding class of persons with the desire and means to read brought forth an increasing supply of reading material which in turn fed the expansion of the market that it served. The gradual expansion of education in this period meant that an ever-increasing proportion of the wider population, and not just the middle classes, became literate.

Another important element of this period was the rise of reform movements in Britain and the USA. In Britain, in particular, movements for social reform were in part a reaction to revolutionary developments coming from the continent, most notably France. Fear of revolution motivated the English ruling classes to make some concessions to the working classes. Movements for reform were fed by two streams: the first broadly coming out of a greater acceptance of the possibility of realising the Enlightenment ideals of social progress through science and technology; and the second fed by a revival of evangelical Christianity with its doctrine that individual salvation was available in principle to all believers. Both of these currents made possible the questioning and rejection of the long-established notion of charity, going back to the Middle Ages and before, which constructed notions of the inevitability of poverty and enjoined those who were well-off to alleviate that poverty through charitable giving (Brown, 2014). This notion of charity saw the poor as a part of the social fabric whose very existence was itself part of a divine order and which it would be futile to attempt to eliminate or even alter in any fundamental way. The new reform movements, by contrast, took the view that scientifically and rationally shaped public policy could understand, alleviate and eventually eliminate a whole swathe of social problems that plagued nineteenth-century Britain, most notably the appalling conditions under which the newly urbanised working classes were forced to live in cities such as Manchester and London (Haggard, 2001).

Social reform produced vast quantities of representation in the forms of official reports, statistics, journalistic accounts, sensationalist accounts, and more. Claybaugh (1997) writes that the 'Novel of purpose' – a work of fiction with a reforming theme – was a fundamental part of that outpouring of representation that was produced as reform expanded. The survey reports that were arguably the characteristic documentary representation that emerged in the wake of and in support of social reform drew upon narrative techniques developed in the novel of purpose in order to constitute the documentation of social ills. There was a feedback loop between the novel of purpose and the contemporaneous social survey report in that not only did typical social survey reports draw upon realist narrative techniques as used in novels of purpose, but many novels of purpose, especially those with explicit campaigning intent, as in the work of Charles Dickens (1812–1870), were also informed by findings reported in social survey reports of that period.

At the same time as social problems were being invented, represented and politicised in the novel of purpose, another textual discovery was taking place in the far-flung corners of the British Empire. Africa was in a very real sense 'discovered' by European travellers' accounts, missionary documentation, and ethnographies produced throughout the nineteenth century (Thornton, 1983). This exploration of exotic (for Europeans) others and colonial spaces was paralleled by the exploration of exotic others 'at home' in London, Manchester and Paris. In most cases the typical explorer was a middle-class educated man driven by an urge to discover and civilise.

Pioneers

The latter half of the nineteenth century was a period when the pioneers of what would become modern sociology and anthropology developed textual forms (ethnographies and survey reports) that employed narrative techniques from realist fiction writing, biography, journalism, travellers' accounts and missionaries tales. These new ways of representing social reality were employed by the pioneering anthropologists and sociologists in order to open space for their new disciplines in the university. As that space opened these textual pioneers addressed existing audiences and created new ones for their writing. Let us take two early urban explorers: Henry Mayhew (1812–1887) and Frederich Engels (1820–1895), both of whom were active around the middle of the nineteenth century. These two did not intend to carve out a disciplinary space in either sociology or anthropology; neither was an academic, though academics would later be influenced by their work. They used their accounts of urban social problems in London and Manchester to raise public awareness of the darker side of urbanisation, with a view to agitating for gradual social reform (Mayhew) or for revolutionary social change (Engels). Mayhew was a trained journalist and satirist and used these skills to produce a multivolume book, *London Labour and the London Poor* (2008), which displayed many of the features of social realism to be found in the fiction of for example Dickens: a detailed description of scenes, character sketches, and quotations of overheard speech, to name just a few. In a similar vein Engels, in his *Condition of the Working Class in England* (1993) employed literary techniques that had much in common with those of the nineteenth-century realist novel: again we have detailed descriptions of places and textual sketches of ordinary people. If narrative was the answer though, then what was the question? What was the problem to which texts such as those produced by Mayhew or Engels were intended to be an answer?

In exploring these questions we have to begin with an overview of the context of industrialising Britain in the mid nineteenth century. In no particular order here are some of the points which are salient to the discussion:

- The latter half of the century saw the emergence of the social sciences and by the end of that period the beginnings of their institutionalisation within the academy.
- The latter decades of the century would witness the consolidation of the European colonial and imperial enterprise which would see much of the world come under the political and economic, if not always a social and cultural, domination of a handful of the most powerful Western European nation states.
- This was also the period which saw the consolidation of nationalism at the capitalist core of the world system.

A vivid account of how Western Europeans saw themselves experiencing modernity is rendered in Marx and Engels's *The Communist Manifesto,* a text that derived much of its impact from narrative technique. Marx and Engels wrote in the middle of the nineteenth century; all around them the Industrial Revolution was changing the physical and human landscape. They vividly evoke the elements which were shaping the emergent modern Europe: greatly increased trade between European nations; the emergence of a world market created by European colonial expansion and supplied by European products; decisive technological advances such as the invention of the steam engine; the expansion of communication and transport; and institutional changes in politics and social organisation. But there was a dark aide to the upheavals of modernity, as Marx and Engels together and separately were to analyse and document in great detail.

Detailed documentation of the problems of modernity that preceded the writing of these two, however, began in the work of 'political arithmetic' (Hacking, 1990) of the early political economists, most notable of whom was Adam Smith (1723–1790). The new science of statistics was developed as a way of supplying 'hard' data on the development of modernising societies (Hacking, 1990). The first modern census of population took place in England in 1801. By the middle of the nineteenth century we have a number of persons going out to survey the social scene in the industrial heartland of England, often, but not always, with a patronising view of those they observed, as many of these pioneering social explorers had a deep commitment to understanding the transformations wrought by the Industrial Revolution in order to develop appropriate social policy with a view to bettering the living conditions for ordinary men and women. Both Mayhew and Engels were very much of this age of reform, and their works were 'narratives of reform' among many such works in fiction and non-fiction that were written in the nineteenth century.

Social and cultural anthropology

Emergence of ethnography in anthropology

An ethnography is a written account of some aspect of human social/cultural life, based on participation and observation, over an extended period of a year or more, usually by a single researcher. It is the characteristic means of generating and reporting knowledge in social and cultural anthropology, and is important for sociology and for some other disciplines, most notably education and cultural studies (Atkinson et al., 2007). Curiosity about others is a general human trait. Responding to such curiosity through producing oral and especially written texts about other people and places can be traced back at least to Classical times (Woolf, 2011).

By the early nineteenth century in Britain, there was an established reading public for two bodies of texts that would feed into what became academic ethnography: missionary accounts of exotic societies and the long-established genre of travellers' tales. Pioneering anthropologists like Tylor, Frazer and Morgan were drawing on these to produce a more 'scientific' ethnography, which was addressed to an audience that considered themselves to be rational empiricists (Thornton, 1983). Another (and larger) audience comprised the church leaders and congregations of the evangelical movement. This audience was from a different intellectual formation, being more attuned to transcendental styles of argument and to the exercise of the individual imagination. Thornton notes that the styles of the two types of text differed in narrative technique: the authors of the diverse body of missionary letters and reports addressed the reader directly, while the early ethnographies were couched in the norms of the scientific report, employing an impersonal third person style of narrative. Similar kinds of accounts emerged out of the early colonial encounter between European-descent settlers and Native Americans. These were initially written by the European settlers in the mode of observations of and about the noble savage. Another source of knowledge about the Native Americans was a re-telling of Native American narratives by European settlers (Hegeman, 1989). Just as the British explorers and missionaries did in Africa, the early North American settlers sought to render knowledge about the Native Americans through texts that constructed the natives as objects of inquiry. Thus, as Thornton argued for Africans, Native Americans were also 'discovered' on paper.

It was towards the end of the nineteenth century that modern social anthropology emerged, enabled in part by the redesign of the travellers' tales and missionary accounts into a new 'scientific' form of writing – the ethnographic monograph:

In effect, the writer On Africa in the period 1850 to 1900 changed from hero to handyman. The image of Africa itself changed from the immense and mysterious to the standardised though enigmatic. Writing about Africa was romantic and imaginative in the early 19th century, since writers of travelogue and the missionary bulletins were interested in attracting an audience for narrative about a new place, new peoples, new problems. Travelogue writers sought to capitalise on their experiences. Missionaries wrote to attract capital for their enterprises. By the end of the century, however, writing reflected an ironic vision of people that had to be explained, both to themselves and to the rest of the world. (Thornton, 1983: 516)

This early anthropological ethnography had its twin in sociology, as I will show later. The parallel emergence of a sociological tradition of ethnography also drew on pre-existing bodies of literature, as the missionaries' accounts of native Africans had their sociological parallel in the 'novel of purpose' (Claybaugh, 2007): the sociological ethnography drew on reports by urban 'explorers' and reformers for whom the mid nineteenth-century underclass of London was as exotic as any tribe in Africa. But before turning to sociology, there is some more to consider regarding social realism and ethnography.

Realist fiction and the ethnographic imagination

One aspect of the establishment of anthropology as a distinct empirical discipline involved setting its work apart from earlier speculative writing that drew more on literary conventions than those of the physical sciences. The establishment of Malinowski's scientific ethnography meant that anthropology moved away from nineteenth-century literary practices and began to shape itself as a positivist discipline. Anthropologists have since tended to develop separate identities as social scientists and as creators of imaginative texts. Time spent on ethnography was (and is) sharply divided from time spent on imaginative writing.

Anthropologists can sometimes struggle to inscribe the more subjective/imaginative aspects of the field experience, but the classic ethnography was perhaps not the best place for such attempts, with its requirement for verifiable evidence. Treating the subjective and imaginative, by contrast, is the special preserve of novelists. The writing of fiction as a 'side line' by anthropologists was one way of meeting a felt need to write imaginatively about the inner worlds of others (Rose, 1993), but few anthropologists have tried to combine classic ethnography with a fictional mode in the same text. In *Writing Culture* (Clifford & Marcus, 1986) several contributors argued that what the ethnographer does when writing ethnography is similar to what the novelist does when writing a novel. On this view ethnographers need to be aware of how literary devices like metaphor, plot, characterisation and symbolism work to construct texts, including and especially, their own ethnographic texts.

Realism, as an artistic and critical sensibility, and as a cultural movement, sought to come to terms with the transformation of social life brought into being by modernity. Realism was the characteristic nineteenth-century mode of novel writing. The realist novel represented people in society, especially the emergent bourgeois societies of Western Europe and North America. Further, it sought to portray people and society in the state of disenchantment that resulted from modernity. The character in a realist novel was one intended to be identified as someone who could be just like the reader, who was the new bourgeois individual. The 'ordinary man' going about his ordinary business came into his own – 'ordinary' here meaning bourgeois – and this figure was usually male. To represent is literally to 'present again': to bring an image of a thing before our consciousness in the absence of the thing itself where the representation of the thing is not the thing itself. This notion of representation underlies realism. When, as with the nineteenth-century novel in English, what is represented is the person in society, the term 'social realism' is often used. The social realist novel seeks to render aspects of society and culture in a given space and time, in a manner that exhibits the quality of verisimilitude. Social/critical realism in literature is parallel to the realist mode of ethnographic writing. Minute observation and recording of persons and events was at the core of Malinowski's scientific ethnography. Grimshaw and Hart write:

> The method of scientific ethnography required the invention of a new literary form. Here, too, Malinowski's lead was decisive. Like the novel in its heyday, the fieldwork-based monograph adopted the style of realism, of being close to life; but, unlike the novel, it abjured any fictional devices, claiming to be an absolutely factual report and explicitly engaging in analytical argument. The distinctive innovation of scientific ethnography was to make ideas seem to emerge from descriptions of real life. (Grimshaw & Hart, 1993)

Realist writing assumes that social reality is amenable to textual representation. The neutral or sympathetic observer, relying on careful observation and inscription, could produce a text which would be both a valid and reliable representation of the social reality studied. The concern of both the realist novel and the realist ethnography was with representation, and indeed faithful representation (Atkinson, 1990).

Sociology

Social surveys

As discussed by Kent in his history of empirical sociology in Britain (Kent, 1981), the early nineteenth century would see the growth of social arithmetic and the social statisticians; the latter are probably better understood if we locate them in the emerging field of political economy rather than sociology. It is at this time that we begin to see social explorers, that is to say, middle and upper class, sometimes but not always well-meaning, persons who set out to explore the mysterious (to them) world of the urban underclasses in England. This social exploration emerged in parallel and has to be understood as the twin of the explorations into the dark and mysterious spaces of Africa and other newly colonised spaces by those persons whose work would come to form the corpus on which modern social and cultural anthropology would be constructed. The Victorian social explorers comprised people who set out to understand the lives of the vastly expanded urban poor. They were responding to a new curiosity on the part of the middle and upper classes towards an aspect of their own societies about which they suspected they knew very little. Modernisation and urbanisation having led to larger cities and rising inequality that expressed itself in greater spatial segregation, the everyday lives of the working and non-working poor were very much hidden from the view of observers higher up in the class structure. The middle-class social explorers studied lives of the urban poor by temporarily becoming one of them. Of their accounts Kent wrote:

> The results were typically presented as a narrative of journey or exploration by a middle-class observer into the unknown culture of the British working class. The urban poor of London and Manchester were seen as 'tribes' of a 'dark continent' that needed to be 'penetrated' like the darkest forests of Africa. (1981: 6)

Outsiders

Mayhew   Henry Mayhew (1812–1887) began his career as a satirist. He tried his hand at many different occupations, including that of inventor, but with no success (Introduction, Mayhew, 2008). He is best known for his multi-volume account of the life of the London underclasses, *London Labour and the London Poor* (first published in 1851). At the same time as Dickens was writing his fictional texts about the urban poor in London, Henry Mayhew set out to study the London poor. He was critical of capitalism, but not as a radical socialist or Marxist: he was a reformer rather than a revolutionary. Of particular interest to the discussion here is the fact of Mayhew moving into self-publishing, and then to writing novels, in order to stave off bankruptcy. His work was of quite considerable scope, but was dismissed by later commentators as mere fact-finding.

Even though his notebooks and questionnaires have not survived, Green (2002) has been able to construct a plausible reconstruction of Mayhew's working methods and motivation from the overall corpus of his work. In

London Labour he employs the realist perspective characterised by a third-party point of view; this is then supplemented by a number of other literary devices that are characteristic of realist fiction: detailed descriptions of settings and detailed character sketches, some of which were supported by line-drawn illustrations. Mayhew presented some of the accounts of the people he interviewed by constructing stories in which he sought to render the actual language used by his informants. Many of these sketches, portraits and stories are supported by statistics and several attempts to develop typologies of the human variety of the London lower classes.

Mayhew's work has much to contribute to contemporary ethnography, concerned as it is to avoid the many well-documented problems with realist representations of social life. Mayhew wrote for a general audience, with a view to enlightening them as to the real-life conditions of the poor in London. That general reading audience was the same one we saw in the earlier discussion of the transatlantic readership for the 'novel of reform' (of which the work of Charles Dickens or Elizabeth Gaskell is a prime example). The writing of the text is as much part of ethnography as is the fieldwork itself, Green (2002) notes. He goes on to point out that the ethnographic text has two moments of truth: the first is the point of contact in the field between the ethnographer and the ways of life that she sets out to understand; and the second for Green is at the point of communicative contact with those 'who are to be vicariously drawn into those experiences and ways of life, the readers of the ethnography' (p. 103). Mayhew employed many of the techniques of contemporaneous realist fiction, in particular his vivid character sketches and the many stories told by his informants which he reported as quoted speech. Van Maanen (2011), in discussing the different kinds of authorial stances adopted in ethnographic writing, asserts that one of the main features of realist ethnography is a narrative stance of studied neutrality on the part of the author. Though his work was squarely in a realist tradition, Mayhew did not adopt this neutral stance because he was committed to reform and intended his work to be a resource for those engaged in reform. Green (2002) notes that Mayhew did not hesitate to deliver policy opinions and moral judgements. For Green, Mayhew's work is of most value to us in finding a way through the opposition of realist versus post-modernist writing perspectives. There is much in so-called traditional realist ethnography that is worth salvaging.

Du Bois   W.E.B Du Bois (1868–1963) was a pioneer sociologist who did groundbreaking work in mixed methods, as evidenced by *The Philadelphia Negro* (Du Bois, 1996), his autobiography, and the mixed-genre *Souls of Black Folk* (Du Bois, 1968, 1994). Du Bois used narrative as a way to represent and understand the racialised city. He was a friend of Max Weber and had greater acceptance as a scholar in Germany than he did in the USA, due to the US racial glass ceiling, which meant that he was unable to secure a

teaching post in sociology at an established university, despite the fact that
his work was comprehensive in scope and groundbreaking in technique. His
Souls of Black Folk is a multi-genre text, using different discourse modes of
narrative, description, and reporting. *Souls* also employed different genres in
its sociological representation of life and poetics to argue that black people
in the USA occupied a unique position in the modern western world, and
that they had developed sophisticated modes of action and understanding
in order to cope with the harsh realities of life in a racially-segregated USA.
The focus on the creative arts in *Souls* was in contrast to his earlier hope
that science would reveal the irrationality of racism. Du Bois wrote in his
autobiography (1968) that he had come to realise that white racism could
not be countered by social science alone, and that he therefore needed
to work in a literary and poetic as well as a social research mode. The
painstaking work of social research exemplified in *Philadelphia Negro* was
not a fully adequate response to the harsh brutalities of lynching: it was
political necessity that led Du Bois to explore different narrative techniques
in his work.

The Chicago School

The City   The city of Chicago looms large in the history of sociology,
and urban sociology in particular. Early twentieth-century Chicago was
a vast social laboratory in which many of the techniques of ethnographic
investigation in sociology were pioneered and refined (Bulmer, 1986).
Chicago was the first university in the world to offer graduate training in
sociology. The researchers who gathered there around the newly formed
Department of Sociology were pioneers in a number of areas: in urban
ethnography, in the use of personal narratives in sociology, and in developing
ecological approaches to understanding how different social groups
occupied different spaces in the city. The Chicago Department of Sociology
was established to aid understanding of the processes that shaped the city in
the wake of mass migration, intensive industrialisation, and the integration
of immigrant groups, many of whom were of different ethnicities (ethnicity
here is largely a matter of different ethnicities understood as different groups
of people from different Western European nations of emigration).

In late nineteenth-century Chicago there was a significant wave of social
surveys that parallelled developments in Britain in the same period. The
settlement house movement, which was transatlantic in scope, was a major
source of data that fed into the sociological knowledge base of the sociology department, but this movement was also a major site of policy, some of
which was based upon work in the Chicago Department of Sociology. Of
significance here is that many middle-class women – often university
graduates – were involved in social work and social surveys in settlement
houses. This was at the time one of the few careers in social science research

open to women. Some of the earliest social surveys in the USA were carried out by members of the settlement house movement, most notably Jane Addams (Deegan, 2010). These surveys were characterised by a strong moralistic overtone.

As one example of the department's pioneering work in sociology, *The Negro in Chicago* (Chicago Commission on Race Relations, 1922) was one of the first social surveys to combine theory and method in a way that would become characteristic of early to mid twentieth-century sociology in the USA. This work was a sociological survey that differed from the work of the social survey movement in that it was scientific in the sense of drawing upon the latest social theories and sampling techniques and also narrower in scope (Bulmer, 1986: 78–80). This is a work that has interesting resonances with Du Bois's *Philadelphia Negro*, but Du Bois was not at the time seen as part of mainstream US sociology, due in part to racism in the academy, and in part to the fact that Robert E. Park, one of the founders of Chicago sociology, had considerable political antagonism towards Du Bois. It is to the work of Park that we turn next.

Robert E. Park   Robert E. Park (1864–1944) was one of the founding figures of Chicago sociology. Park studied philosophy and social theory in the USA and in Germany and was influenced by the work of the German social theorist Georg Simmel (1858–1980). He also worked as a reporter and publicist for the anti-racist campaigner and educator, Booker T. Washington (1856–1915). Park was a contemporary of Du Bois, who like Park was influenced by German philosophy and social theory. Both men studied for a time in Germany. Despite both Du Bois and Park carrying out research on the status of blacks in US cities, and despite both being committed to the ending of US racism, there was no collaboration between the two, and indeed there was considerable antagonism between them, with Park taking a gradualist approach as against Du Bois's more militant politics.

Park, through his work as a journalist, became a major proponent of the human interest story. This was significant in light of the fact that in the nineteenth century in the USA the journalist was often seen as a disreputable figure (Lindner, 1996). In order to combat this, Joseph Pulitzer founded a College of Journalism in 1908, to raise journalism to the rank of a profession. Park was a pragmatist and had read and taken on board the work of John Dewey. He 'held do-gooders at arm's length', and was opposed to the moralising tone of the settlement house and early social survey movements (Lindner, 1996: 137). He was keen to establish social research on a sound scientific footing, which for him meant that the value of social research was to be found in the evidence of the research findings themselves and not in a moral framework (Lannoy, 2004). Park engaged in fieldwork through participant observation, drawing on his journalist's skills, and was one of the pioneers of the use of biographical research methods (Park, 1915, 1970). For him, biographical and related narrative materials supported putting oneself in the position of other people, leading to mutual understanding, or as Max Weber put it, *verstehen*.

Social Science and the Stories that People Tell

Sociological interest in and use of narrative goes back to the very beginning of the discipline, with pioneering work by some founding members of the sociology department in Chicago (Plummer, 2001; chapter 5), and especially figures like Du Bois and Park making the case for the collection and analysis of narrative material. Sociologists use narrative texts to gain insight into the lived social world. As Franzosi (1998: 519) notes, narrative texts are rich in sociological information. Sociologists working with narrative draw on the work done by linguists and sociolinguists in theorising narrative and narration, and move on to focus on the social relations that are actual and implied in narrative texts as discourses and in narrative acts as social performances. And more sociologists are becoming aware that the communication of sociological knowledge entails narration to a greater or lesser degree. Contemporary sociology has seen an expansion of work based on various forms of discourse analysis, within which we find narrative analysis (Berger and Quinney, 2005).

Anthropologists bring very similar concerns and perspectives to narrative as those of their sociological colleagues. What is arguably distinctive about anthropological approaches to narrative is the close attention that is paid to the symbolic work of narration. Linguistically oriented anthropologists bring the plethora of linguistic theory to bear on narrative, and move on to pay special attention to the collective work of meaning making and interpretation in narrative text and performance. Compared to sociologists, anthropologists have more highly developed tools for studying narrative in non-western settings, as well as for comparing narrative texts and narration across cultures (Langness and Frank, 1981).

Summary

In this chapter we looked at the use of narrative in the early work of sociology and of social and cultural anthropology. The narrative turn in social science may be fairly recent, but narrative has been present, if not always acknowledged, from the very beginning of academic social science. Social realism was a defining feature of much nineteenth-century fiction. For the first time in the history of literature, ordinary people (at least ordinary middle-class and to a lesser extent working-class people) were the subjects of fiction. This development was the literary parallel to the consolidation of capitalism in the economic sphere and of liberal democracy in the political sphere. Social reform was fed by liberal projects to redress the negative consequences of capitalism, and the work produced by many of its leading figures drew on techniques and forms that were developed in social realist fiction; the development of academic social science in the USA and the UK proceeded hand in hand with projects of social reform.

Questions to consider

1. Read any of the introductory texts on social realism that are listed in the 'Further reading' section below.

   a. What are some defining features of social realism?
   b. Identify social realist features in any classic work of anthropology or sociology with which you are familiar.

2. Read Mayhew's *London Labour and the London Poor,* and Dickens's *Hard Times.*

   a. Compare the representation of people and social relations in the two texts.
   b. How important is description of places in these two texts?

Further reading

Atkinson, P. (1990) *The Ethnographic Imagination: Textual constructions of reality.* London: Routledge.

Bulmer, M. (1986) *The Chicago School of Sociology: Institutionalization, Diversity and the Rise of Sociological Research* (new edn). Chicago: University of Chicago Press.

Claybaugh, A. (2007) *The Novel of Purpose: Literature and Social Reform in the Anglo-American World.* Ithaca: Cornell University Press.

Mayhew, H. (2008) *London Labour and the London Poor* (Wordsworth Classics of World Literature). Ware, Hertfordshire: Wordsworth Editions.

Morris, P. (2003) *Realism: New Critical Idiom.* London: Routledge.

Park, R.E. (1915) 'The city: suggestions for the investigation of human behavior in the city environment', *American Journal of Sociology,* 20(5) (March 1): 577–612.

Phoenix, A. (2008) 'Analysing narrative contexts'. In: Andrews, M., Squire, C., and Tamboukou, M. (eds), *Doing narrative research*, London: Sage, pp. 64–77.

Rapport, N. (1994) *The Prose and the Passion: Anthropology, Literature and the Writing of E.M. Forster.* Manchester and New York: Manchester University Press.

Thornton, R. (1983) 'Narrative ethnography in Africa, 1850–1920: the creation and capture of an appropriate domain for anthropology', *Man, 18*(3): 502–20.

2

NARRATIVE WAYS OF KNOWING

OVERVIEW

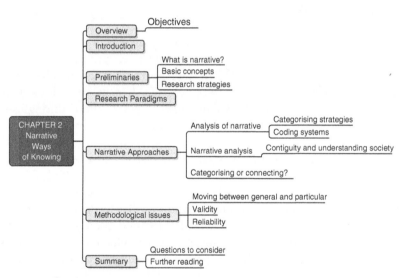

Figure 2.1   Chapter map

Key learning objectives

- To review key ideas in the methodology of social research.
- To outline the main positions in ontology and epistemology.
- To outline four research strategies: induction, deduction, retro-duction, and abduction.
- To present the key features of narrative analysis and analysis of narrative.
- To present issues that are relevant for making generalisations from narrative research.
- To review issues of validity and reliability from the perspective of the narrative researcher.

Introduction

In this chapter I present a survey of some key concepts in the methodology and philosophy of social science that are most relevant to the narrative researcher. Taken together, these form the basis not just for the chapter but also inform much of the rest of the book. We then move to look at the influential work of Donald Polkinghorne (1988), who distinguished between 'analysis of narrative' and 'narrative analysis'; these two terms are at the heart of the approach taken in this book. In analysis of narrative, the narrative is the object to be analysed; the social scientist begins with the narrative, reading it in order to draw out generalisations, looking for connections to be made to themes and issues drawn out of other narratives. In narrative analysis we connect events into stories that form the basis for our findings on the social world. We will discuss methodological issues that impact on narrative approaches in social research, which entails our plunging into the classic methodological problems of reliability and validity and moving between the particular and the general.

Preliminaries

What is narrative?

As we saw earlier, there are many and varied usages of narrative and of the closely related concept of story. I will follow Polkinghorne's (1988) direction and rely upon the context of discussion to make clear in which sense the term 'narrative' is being used. So when I write, for example, of ethnography as a kind of narrative I am using the term 'narrative' in a very loose sense in order to capture the characteristic of an ethnographic text as containing many narrative elements which contribute to its overall structure. In many cases ethnographies will also contain narratives in a more strictly defined sense of sequences of interconnected events and characters. The smaller narratives contained within the broader text and ethnography can be ones authored by the social researcher herself, collected from the field and quoted verbatim, or various combinations of these (Roberts, 2002). This book also deals with other kinds of narratives, those which we call personal narratives, such as autobiographies or life histories. These can sometimes be the objects of analysis, or they can be data that are drawn upon to create another kind of text, particularly in the case of life histories, which social researchers create as the main means of communicating the findings of research projects. Thus narrative in this book does a great deal of work and it shows up for this work dressed differently and displaying different capabilities.

In places I will use 'story' and 'narrative' interchangeably, where my main concern is with focusing on discussing the creation or analysis of a text that is strictly focused around a chronological recounting of a series of events. When I want to shift my focus onto the textual strategies employed in conveying messages or world views through stories I will treat these strategies under the general umbrella of 'discourse'. Consider the extensive body of work on women's personal narratives (as discussed in Stanley 1995). Imagine that we are reading an autobiography written by a person who was middle-aged, female, racialised as White, culturally Catholic, well-educated through self-study, and living in New York in the early twentieth century. Her autobiography is about her work as an activist for women's rights. The text of the autobiography – considered as a connected sequence of events which the subject of the autobiography recounted – would be the life story of the subject of the autobiography. We could then turn to the use of language in a strict grammatical sense and to the use of metaphor and imagery in the autobiography in question as elements of the discourse of that autobiography. After that we might place that autobiography alongside other texts written by people in similar positions in similar societies in the same historical period, and in so doing decide that the autobiography we are reading is a kind of 'narrative of vindication' in which we propose that this kind of text sets out to counteract social and political injustices that have been suffered by the author of the autobiography and by people similarly positioned to that author (Mostern, 1999; Stanley, 1995). We then find that there are characteristic techniques of assembling and presenting a 'narrative of vindication'. The analysis of these techniques would involve drawing upon methods of analysing narrative texts, which we apply to these autobiographical texts

that are here termed 'narrative discourses'. These points will all be fully
developed in subsequent chapters.

Box 2.1   How case studies are used in this book

What is a case, and what is a case study? In its simplest sense,
a case is any bounded unit of analysis, and by bounded I mean
clearly located in time and/or space (see the definition and discussion of case studies in Creswell, 2012). In thinking about cases
for your own work, you might find it useful to reflect on the main
people, places and events in your research. What are the people,
objects, events, periods or places that you want to single out for
description, comparison, or any other kind of analysis? In personal narrative work, for example, it is often clear that the person
who is the subject of the personal narrative is the case under consideration. But then you might want to focus on different critical
events in the overall life story, and so at another level these events
themselves become the cases. You may also want to compare several individuals in terms of how they constructed stories around
a key life event such as marriage – here the people would be
cases, and so too would be their marriages. From another point of
view, you might be interested in studying narratives drawn from a
series of interviews, or from web-based research on a social network site such as Facebook. Each interview could be a case, or
each Facebook profile could be a case. There are no hard and fast
rules for deciding on what is a case, and you should allow time for
reflection and initial analysis to test if the cases you identified will
actually facilitate the kinds of data organisation and analysis that
you require. Moreover, you should not assume that the cases you
choose in order to help you organise your data would be the same
cases that would serve best as units of analysis. We will return to
identifying and analysing cases at various points in the chapters
that follow.

Throughout this book I use the terms 'case', 'case study', and
'exemplar work' interchangeably to refer to research that illus-
trates some particular aspect or technique of narrative research.
I present these cases or exemplar works as summaries of narrative research either done by others or from my own work. My
exemplars and case studies all follow a standard format in which I
present some background to the study, indicate the data on which
the analysis is built and the analytical technique employed, and
present a summary of the findings coming out of the analysis.

Basic concepts

I assume you would already have taken an introductory course in social research methods (if you have not then see the suggested readings at the end of this chapter). The advanced undergraduate and many postgraduates might wish to skim the next few pages and return to reading from the section titled 'Narrative Approaches'. For those new to social research methodology or wanting a refresher, I will present some key concepts in social research (for a comprehensive treatment of social research methodology see David and Sutton, 2011). **Research** is concerned with carrying out a disciplined investigation into the social world. Researchers are guided by theory, which we can understand as a set of ideas about how the world works. It would be naive to imagine that you can approach research without some kind of preconceived notions, and these notions whether 'common-sense', intuitive, or based on disciplined reading in the social sciences, would constitute your own theoretical understanding of the issue that you want to investigate. Research is a process, a way of generating knowledge about the world. Research is also a product, a body of other people's prior research into the social world. A **research question** is a way of formulating what we want to learn about the social world. The most common forms of research questions in the social sciences are 'what' questions that seek descriptions; 'why' questions that seek explanations for events in the social world; and 'how' questions that seek to find ways to bring about change in the social world (Blaikie, 2007; Mason, 2002; Maxwell, 2012a).

Methodology is concerned with higher-level approaches to studying research topics, e.g. qualitative or quantitative, feminist, social constructionist. Methodology will comprise a set of theories about how the world is, one or more theories about how to find out about the world, or how to generate knowledge about the world, and from these a set of guidelines which will indicate in a general sense how to go about pursuing a research project. **Methods** by contrast are about specific research techniques, e.g. social survey, participant observation, biographical interview. There is no simple one-to-one correspondence between a given method and a given methodological position, though some methods are more usually associated with particular methodologies, for reasons which have to do with philosophical questions about the nature of reality and how to generate knowledge of that reality.

Narrative approaches in social research make use of already existing ways of generating and assessing knowledge of the social world. Narrative approaches use and sometimes adapt established methodologies and methods; narrative approaches are primarily *qualitative* though not exclusively so. Simply put, qualitative research is concerned with generating knowledge of what the world means for us, while quantitative research is aimed at measuring in discrete units various aspects of our social world. Put another way, qualitative research aims to provide accounts that are rich in meaning, which cannot be expressed mathematically, while quantitative research provides accounts that are rich in precision, which can be expressed mathematically.

Ontology is that part of philosophy that concerns itself with questions of what is the world like, and how is it constituted? Ontological questions are fundamental to social research because how we go about answering them will have a major impact upon our methodological choices, and at a lower level, decisions around particular research methods and techniques of analysis and indeed the presentation of findings. Very broadly speaking we can think of two opposed ontological positions, with the first materialist and the second idealist. For a materialist – and I have in mind here the social sciences – the social world has an existence that is in key respects independent of, or prior to, human knowledge. Another way of putting this is to say that many, most, or indeed all aspects of the world are fundamentally independent of our ideas of the world. By contrast, for the idealist, the social world is largely constituted by human thought and reflection. The world then is mainly what we as human beings think it to be. As stated here materialism and idealism are no more than abstract ideal types intended to help us think through fundamental issues that will affect our research. *How* real-life researchers address ontological questions is a complicated process, involving a great deal of reading, reflection, and inter-action with other researchers. Where we might find ourselves on an ideal continuum of realism/materialism versus idealism will partly depend on our own personal and political outlooks, our biography, and what we understand ourselves as wanting to achieve in pursuing social research.

Epistemology concerns itself with the question of how do we generate knowledge of the world? A related question is that given two different ways of generating knowledge of the world how do we assess their competing claims? Here are some of the main epistemological positions adopted in social research:

- Empiricism: knowledge is seen to derive from sense experience or observation.
- Rationalism: knowledge is derived from thought and reason.
- Relativism: knowledge is culture-bound and relative to perspective; sees the world as socially constructed (overlaps with ontology).
- Realism: there is reality external to thought (an ontological assumption), but knowledge of that reality is generated by human thought and activity.

This is a necessarily simplified presentation of the some of the key issues in philosophy of social science. In practice it is not so easy to tidily separate out one perspective in ontology or epistemology from another, and working social researchers will often develop a programme of work that draws on overlapping positions. So, for example, while based in some of the positions laid out above, a working epistemological position may not neatly map onto the typology given above, and a researcher has to think about epistemology with regard to questions of the nature of the social world – ontology.

Box 2.2 Ontological and epistemological positions

Ontology is concerned with fundamental questions regarding the character and conditions of existence. Epistemology is concerned with how we know about the world. All social research is framed around identifiable ontological and epistemological assumptions.

For ontology, we can identify two poles around which we find answers to ontological questions: realism and idealism.

- All there is is what we can observe and experience (often termed naive or uncritical realism, because from this perspective we assume that reality is 'out there' and depends little if at all on what we think);
- The world is largely independent of our thought but we can come to knowledge of it thought rational activity (critical or cautious realism);
- At the other extreme from forms of realism we have the view that that the world is largely what we think it (idealism).

With respect to epistemology, the fundamental polar positions are rationalism (we know the world through the disciplined exercise of our powers of reason) and empiricism (we know the world largely through observation and experience). We have variations ranging across:

- Empiricism – knowledge is mainly the result of sense perception.
- Rationalism – behind what we sense there are fundamental structures, which we can know by examining the structure of thought.
- Realism (which crops up here in its epistemological guise) – seeks to explain observed regularities by making reference to underlying mechanisms, which are not directly observable.
- Constructionism/constructivism – this one is anti-empiricist, and comes in individual and collective variants, focusing on either the individual construction of the social world, or the collective construction of that world.

A note on the 'ontological turn'   As I have presented them above, most of the perspectives on epistemology and ontology presume some kind of separation of subject and object. For a critical realist such as Maxwell (2012b), our knowledge of the world is to some extent distinct from the world; the same holds true for a social constructionist such as Becker (1998). Indeed, the classical social science tradition as represented by the works of Durkheim (1966), Marx (1976) and Weber (1930) is characterised by an insistence that the researcher must focus on epistemology so as to generate defensible accounts of a social reality that is assumed to be relatively independent of the mental activity of that social researcher (for a contextual discussion of classical social theory, see Craib, 1997; Ritzer, 2007). The so-called 'ontological turn' (Castro, 1998; Latour, 1993; Law, 1991) in social science questions this very distinction between the social world as object of knowledge (ontology) and our work, as subjects, as knowers, in generating knowledge of that world (epistemology). Rather than conceiving different perspectives on a relatively autonomous social reality, the ontological turn asks us to consider that we are in effect living in multiple realities, in multiple ontologies, only one of which is the view that we can clearly distinguish different epistemologies with regard to their object. For radical ontologist John Law, narratives do not as such represent a relatively autonomous reality, but in fact help to constitute reality. We can see this at work in his *Aircraft Stories* (Law, 2002), where he discusses the design of a military aircraft in terms of an interconnected web of stories, practices and texts. For Law, the TSR2 military aircraft is a network of objects and discourses that shifted over time and depending on the position of the human agent considering it. The aircraft that lies at the core of the book is not a single object; rather, it is/was a web of stories about the aircraft, a range of practices and narratives that together reveal the aircraft. Though Law rejects the classic modernist subject-object distinction, he does not embrace a radical postmodernist relativism: he assembled his text from archival materials and from interviews, and his published account is recognisably a variety of ethnographic and historical text, one that employs many of the narrative strategies of social science.

Research strategies

There are different ways to think about social research, different styles of reasoning and approaches to inquiry. Blaikie (2007) presents four research strategies, which are ways of addressing research questions. Each research strategy has a distinctive logic of inquiry as well as ontological and episte-mological assumptions attached; each research strategy has strengths and weaknesses, and offers strong or weak answers to 'what' and 'why' type research questions. Blaikie's concern as a social scientist (which is one that I share) is with how these ideas can be made to inform social research.

Induction: The logic here involves moving from singular statements and observations about the world to general statements about how the world works. Starting with one observation of some aspect of the social world, expressed as a singular statement, you accumulate a number of observations from which you move to develop a generalisation about the broader social domain from which you initially gathered your data. The logic here is linear, i.e. from particular observations to generalisations about the social world. There are however problems with this strategy. One, as identified by David Hume (1711–1776), is that there is no logical basis – no matter how many observations you make – for believing that what you have so far found as a pattern in these observations will be repeated in the future. There is also a question here, namely how many observations are sufficient? The inductive research strategy is based on a shallow realist ontology and an empiricist epistemology. Blaikie notes that a revised version of this strategy would confine its aims to describing the characteristics of social patterns. It is best for answering 'what' questions.

Deduction: Your starting point here is a pattern or regularity that has already been observed or discovered. You develop some hypothesis as a proposed explanation for these regularities and you set out to test your hypothesis against appropriate data. Deduction enters into the formulation of your hypothesis in the predictions of what events would follow from certain pre-existing conditions. You deduce that if there is condition A and condition B then event C will occur. You then devise an experiment to test this, and if you find that C does occur when conditions A and B precede it, allowing for intervening factors, then you provisionally accept that you have an explanation for C. This strategy is widely known as the hypothetico-deductive strategy and is famously expressed in the 'falsificationism' of Popper (1972), who argued that we can never prove a theory to be correct, but instead we must design theories so that we specify the conditions under which any theory could be proven false (falsified) and then constantly test our theory against these conditions; if the theory withstands our best efforts to disprove it, then we may provisionally accept the theory. Based upon the results of these tests you may have to reject or rework your hypothesis, or decide that it does in fact constitute a suitable account of your observations, in which case you will accept it as it stands. Hypothesis testing and data gathering are processes of trial and error. This deductive strategy has been criticised on various points: that it does not properly address the problems of finding suitable data to test a theory; that it is somewhat naive about the impacts of culture and politics on scientific communities; and that what counts as evidence and appropriate experimental design is not a matter of universal agreement. Contestation between rival theories is a constant feature of all sciences. The deductive research strategy is based on a cautious realist ontology and a falsificationist epistemology. A revised version would seek to explain the pattern of variation between two concepts, with that observed pattern resulting from research based on the revised version of the inductive strategy that we discussed earlier. Tentative theories would be posed in the form of a deductive argument in which the conclusion states the association you are seeking to explain. This strategy is only appropriate for answering 'why' questions.

Retroduction: Here you are again trying to account for observed regularities, but you are doing so by seeking to identify underlying structures and/or mechanisms, the operation of which would account for the regularities that you observe in the world. You make conjectures as to what would have to be the case in order for the observed regularities to exist, and you try to come up with underlying structures and mechanisms that would produce the observed phenomena. You proceed by building abstract models, specifying their properties, and then seeking to account for observations in terms of these models; critical realists have elaborated these ideas to a great extent (Collier, 1994; Sayer, 1999). The logic of this strategy is iterative. The main problem with the retroductive strategy however is that there are no agreed views on how to arrive at the underlying structures and mechanisms that are proposed as explanations of the observed phenomena. There is guesswork and intuiting involved that may be difficult to systematise. This strategy is good for answering 'why' questions (Blaikie, 2007: 82–8).

Abduction: This strategy is distinguished from the preceding three in how it is applied in social sciences because it starts from the lived reality of the social world and social actors being investigated. It is based on an interpretive strategy that takes as 'data' the inter-subjective network of meanings that people give to their worlds. As a researcher you have to enter the web of meanings of the milieu you want to study in order to become familiar with the codes and norms of the social actors there. In this strategy there is a key distinction made between the language people use on an everyday basis, which partly constitutes the social world, and the language of social science. Moreover, this strategy pays great attention to specialist language used in specialist fields (Berger & Luckmann, 1967; Winch, 2008). A focus on interpreting and translating among different language-worlds is what is distinctive about this research strategy when compared to the others. This strategy assumes an idealist ontology (but a subtle realist ontology is quite compatible with a constructionist epistemology, and its logic is iterative: see Blaikie, 2007: 101). The main problem with this strategy is that there is little agreement on specific procedures beyond basing data on the language and categories of the social actors; how to render findings in a social scientific language and what are the 'rules of translation' from one domain into the other are matters of dispute among those who use this research strategy. This strategy is often combined with the revised versions of the other three strategies and is useful for both 'what' and 'why' questions (Blaikie, 2007: 88–104). The abductive research strategy is arguably the most influential in qualitative research. While there is no essential link between any of these research strategies and any one of the various narrative approaches, the observant reader may have found that the abductive strategy does stand out somewhat – which is not surprising as it is the one most often favoured by ethnographers and many qualitative researchers. It is common to have elements of more than one of these research strategies informing the design and execution of a single project. As we shall see in later chapters, it is quite common in working with narrative texts to have an overall strategy that in effect combines two or more of these strategies, most often the abductive with one or more of the others.

Research strategies as I have summarised them here, and indeed all of the philosophical and methodological issues discussed in this chapter, are not rigid, take-it-or-leave-it tools. They are conceptually distinct but less so in application. You should aim to use these ideas flexibly as you plan and progress through your narrative research project(s), always remaining aware of the strengths and limitations of particular research strategies.

Research Paradigms

A research paradigm incorporates general philosophical assumptions about the nature of reality–ontology, and of knowledge–epistemology (May, 1997: chapter 2). At a more concrete level a research paradigm will align more or less closely with particular methodological approaches. Persons working with a research paradigm are in general agreement about the nature of the social world, what counts as a proper way of posing questions of that world, and how to go about judging the answers emerging from research based on these questions. As Maxwell points out (2012a, Chapter 2) at one level we may distinguish a qualitative paradigm, and within that we can identify critical theory or phenomenology as themselves paradigms within an overarching 'qualitative research paradigm'. You might have encountered Thomas Kuhn's (1970) famous use of the idea of a scientific paradigm as a relatively stable and ordered way of conducting scientific research which shapes fundamental questions, procedures, theories and teaching curricula during a period of normal science. The notion of a research paradigm owes much to Kuhn's work, even given that he was writing of science in a wider sense than social science and most of his examples are drawn from the physical and biological sciences.

Research strategies are located within broader paradigms. We can consider a Marxist research paradigm (there is more than one) to entail some form of realist ontology, which would be required in order to work with the fundamental Marxist concept of false consciousness, where a view of the world is held that is contrary to how the world is in reality: the epistemology of a generic Marxist research paradigm could range from weak forms of constructionism to neo-realism. A Marxist research paradigm would likely favour a retroductive research strategy, because at the heart of Marx's model of capitalist political economy there is the structure of class and the processes of class conflict, accumulation and exploitation: these are all layered, from the higher visible manifestations down to the underlying structures and processes that Marxists argue to be the causal explanations for what we observe and experience as the everyday features of capitalist society. To take another example, symbolic interactionism as a research paradigm entails some variant of an idealist ontology since at its core it sees social reality as made and remade in the linguistic and practical activities in which we engage as social beings. The epistemological assumptions of symbolic interactionism are relativist and constructionist. And while any research strategy could in principle be adopted by symbolic interactionists, who are after all famed for their pragmatism, most researchers working within this paradigm have favoured some variant of the abductive research strategy. Let us turn now to narrative-based research.

Narrative Approaches

Jerome Bruner (1986; 1991) has argued that humans make sense of the world in two fundamental ways, in two cognitive modes: paradigmatic and narrative. In the paradigmatic mode the human mind recognises elements as belonging to categories in a classifying operation. So in this cognitive mode, when we encounter an object we seek to map it onto already existing classificatory schemes of objects, trying to work out *what kind* of object it is. We map characteristics of the object in terms of differences and similarities to other objects that themselves are already mapped onto ideal types in our already existing scheme. This implies that we have in our minds 'template' or 'prototype' models of mammal and of dog or cat, or of plants and flower, which are collections of characteristics and properties of an ideal concept of a dog or a flower. In the paradigmatic cognitive mode we make decisions as to whether an object that we encounter is a type of some ideal object in our mind. For Bruner, this mode of cognition is most characteristic of modern science.

In the narrative mode of cognition we seek to connect people and events into a temporally coherent whole. The passage of time is important in this mode. As Paul Ricoeur (1984) argued, some sense of the passage of time is quite fundamental to how humans understand themselves and the world around them. The narrative mode of cognition is one which organises ideas and experiences into stories and is seen to contrast with the paradigmatic, scientific mode in that it operates in an emotive or emotional and expressive register as opposed to the rational register of paradigmatic cognition. These ideas are obviously abstract ideal models of cognition and cannot always be easily separated from one another in seeking to account for how people go about making sense of the world.

This framework of two contrasting approaches to cognition has a lineage that goes back to David Hume's discussion of the ways in which ideas may be associated: by resemblance/similarity; by contiguity in time or place; and by cause-and-effect. Of these, the first two, resemblance/similarity and time-space contiguity, map onto the 'analysis of narrative' and 'narrative analysis' respectively. According to Maxwell (2012b: 53) the distinction was then further developed apparently independent of Hume's work by Saussure and Jakobson. He notes that this distinction maps onto the classic structuralist distinction between the paradigmatic (concerned with similarity/difference) and the syntagmatic (concerned with contiguity). It is a distinction also found in work on the structural analysis of myth and other forms of narratives, and is in fact a fundamental idea in work on structuralist linguistics that goes back to the end of the nineteenth century, as we shall see in the next chapter.

Donald Polkinghorne (1988) drew upon the work of Bruner in order to develop a conception of two differing modes whereby narratives are implicated in generating knowledge of the social world. He makes a distinction between the cognitive–knowledge generating versus the emotional–expressive. Polkinghorne writes of the analysis of narrative that it is a paradigmatic-type enquiry that gathers stories as its data and uses analytical categories to produce taxonomies out of common elements that occur across a range of the stories. By way of contrast, for Polkinghorne, narrative analysis involves gathering events and happenings as raw data and uses analytical procedures that aim to produce temporal sequences that yield explanatory stories.

Analysis of narrative

In analysis of narrative, the narrative is the object to be analysed; the social scientist begins with the narrative, reading it in order to arrive at a generalised understanding that is applicable in terms of its similarity or difference to other narratives. In this kind of work it is normal either to begin with, or as a result of working with, collected narrative texts to produce some kind of framework into which the individual narratives as cases can be fitted. The procedure here is to analyse different kinds of narrative in terms of structural features, or genre, or content. This is a catagorising strategy in that it seeks to isolate elements of narrative and realign these to fit into nodes in a classificatory scheme.

Categorising strategies

Categorising strategies work by comparing and contrasting the analytical objects of interest. The connections between the items being compared are virtual because there is no intrinsic connection between the objects of comparison in either space or time. The aim is to abstract some aspect of the objects being compared and then use that abstraction as the basis for categorising and comparing these objects. This kind of strategy is sometimes referred to by sociologists and anthropologists as *nomothetic,* which means that the object of research is explored and explained in terms of general characteristics. In this approach the object of interest – a narrative in this case – is analysed in terms either of the properties or characteristics that it shares with other narratives, or the properties/characteristics that differentiate it from other narratives.

In analysis of narrative we must have some prior framework of theory and concepts as a starting point for our selection and analysis of narrative texts. That prior framework may be built from a general review of literature in the areas in which you want to do research, or more specifically from a particular perspective.

Box 2.3   A research problem – young people and apprenticeship schemes

Consider the following (see the book's website, www.narrative networks.net, for a fully worked-up project design): let us say we wanted to study young people's experience of work apprenticeship schemes, and our work was informed by a radical social science paradigm that we might begin with a particular perspective on this problem, such as seeing the labour market as skewed more toward the interests of employers rather than employees. Having a particular perspective is not being biased, rather it is recognising that every researcher has a view on how the social world works at a fundamental level. At the early stage of your research planning, you may or may not have made a decision about a research strategy, methodology or methods: all of the research strategies that I discussed earlier would be broadly compatible with an analysis of narrative project informed by a radical critique of labour policy on apprenticeships for young people, as would any of the research paradigms. So a first step in formulating a research project is to document your own prior assumptions and perspectives on the problem. As that first step let us set out some initial ideas, which are by no means a complete research design; we will then use this research problem to illustrate the varieties of narrative approaches in what follows.

- Research problem: what are the experiences of young people in unpaid apprenticeship schemes?
- Overall approach: narrative methods (but at this brainstorming stage we do not know which ones).
- Data sources: official records; interviews with young people on an apprenticeship scheme; possibly, access to the electronic communications of the young people on the scheme; (perhaps) access to individual diaries kept by young people on the scheme; (perhaps) undertaking interviews with employment agency employees and organisations that take on apprenticeships.

Let us explore this research problem with a view to using narrative methods to enhance our understanding of youth apprenticeship schemes. If you were interested in analysing narratives about the experiences of young adults in unpaid apprenticeship schemes from a radical perspective, you might begin by reviewing literature on the labour market and young adults. You would likely have to decide on a definition of 'young adult' in terms of an age group. You might then choose a location (a region, city or neighbourhood) so as to make your task manageable. Suppose you decided that a good place to locate them would be at a local employment office. All of these decisions – on an age profile, a local area and a particular place – lead to the outlines of a categorising framework. The age group, local area, and being registered at a particular employment office, are all attributes of the people that you want to ask to tell you stories of their experiences in unpaid apprenticeship schemes. As you decide on the generic profile of the kind of person whose apprenticeship story you want to research, you are developing a kind of generic profile of the person in your study. This profile is a set of attributes (age, residence, whether registered with a local employment office) that will help you in your selection of real persons who would be good candidates for your proposed narrative interview (we will look in detail at sampling for narrative approaches further on in the chapter). These attributes are abstract and virtual in the sense that they are used to group people together only for the purposes of your study. They allow you to make comparisons between the people you actually interviewed, or more accurately between the recoded narratives of the people you interviewed. As you collect and analyse narratives, you will make decisions on what is significant based on your *conceptual framework,* that 'system of concepts, assumptions, expectations, beliefs, and theories that supports and informs your research' (Maxwell, 2012a: 39), which will then give you directions as to which elements in the narratives are significant for your project.

As the work of the analysis of narrative proceeds, a system of classifying concepts and categories is elaborated which can be used as a kind of mapping tool with which to assess where in the existing scheme the narratives, as objects of interest, are to be placed, and/or to assess if the existing scheme of categories has to be expanded or modified so as to accommodate new narrative text. Some of these categories might include: gender, which could be one fundamental criterion for grouping the narratives we analyse; age grouping, as it could be useful to divide up the narratives according to the age groups of the apprentices; the type of workplace, in terms of industrial sector; systematic differences in the vocabulary used in the narratives. We could then seek out some concepts that would capture these differences in a systematic way. The most common way that categorising strategies are used in qualitative research is in the ubiquitous process of *coding.*

Coding systems

A coding system is a tool of qualitative research that comprises an organised scheme of concepts which are used as a basis for comparing and contrasting the objects of interest to the qualitative researcher. A coding system can be derived from existing theory and prior work—that is to say, it may be developed deductively, or it may be developed as a result of close reading and reflection on field research data, in which case we would say that the coding system was arrived at inductively. In actual practice many qualitative researchers will draw upon both induction and deduction in elaborating and modifying the coding systems that they use in their work (Bazeley, 2013: chapter 5).

Analysis of textual material by means of coding is one of the most widely practised techniques in narrative research. Discussions of this method range from the detailed treatment of theoretically driven deductive coding in Miles and Huberman (1994), to the grounded theory of mainly inductive coding as developed by Strauss (1967), to the approach of Coffey and Atkinson (1996) and Layder (1998), for whom inductive and deductive approaches are to be seen as mutually reinforcing and enabling the qualitative researcher to address the problem at hand from either a theory-first or field-data-first perspective. Dey (1993), one of the early developers of specialised software for qualitative data analysis, presented the qualitative research process as involving description, classification *and* connection.

There are well-recognised drawbacks to the categorising strategies employed in analysis of narratives. In coding narrative data we are in effect breaking the narratives up into smaller chunks which we then categorise and combine or contrast with other chunks which we have also categorised. In doing this there is a danger that the originating context of the segments to which we assign codes will be lost. This decontextualising consequence of coding data may mean that particular relations within the individual case/individual text/individual narrative may be lost sight of as we code, extract and analyse sections drawn from a range of narratives. Given that it is intrinsic to the methodology of analysis of narrative that we do in fact develop categories that allow us to make comparisons across cases, it is difficult to see how we can avoid decontextualisation as we proceed in our analysis of narrative. Before the widespread availability of personal computers, a minimum safeguard in this kind of work was to ensure that narrative texts (physical manuscript or typescript) collected and assembled in the field were copied and stored somewhere in their original integral form; subsequent analysis would then work on copies. With computer-assisted research, this is no longer a salient issue as it is quite trivial for even the most basic computer software used for textual analysis to preserve input texts in their integrity while allowing segments to be coded and analysed across textually-based cases. When using computer-assisted data analysis, as do most researchers nowadays, the integrity of one's original source data will be preserved by the computer program, but it remains the responsibility of the researcher to think through, as sensitively as possible, the consequences of decontextualisation as a result of coding operations. In other words you, and not the computer, must do the thinking—a theme to which we shall return at several points in the chapters that follow.

Grounded theory as developed by Strauss and Glaser opened the way to the widespread use of coding techniques in social research. Given that grounded theory is seen to emerge from the data (at least on a superficial look at grounded theory), the approach would appear to be based in an inductive research strategy. As Strauss (1967) shows in the classic work, grounded theory is 'grounded' in data through an interactive process of coding, reflection, and data gathering. Coding is widely used in narrative work, so it is worth making the point here that grounded theory has more in common with an abductive research strategy than it does with a classic inductive strategy (Blaikie, 2007: 100): going from data analysis to coding to reflection to more data gathering and so on provides a sound and tested way of addressing the key requirement of an abductive strategy, which is that you engage with the meaning of the world for the people you research. Writing memos is a fundamental aspect of grounded theory research, and it is normal that the researcher's pre-data-gathering expectations are recorded in memos that become part of the overall information system of the research project (Corbin, 2008).

Narrative Analysis

In narrative analysis we connect events in order to produce accounts in the form of narratives, rather than seek to fit each case or observation under a broad scheme of classification. As Riessman put it, 'narrative analysis keeps the story together for analytical purposes, while grounded theory approaches tend to pull the text apart into discrete, coded segments' (2008: 77). Some typical kinds of text produced in this mode, for example biographies and autobiographies, are often written by people who are not social scientists. But there is also a social scientific perspective as it were, on narrative analysis that we can see when we turn to look at the life and case histories produced in the psychological disciplines, or the life histories produced by ethnographic work in sociology and social/cultural anthropology. In a more experimental vein some recent work has sought to question formal distinctions between the fictional and non-fictional in 'evocative' forms of new ethnography (Banks & Banks, 1998). We also have the field of creative non-fiction or new journalism, in which stories are told by drawing upon well-established conventions from fictional genres (Berger & Quinney, 2005).

Contiguity and understanding society

Van Maanen in his highly regarded *Tales of the Field* (2011) writes of the 'realist tale' that this kind of ethnographic text is self-consciously informed by many of the conventions that have long shaped fiction writing (and indeed some kinds of journalism in recent decades). For him fieldwork is no longer the exclusive preserve of anthropologists or sociologists. One important implication to be drawn from Van Maanen's rendering of the 'realist tale' in ethnography (and of Polkinghorne's formulation of narrative analysis) is that a writer must always be aware of crafting a plot, of the building of a causal chain of events, even in non-fiction writing. While plotting is used explicitly in fiction and creative non-fiction, it is used more implicitly in many forms of social scientific writing.

Maxwell (2012b:115) writes that while narratives and case studies are often included in social research texts these narratives are largely 'presentational rather than analytic'. Maxwell would like to see more of the kind of connecting strategies that typify narrative analysis. He notes as well that much narrative research, when defined broadly, can be shown to include both categorising and connecting strategies. For him the two most common analytical approaches that pursue connecting strategies are discourse analyses of narratives and the profile case study that has been used in sociology, anthropology and clinical psychology. I will discuss both of these in greater detail in subsequent chapters and illustrate how they work by drawing upon some of my own work as well as that of others.

The term 'ideographic' is used by anthropologists and sociologists to refer to an analysis that is focused on the unique characteristics of an individual case. Return to our imaginary project of research into the experiences of young people in unpaid apprenticeship schemes. In that project a narrative analysis could be based on constructing a narrative of one person's experience of an unpaid apprenticeship scheme. The events we connect into a narrative could be those related by the subject or they could be event data collected from other sources, such as a set of data collected by employers and labour agencies each time the individual was placed on an apprenticeship scheme, over the course of the apprenticeship, and each time the individual left a scheme. Official data collected on each person in the apprenticeship system might not appear at first to have much to do with narrative, but consider that the fundamental items of data out of which stories and ultimately narratives are constituted are in fact events. Consider the kinds of official data likely to be collected on an apprenticeship, and imagine combining these with the data resulting from the prevalence of digital communication: young persons on the apprenticeship scheme would likely post entries on their experience on Twitter or Facebook, and would also be likely to have accumulated text/SMS and email correspondence; all of these contain event data and can be used to form a storied account, so we need not rely on the individual explicitly recording their own life story in a journal as they work through the apprenticeship. Of course, it could also be the case that the work apprentices keep a detailed journal, but that is not necessary in order for the research imagined here. The key point here is that the researcher is the one who ultimately organises the material, who plots it and produces a story. It is worth noting that, with the above in mind, a narrative study can also be based on event data from different individuals and the final narrative account would be that of a typical 'career', as an unpaid apprentice, in this case.

The individual narrative might have come out of a research project in which a number of individuals recounted their stories of unpaid apprenticeship, and these stories then became the object of the kind of analysis of narrative that we discussed in the previous section. The difference in this instance is that we are focused on exploring the meaning of one individual's experience of unpaid apprenticeship from the point of view of that single individual. We are not concerned with drawing out particular attributes of that individual as a basis for making comparisons to other individual stories of apprenticeship (the nomothetic approach). Narrative analysis is characterised by an ideographic approach, which focuses on the individual narrative of apprenticeship, on how events in that individual's experience were connected in that person's story of apprenticeship. Some of the questions that we might ask in this narrative analysis could be how does this person account for their present position in the labour market in terms of key events in their apprenticeship story, for example when they decided to leave school and what were reasons they gave for deciding to leave, and how did they explain their satisfaction or dissatisfaction with an unpaid apprenticeship scheme in terms of previous life events in the story that preceded their entering the apprenticeship scheme?

In this kind of analysis relevant a priori theory, for example radical theories about the exploitation of young people's unpaid labour as being functional for neoliberal capitalism, does not direct the analysis in the way it might have done in an analysis of narrative. This is because we are not seeking to extract elements of this individual narrative as evidence for or against a particular theory. Concepts from the radical theory of young people's exploitation in a neoliberal labour market are what we can refer to as 'etic' concepts, that is a say, concepts that are brought to the analysis by the researcher, and which may be used as a basis for comparison across cases. In narrative analysis we want to bring the concepts and language of the individual subject of the narrative to the foreground; the concepts and language of the individual narrating their story are what we call 'emic', and these are important for understanding the meanings given to events by that individual. So, analysis of narrative is a nomothetic approach that uses etic concepts, while narrative analysis is an ideographic approach that seeks to interpret the narrative in emic terms.

The connecting strategy of narrative analysis works *within* the text rather than *across* texts. To return to the hypothetical research programme on young people's experiences of unpaid apprenticeship schemes, narrative analysis would focus on an individual text, paying close attention to how the story events in that text work together. Here we would pay attention to the narrative discourse of such a text, to the features of the textual vehicle through which the story is conveyed: vocabulary; the representation of other people, places and objects; grammatical features; the rendering of time; and more that we shall discuss in the following chapter.

It is worth stressing that narrative analysis, as based on a connecting strategy, does not rely entirely upon contiguity. Many studies in this vein do in fact draw upon categorisation (Maxwell, 2012: 116). It is mainly for this but also for other reasons that Maxwell, Polkinghorne (1995), Atkinson (1990), and Coffey and Atkinson (1996) all advocate categorising and connecting strategies as complementary tools in the analyst's overall toolkit. These two strategies can be complementary in a very obvious sense that paying close attention to how various elements are connected in the individual narrative can serve as a counter to the decontextualising effect of categorisation. At the same time, it is difficult to generalise from the individual cases of narrative analysis, and it is often the case in social research that we would wish to have some basis for comparing cases and also to have grounds for making informed guesses as to whether what we have found in our research might hold true for the wider population from which the narrative texts that we have analysed have come. Even within the same research project we can shift between categorising and connecting 'moves', drawing upon their respective strengths while seeking to counteract the weaknesses of either approach (Maxwell, 2012b, Chapter 7). Of course, in order to shift between these two analytical strategies you will need to have appropriate data: in order to carry out analysis of narrative you would require either several narratives or some other data which, through triangulation, can be used as a basis for a categorical comparison of aspects of the selective narrative(s) with others; in order to do a narrative analysis you will need to have a text in which there are several events that are interconnected in some temporal order. So in both cases the researcher needs to have some form of diachronic textual data – that is, data that are time sequenced.

The relationships explored in narrative analysis are real in the sense they are comprised of events that are connected in a temporal sequence, i.e. these are narrated in terms of earlier events causing later events. This is unlike analysis of narrative where the relationships between the elements of the narrative are virtual in the sense that there is no necessary connection between them. Due to its (ideographic) emphasis on understanding through the subject's (emic) categories, there is a clear affinity between narrative analysis and the abductive research strategy, which is not to exclude other kinds of research strategies from being useful for narrative analysis. The focus on the meaning of events for, and in the terms of, the narrating subject is fundamentally interpretivist, hence the affinity of narrative analysis for abductive strategy.

Categorising or connecting?

We looked at analysis of narrative (categorising) and narrative analysis (connecting) separately in order to make clear the distinctions between them. In many real-life narrative research projects the two strategies will both be present. Consider a project in which several narratives are analysed comparatively in order to identify common elements of, for example, use of language and imagery, or of themes, such as personal fulfilment. The common elements or themes would be identified by codes, and the relevant passages of text would be assembled under the corresponding codes. This is a classical paradigmatic or categorising strategy. The researcher could then decide to write the report on these findings in narrative form, as a story in which the connections among all of the similar events in the analysed texts would be explored together as forming a story. Here the categorising comes first, and is followed by the connecting. By way of contrast, consider a workflow in which a narrative strategy comes first, the outcome of which is story text, followed by an analysis that compares and contrasts based on the findings of the earlier narrative stage. Maxwell (2012b) points out that many qualitative researchers employ both categorising and connecting strategies in their work, with the differences turning on which is given greater emphasis and which is done before the other. Maxwell quite rightly suggests that we think of categorising and connecting as 'moves' rather than as purely alternating or strictly sequential strategies (2012b: 119).

Let us sum up the discussion of the two sides to narrative research. I have set out the contrasting features and characteristics in the following table. It is important to keep in mind that an actual narrative research project will always see the researcher drawing on both analysis of narrative and narrative analysis: you might think of the contrast as lying at both ends of an ideal continuum, with real-life narrative work always sitting somewhere in between the two extreme points. You might also find it useful to think about the items set out in the table following in terms of their significance for your own project; not every element will be relevant in any given project.

Table 2.1   Two sides to narrative research

Analysis of narrative	Narrative analysis
Paradigmatic	Narrative
• rational • objectivist	• expressive • particularistic
Categorising (coding)	Connecting
• Deductive: psychoanalysis, statistical analysis, Propp on fairy tales • Inductive – grounded theory is a good example of this.	• Telling a story. • Narrating.
Similarity/difference	Contiguity
Nomothetic	Ideographic
• Explore general characteristics • Abstract discourse (etic)	• Focus on unique characteristics of individual case • Context-bound discourse (emic)
Compare and contrast	Look for antecedents and consequences

Methodological Issues

Moving between the general and the particular

A perennial problem faced by all social science researchers is that to do with moving between the general and the particular. In quantitative research there are a number of well-tested procedures which when followed will support making generalisations from a set of sample data. In qualitative research the matter is not so clear cut. Most qualitative research projects are based on small-scale and intensive fieldwork or focused document analysis. Most often the basis on which a sample of informants or documents was chosen relied upon theoretical considerations, perhaps snowball sampling in situations where little is known in advance about the field of study, or sometimes even convenience sampling where the people or documents with which the research started working were those that were most readily to hand.

Regarding the specific kind of qualitative research with which this book is concerned, namely narrative approaches, then two distinct sets of possibilities present themselves. If you are carrying out an analysis of narrative, that is to say a paradigmatic type analysis or categorising strategy, then you will most likely be concerned with making comparisons across texts or cases or informants. The sampling strategy that you used to locate these texts or cases or informants will then determine what kinds of generalising inferences you can make with confidence. With respect to narrative analysis – where what you are trying to do is to use a connecting strategy to combine events into a narrative form – you would have to give consideration to how you selected the events that constitute the time-based data that are the base for your analysis.

Validity

It is quite common in qualitative research writing to see an author call for a reconsideration of validity and reliability, a call which is based on the assumption of a fundamental difference in the kinds and quantities of data used in a qualitative study as opposed to a quantitative study and the sampling procedures from which these data were generated. Let us deal first with validity. In formal logic a valid conclusion is one that has been arrived at in such a way that it can be shown to have been correctly drawn from its premises. Polkinghorne (1988: 175) notes that in measurement theory validity is concerned with the relationship between the measuring instrument and the concept that it is attempting to measure. Webster and Mertova (2007) follow Polkinghorne quite closely on this and they agree with him that a formal logical understanding of validity is unsuitable for many kinds of narrative enquiry. They note that for many types of narrative enquiry, using other sources of data to test or confirm or corroborate the main narrative data (triangulation) may be almost impossible to achieve (2007: 91). So instead of triangulation they propose for narrative enquiry an analytical framework which focuses on events: critical, like, and other. Triangulation aims to improve the validity of qualitative research findings, but the problem as they see it is that the very data that are drawn upon to triangulate the narrative materials which are of primary focus, are most often data that are derived from contexts quite different from those of the data of primary focus, which raises the vexed question of using any kind of qualitative data out of context. They argue that multiple interpretations can be shown to be valid but that the establishment of this validity requires us to rework the very concept of validity itself.

Polkinghorne (1988: 175–6) offers a productive reworking of validity for narrative inquiry. He notes that validity in narrative research revolves around a well-grounded conclusion, which is generally defended by 'informal' reasoning. For him, the search for validity in narrative inquiry produces likelihood rather than certainty. He maintains that a valid argument based on narrative evidence is 'strong and resistant to challenge'. Such an argument depends in part on the trustworthiness of the field-notes and transcriptions on which the findings are based. The implication here is that the narrative researcher makes these materials available for scrutiny by others (which, I should add, is technically quite easy in this age of near-universal web access, though issues of informant confidentiality have still to be considered). Bold (2011) takes a position on validity that is in broad agreement with Polkinghorne's, as do Mertova and Webster (2007) as well as Elliott (2005). Mason (2002) advocates treating validity in terms of validity of methodology, where you explain the logic of how you worked toward and through your intellectual puzzle (and I would add your research strategy and research paradigm), and validity of interpretation, which revolves around cautious and well-supported claims.

The main reason why I agree with these authors that the validity of narrative enquiry needs to be fundamentally rethought, is that many kinds of narrative, particularly individual life stories, are of interest precisely because of their individuality. To decontextualise such narratives would be to go against Sartre's (1963) injunction that we treat the individual as a universal singular. Sartre's humanism however might not persuade some readers, who could go on to ask: can the narrative represent anything beyond a narrow individualistic rendering of events? There are several ways we might go about responding to this question. First, we have the fact that many social science texts make extensive use of the 'narrating discursive mode' (Bax, 2011), a mode of writing which works by rendering findings in terms of a sequence of related events, as in many ethnographies and life histories. There is also the related fact that there is widespread use in social science of general narrative techniques shared with novelists and journalists, such as detailed description of places and people, use of different narrating points of view (first as against third person, for example), foreshadowing and flashback (we shall discuss these in more detail in Chapter 5), the point here being that if we have long been using the forms and techniques of narrative in social science, then there must already exist strategies to address validity concerns; we discussed some of these earlier. Second, most of us have engaged with the issues raised regarding the politics and presuppositions of textual representation in social research in the wake of *Writing Culture* (Clifford & Marcus, 1986). Whether you fully reject the claims of realist representation (Rosaldo, 1993), or if like me you work from a revised and cautious or critical realist approach, or even if you want to hold onto narrative for some other reason, you cannot claim innocence of the use of narrative to create truth in social science, and of its consequences (Richardson, 1990). Perhaps some economists can, but not the rest of us.

On a more practical level, there are well-tested strategies for dealing with the 'factual' content of narrative non-fiction: we can verify factual items in the narrative by cross-checking against other narratives and in official documents, and we can analyse a narrative for internal consistency. While it is possible to employ narrative approaches from across the range of onto-logical and epistemological positions we discussed earlier, I would argue that as social scientists we cannot approach narrative from a perspective of naive empiricism, by which I mean taking a position that the literal text of the narrative is a self-contained truth of some kind.

Reliability

With regard to reliability, Elliott (2005) writes that it is concerned with the replicability or stability of our research findings. For Polkinghorne (1988) reliability is about the dependability, consistency, and stability of the meas-uring instrument. Both see these formal conceptions of reliability as problematic when applied to narrative enquiry. Mason (2002), in a similar vein to Polkinghorne, points out that in qualitative research we do not have instruments that can be tightly specified, so thinking about reliability in terms of instruments is problematic. She suggests instead that we aim to offer an explanation of and reasons for why our audience should believe our work is reliable and accurate.

Box 2.4   Reliability and validity in narrative research

Webster and Mertova (2007) seek to rethink reliability and validity along the following lines:

- Access (of others apart from the researcher) – to real milieu, to recordings, notes and transcripts.

- Honesty – trust in the human instrument, refining the human instrument, trustworthiness.
- Verisimilitude – resonance, likeness.
- Authenticity – convince the reader.
- Familiarity – critical elements throw the familiar into focus.
- Transferability – can be adapted.
- Economy.

Narratives are produced, in situation-specific ways and in varied contexts, by people pursuing myriad agendas and with varying abilities to realise these agendas. As such, we must assign primary importance to the individual character of the narrative. This is not at all to say that we cannot generalise from one narrative, or a few narratives (Maynes et al., 2008: chapter 5).

Summary

In this chapter we reviewed some fundamental issues in the methodology of social research. We distinguished two modes of knowing: the paradigmatic or deductive-nomological, which organises knowledge according to systems of classification; and the narrative mode of knowing, which creates meaning by organising knowledge into connected sequences of events or stories. We also differentiated between analysis of narrative, in which we organised narratives and their elements according to categories and classification criteria; and narrative analysis, where we organised observations and events into stories by plotting them. We saw that the two modes are analytically distinct, but do overlap in practice. We closed with a discussion of generalising from narrative materials, and of validity and reliability as these impact on the work of the social researcher using narrative.

Questions to consider

1. Compare 'analysis of narrative' and 'narrative analysis'.

   a. What kinds of data are used in these two approaches?
   b. Contrast the methodological approach of these two types of analysis (consult Polkinghorne, 1988).
   c. What does the end product of analysis look like in either case?

(Continued)

(Continued)

2. With regard to abduction, consider the following

   a. Why is there a close fit between abduction and narrative analysis (pay attention here we mean 'narrative analysis' not generic narrative approaches)?
   b. Explore 'grounded theory'; what are the connections between this approach and narrative research?

3. Even though categorising and connecting are analytically distinct, they will often be part of a typical narrative research project.

   a. Do you agree with the above statement? Why?

Further reading

Abbott, H.P. (2008) *The Cambridge Introduction to Narrative* (2nd edn). Cambridge: Cambridge University Press.

Atkinson, P. (1990) *The Ethnographic Imagination: Textual Constructions of Reality.* London: Routledge.

Atkinson, P. and Delamont, S. (eds) (2006) *Narrative Methods* (Sage Benchmarks in Social Research Methods). London: Sage. (This is a multivolume collection that brings together work by key authors.)

Blaikie, N. (2007) *Approaches to Social Enquiry: Advancing Knowledge* (2nd edn). Cambridge: Polity.

Cobley, P. (2001) *Narrative.* London: Routledge.

Herman, D., Jahn, M. and Ryan, M.-L. (2005) *Routledge Encyclopedia of Narrative Theory.* London: Routledge. (This text offers comprehensive coverage of the full range of narrative theory and methods.)

Maxwell, J.A. (2012) *A Realist Approach for Qualitative Research.* Thousand Oaks, CA: Sage. .(See Chapters 3, 4, and 7 on categorising and connecting strategies.)

3

ANALYSING NARRATIVE

OVERVIEW

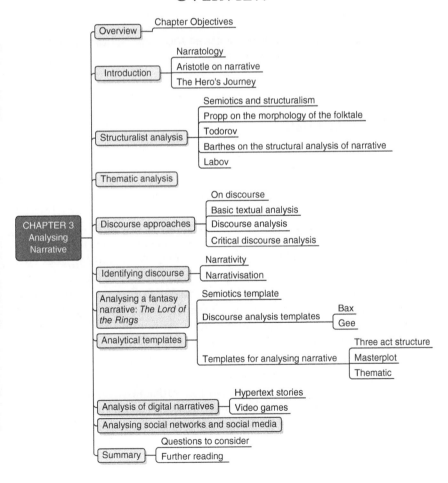

Figure 3.1   Chapter map

Key learning objectives

- To introduce the key concepts of narratology – the analysis of narratives.

- To introduce the structuralist analysis of narratives, and relate this to semiotics.

- To introduce the thematic analysis of narratives.

- To introduce key concepts of discourse and discourse analysis, and to show how these are important for the analysis of narrative.

- To show how narrative may be identified and described in terms of the quality of narrativity and the process of narrativisation.

- To introduce methodological issues that arise when analysing social networks in terms of their narrative elements.

- To introduce methodological issues that arise when analysing hypertexts and videogames as narratives.

INTRODUCTION

Narratology

Narratology is the formal study of narrative, both as object and as process/act. The term was first used by Tzvetan Todorov. In the widely-read *Narratology*, Bal (2009: 3) writes that narratology is 'the ensemble of theories of narratives, narrative texts, images, spectacles, events; cultural artefacts that "tell a story"'. For Genette (1990: 16) narratology has two aspects: the first to do with a thematic analysis of 'the story, or the narrative content'; and the second to do with analysis of narrative as a mode of representation of the story, of the formal properties of the narrating mode. Genette argues that the second one is more important because the distinctiveness of narrative lies in it being a mode of representation rather than in its content. A researcher might approach narratives in different ways, paying attention to different aspects, such as textual structure, genre, or theme, to name just three. The study of narrative involves consideration of the structure and formal properties of narratives, and the functions of narrative (that is, we intend to do *and* do actually something with narrative). The auto/biographical aspect of some narratives may be considered a distinct sub-area of narratology and we will look at this aspect on its own in a later chapter.

Aristotle on narrative

Aristotle (384–322 B.C.E.) developed perhaps the earliest scheme for analysis of the structure of narrative. His system focuses on change of state as time passes and as the story unfolds. The first stage or Act I comprises a stable beginning/setting, followed by disruption in the second stage (Act II), and then the sequence ends with a return to stability in Act III, which is not necessarily (and indeed is not usually) a return to the exact state that held at the beginning of the story. This scheme was designed for critique of dramatic works, the prose and indeed the novel form of storytelling being unknown to Aristotle. Moreover, his system was conceived for critique of poetics – for judging what was good, beautiful and worthy – and not for formal analysis of story texts. Aristotle's approach formed the basis for more elaborate frameworks for the analysis of narrative developed from the early twentieth century, and has been adapted to analyse and to construct narratives in a variety of media.

The Hero's Journey

Another way of thinking about the tripartite scheme developed by Aristotle is in terms of what is often referred to simply as the generic three-act narrative, which has become a staple form across a range of media. The three-act narrative structure formed the basis for the more elaborate monomyth, a template for a whole range of myths found in different cultures as developed by Campbell in his famous (1993) book *The Hero with a Thousand Faces*. Campbell argued that this basic structure was found in a range of stories and myths told in societies around the world, and indeed we see this structure employed in film, literature, drama and videogames. Campbell assigns distinct functions to the beginning (Act 1), middle (Act 2) and end (Act 3).

The story begins in Act 1 with the Hero in the Ordinary World, which is the stable normal setting. Then the Hero is called to adventure by something that tasks the Hero with some difficulty. The Hero initially refuses, and then has a change of heart due to the intervention of some mentor or special device; then the Hero decides to heed the Call. This brings Act 1 to a close. In Act 2 the setting is the Special World, in which the Hero is tested and challenged and must engage in combat and endure setbacks before achieving the goal at the end of the act. Act 3 has our Hero return in triumph to the Ordinary World, which may itself have undergone some change. The narrative is now complete. Campbell's work was adapted by Vogler (2007) to the needs of contemporary screenwriters.

Box 3.1   The Hero's Journey

Vogler (2007; www.thewritersjourney.com) constructs a story model of twelve stages in four major acts, in an expansion of Aristotle's three-part classical story scheme. The action moves between an ordinary world, where the story begins and ends, and a special world, where the Hero [sic] confronts challenges and is changed. The first four stages serve to introduce the Hero in his/her normal world; then the major obstacle/challenge is introduced. This challenge is rendered all the more starkly because our Hero is in their normal world, and so we can see that in order to confront the challenge, the Hero must leave the ordinary world. Sometimes leaving the ordinary world can entail embarking on a physical journey, but in some stories the departure from the ordinary world can entail the Hero interacting with new situations and people in a familiar setting. The ordinary world is ordinary in one or more senses: physical, emotional, social or cultural.

Vogler has the Hero coming to awareness of the challenge and then refusing or hesitating to take on the challenge, and then deciding to or being forced to accept the challenge. In taking on the challenge, the Hero often has a human or nonhuman helper. Then in the second major act, the Hero crosses into the special world and there confronts enemies. The Hero will suffer at least one major defeat or setback, and will have to endure many trials. Then in the third act, which also takes place in the special world, the Hero overcomes their greatest challenge - perhaps a climatic battle or confrontation with the main enemy - and goes through some kind of rebirth/regeneration before starting on a physical or symbolic journey of return to the ordinary world.

In the fourth and final act, the Hero is back in the ordinary world, having overcome challenges and been changed in the process. The ordinary world may be the same, but the Hero has changed, and he/she sees the ordinary world through new eyes.

Vogler also maps the Hero's 'Inner Journey', ranging over the Hero's growing knowledge of the challenge in the opening ordinary world, the Hero's fear and unwillingness to take on the challenge, and the inner struggles and emotional transformations and the suffering that the hero experiences.

Vogler drew on plots and character archetypes from a range of long standing and well-known sources, including Homer's epics and folk/fairy tales. What stands out most in Vogler's scheme is the familiarity of various challenges, situations and characters, and the ultimate emotionally satisfactory conclusion.

Campbell's monomyth has had great influence in Hollywood and in popular genre fiction, but his ideas are male-biased and ethnocentric (the myths that have the greatest influence in his system are those that most deeply inform ideas of 'western culture', i.e. the Homeric epics and the Judeo-Christian origin stories). Moreover, Campbell's work has thin ethnographic support and is pitched at so general a level that by the standards of contemporary social research on myth Campbell comes across as a populariser. Vogler's (2007) more recent adaptation of Campbell's ideas does attempt to argue that the monomyth need not be sexist and ethnocentric, but Vogler's approach is itself not analytical in the way in which many social scientists would understand analysis. That said, any social researcher who will work with popular fiction, film or video-games, and the creators and audiences for these, must be aware of the monomyth and especially of Vogler's work, since these ideas have been widely employed in creating hugely popular films such as *Star Wars* and numerous videogames.

Stories do not always adhere to the strict sequence of the three-act structure: many stories will open in Act 2 and use flashbacks to narrate Act 1. Moreover, many stories will use flash-forwards to foreshadow events in a later act. We identify an act by its constituent elements, not by its sequential location in the unfolding story. Different narrative discourses will treat the acts in different ways and use different kinds of devices to connect them, which reiterates the point that there is more than one way to tell a story. Later we will see variations on this three-act narrative structure in the work of Propp and Todorov.

Structuralist Analysis

Structural approaches to the analysis of narrative focus on identifying the building blocks of narrative and describing how these work to create a narrative text. Here, the emphasis is on the form of narrative rather than its content—that the structuralist analyst pays attention to how the content of narrative is organised. The pioneering work in this field was done by the Russian scholar Vladimir Propp (1895–1970), a key figure in what is known as the Russian Formalist school of literary criticism, and whose work on the morphology (forms) of the Russian folktale has become a classic text (Propp, 1968) which we will discuss shortly. Structuralist analysis of narrative draws on linguistics and literary criticism and has a large technical vocabulary. For a social scientist wishing to work with narratives from a structuralist perspective, a basic grasp of key concepts in linguistics is essential. The list of further reading at the end of this chapter will give detailed guidance; if you have not studied linguistics before, then a good introductory text is David Crystal's (2005) *How Language Works*.

Semiotics and structuralism

According to Umberto Eco (1976) 'semiotics is "concerned with everything that can be taken as a sign"'. The foundation of semiotics is the linguistic theory that language is a system from which meaning is produced through a network of relations and binary oppositions. In order to grasp semiotics we must go back to its roots in structuralist linguistics at the turn of the twentieth century, which rejected the then widely accepted idea that language is a mirror of reality. As pioneering structuralist linguist Saussure (1857–1913) saw it, meaning is produced within language rather than reflected back to language from an external reality (Saussure, 1966). General linguistics has drawn our attention to the special generative quality of language, whereby from a finite set of words (a lexicon) and a finite set of rules (grammar) a virtually infinite number of meaningful statements can be produced. Structuralist linguistics differentiated the overall system of language from the specific articulation of acts of communication by using two key terms: *langue* (language) to refer to an overall system of utterances, words, written signs and the rules of their combination and articulation; and *parole* (speech), where langue is put to use in order to communicate as in actual speech.

For Saussure, communication was fundamentally about signification, i.e. the process of producing, sending and receiving signs. The sign is at the core of Saussure's theory. The sign comprises two elements: a signifier, which is a sound pattern, a word or phrase; and a signified, which is a concept to which the signifier is linked. The signified concept can be either an abstract notion such as 'love', or an idea that indicates a physical object in the world. He identified three key characteristics of signification in his theory: first, that signs are arbitrary, which means that there is no necessary connection between a signifier and the idea or thing that it signifies; second, that language is relatively autonomous from reality, which means that the same reality can be represented by means of different signs; and third, that despite the arbitrary overall character of signification, there are limits to the arbitrary character of signs because conventions develop around shared usage that 'fix' signs to some degree in society, but not permanently. These three points become clear on reflection: as anyone who has studied a language other than his or her own native language knows, there is usually no obvious reason why things are named the way they are in the new language, which in turn can cause us to realise that there might well be no essential reason why things are named as they are in our own native language! Things are named as they are by long-established usage or convention. On grasping this it then becomes obvious that there would be little point, apart perhaps from personal pleasure, in inventing a personal private language.

Structuralist linguistics distinguishes two types of meaning: denotation – strict formal meanings, the kind you find in a dictionary; and connotation – a more elusive meaning that shifts away from a formal definition as is more related to context. This distinction is important for narrative researchers because we will often want to consider how meaning is constructed in a narrative text or performance. We need not be committed to all of the tenets of structuralist linguistics or of semiotics in order to take seriously that the words and clauses in a narrative cannot be taken as offering transparent reference to a real or imagined world. All narratives require interpretation, and semiotics offers a set of tools that can aid narrative researchers in this task. Charles Peirce (1839–1914) suggested that there are three modes of signification – making meaning by linking signifiers to things and concepts. These are: symbolic, where the signifier is arbitrary and conventional; iconic, where the signifier resembles or imitates that which it signifies; and indexical, where the signifier is directly connected in some way, physically or causally, to that which it signifies. A map is indexical in pointing to the locations of things; and it employs iconic signification as when a simplified drawing of a cup, knife and fork signifies a café or restaurant.

Another key structuralist analytical device is that of the axes along which meaning is made in a text. One axis is termed syntagmatic and proceeds along a sequence. This is how we read a sentence: in following a sentence from its beginning to end, we are proceeding along a syntagmatic axis. The same holds true for any text: the meaning of the text is derived in part from the sequence of elements in that text. This is indeed another way of refer-ring to the narrative mode of knowing that we discussed in the previous chapter. The other axis of signification for structuralists is paradigmatic, which is concerned with categories of things and concepts in the text which can be substituted for one another. It is indeed another way of refer-ring to the categorising mode of knowing, which itself is also termed paradigmatic, as we saw in the previous chapter. Structural analysis of myth (a kind of narrative) yields two distinct but complementary bodies of knowledge due to the difference in these two axes of signification (Lévi-Strauss, 2001). Syntagmatic analysis reveals the manifest (or overt) content of a narrative, while paradigmatic analysis revels the latent (hidden or underlying) content of a narrative. Structuralist analysis of narrative draws upon the structuralist linguistics of Saussure and the semiotics of Pearce, and this explains the emphasis on formal description as against interpretation and evaluation.

Propp on the morphology of the folktale

The work of Vladimir Propp (1895–1970) on the morphology of the Russian folktale (1968) pioneered the modern discipline of analysing narrative. He built on Aristotle's three stages of equilibrium, disruption and the restoration of a new equilibrium, through which he saw the events of the folktale proceeding. The fundamental elements of Propp's analytical approach are functions and sequences that connect these functions. He identified 31 functions in total, which along with the actions that connect them, were identical across the folktales. Propp's analysis is fundamentally concerned with connections as sequences and is largely syntagmatic, though he was also concerned with how oppositions worked in the folktale (Berger, 1997: 24–8). The connecting structures of folktales were for him embedded deep in culture: we learn how to make sense of a folktale through being socialised into the functions and characters and the ways that these were connected, so the acts of telling, writing, hearing and reading of folktales were exercises of narrative competence in a shared culture.

These functions identified by Propp are stable and fundamental elements in the folktale, and involve the same set of actions irrespective of which character performs the function, though some functions are typical of some kinds of character rather than others. A folktale need not and usually will not contain all 31 functions and those functions that do appear in strict sequence; they may be linked in different ways and repeated in the story. Propp organised the functions in scenes, moving from the beginning to the end of the folktale. The folktale begins by presenting the beginning state of affairs and then proceeds through four functional groupings.

The first substantial group of functions serves to introduce the main characters. These functions include the warning of the hero (*interdiction*), the hero obtaining information (*delivery*), and the villain attempting to trick a victim (*trickery*). The second group of functions make up the main body of the story, where the hero makes a choice (*counteraction*) and sets out on their mission (*departure*). In the third grouping, the hero is tested (*testing*), fights the villain (*struggle*), or defeats the villain (*victory*). The fourth and final grouping of functions involves the return of the hero and the restoration of order; some of the functions here are *return, rescue, solution* and *recognition* among others.

Propp identified characters that served one or more of these functions. The character is a human being, an animal or a supernatural being, but all characters have human qualities and characteristics, such as the facility of speech. He directed attention to the actions of characters and the consequences of their actions, as well as examining how characters provide information to one another. He proposed seven types of character, some of which are instantly recognisable to us, such as hero or villain, because they are recurrent across a wide range of narratives that permeate contemporary cultures. For each type of character there is a typical function (but a character may perform more than one function).

Box 3.2 Propp's characters and functions

- **Hero,** the central person in the narrative, whose chief function is be either a seeker or a victim.
- **Hero's helper,** whose main role is to assist the hero in restoring equilibrium.
- **Villain,** whose main function it is to disrupt the normal order of things, and to hinder or threaten the hero and other characters in the story. The villain is the agent of the major disruption.
- The **donor's** main function is to provide the hero with information or objects that will assist the hero in resolving disruption.
- The **victim** (princess) is threatened by the villain and is eventually saved by the hero; the victim's function is largely passive, i.e. to be a victim.
- The **dispatcher's** function is to task the hero with a challenge.
- The **false hero's** function is self-explanatory, i.e. to appear to carry out the hero's function without actually doing so.

Propp's work pioneered the systematic analysis of narrative, and his ideas have been useful for working on all kinds of narratives and not just folktales. Many fantasy and adventure videogames have characters and functions that can be mapped onto those developed in Propp's work. Take for example the hugely popular subgenre of videogames derived from the *Dungeons and Dragons* board games, of which *World of Warcraft* is a prime example. On starting as a new player, you have to choose a 'race' which is a type of being with set characteristics and skills; often your player character will tend toward either good or evil, which maps well onto Propp's distinction between Hero and Villain. In many of the games within this genre you can band together with others, who from your perspective will take on the character and functions of Propp's Hero's helper.

Todorov

Not all of the functions identified by Propp are necessary, according to Todorov (1969), and the functions themselves can be more effectively used if they are organised into some kind of hierarchical order, partly because not all of Propp's actions have the same status and significance. Todorov distilled Propp's system into five obligatory elements, which directly map onto Propp's conception of a folktale narrative comprising a scene-setting function and four substantial groups of narrative functions as we discussed in the previous section:

Setting—equilibrium (parallels Propp's scene set-up and Campbell's Act 1).

Disruption (as with Propp's 'Introduction' grouping; Campbell's Act 1).

Recognition of disruption (parallels Propp's beginning of mission; Campbell's Act 1).

Attempt to resolve disruption (as with Propp's hero struggling and overcoming the villain; Campbell's Act 2).

Final equilibrium (Propp – the hero returns; Campbell's Act 3).

The narrative structural schemes are all familiar to us from fiction and film, as they shape many of the stories that have become part of a shared cultural stock. While Todorov agreed with the classic early formulations of narrative that stressed the succession of events (as in Propp's and Campbell's frameworks), he also argued that another fundamental feature of narrative is that one or more transformations take place over the course of a narrative. These transformations can take the form of turning something into its opposite or of realising an intention. The movement from setting through to final equilibrium is clearly one of succession, but it also involves various kinds of transformation, both of the characters and the settings.

An interesting question that comes up here is to do with just how widely shared are the narrative schemas identified by Propp and Campbell: are they universal or are they common to 'western' societies and cultures, but less so for others? One might respond along two lines. First, by conceding that while a globalised media culture has spread western storytelling conventions in literature, television, film and computer games to places beyond the West, people read these stories in ways that are shaped by their local social cultural contexts. And one should in any event be cautious about assuming a monolithic western social and cultural context: even within western societies differentiation and stratification around social class, gender, ethnicity, sexuality and disability, among others, mean that story schemas are not received and read in the same way by everybody. It would seem sensible to concede a degree of trans-cultural reach for some narrative schemes, while at the same time being aware of the socially and culturally specific ways in which these are read. Second, we might wish to consider that while humans everywhere create and share stories, time, the passage of events and how people and places are placed within time and space have been found to vary considerably. This would mean that even though narratives are found everywhere, the analyst would have to do a great deal of work in order to identify and consider if and how the effects of local culture and social relations impact on how stories are made and shared.

While semiotic analysis, especially the structuralist variant deployed by authors such as Barthes and Todorov, is primarily a categorising strategy, there are also elements of connecting involved because a narrative must be read as a syntagmatic structure of signification, along which the analyst uncovers chains or sequences of meaning that make a text a narrative. To put it another way, exploring story elements along a syntagmatic axis is a way of examining how those elements combine to make a story, and ultimately a narrative.

Barthes on the structural analysis of narrative

Roland Barthes (1915–1980) claimed that there are 'countless forms of narrative in the world' (Barthes, 1993). At the same time, he noted that narrative is neither fundamentally random nor the product of individual genius. In the previous section we saw the structuralist principle of a universal human capacity for language that underpins actually existing languages. Barthes applies this principle to the narrative, arguing that every narrative draws on pre-existing structures and forms. In order to distinguish between different kinds of narrative, such as novels and films, we must make reference to some common model of narrative, of which novels and films are variations. Thus he asked: what are the fundamental units of narrative, what are its basic structures and functions, its rules of combination? In short, what is the grammar of narrative? It is the task of the analyst to seek answers to these questions.

Should the analyst proceed from a prior set of concepts and theoretical questions (deductively or theory-driven), or should she seek to derive her concepts and questions from a close reading of multiple narratives (inductively or data-driven)? Barthes thinks it is naive to attempt inductive analysis of narrative because there are too many narrative texts in existence, so we have to work deductively, making and testing hypotheses. But where do these hypotheses come from? Barthes offers an elegant answer: we develop deductive principles for analysing narrative by drawing on the work done in linguistics, especially structuralist linguistics.

Barthes' structuralist analysis of narrative works on texts above the level of the sentence, and given that one common definition of discourse is that it is text at a level above that of the sentence, analysis of narrative for Barthes is thus a form of discourse analysis, which is a position that is generally accepted today. We will look in more detail at discourse analysis shortly. For Barthes (1993: 240) discourse could be seen as a large sentence, while a sentence could be seen as a small discourse.

Barthes proposes three levels of analysis:

1. The first level is the level of function (in the sense in which Propp used it). Functions are fundamental elements in the narrative that carry meaning and correlate with at least one other element in that narrative, so 'the woman opened the window' will correlate with some other function in which for example someone enters through the window, or the woman calls out to someone outside. Some functions can be mapped onto linguistic units: 'the woman opened the window' is a simple sentence in addition to being a basic linguistic unit, but some functions do not map onto linguistic units. The meaning of a function can have both denotative and connotative aspects. For Barthes there are two major classes of function: distributional and integrational. He terms the first class a 'function' and the second an 'index'. The meaning of a function is directly connected to the other function(s) to which it is correlated; functions make chains along the syntagmatic axis, as we read the narrative text. Indicies [sic] are concerned with being, and derive their significance metaphorically and have to be decoded along the paradigmatic axis. The woman who opened the window is wearing running clothes and shoes, which could indicate that she is very fit or wishes to become fit, or she prefers to dress casually in sports clothes throughout the day. Which of these or some other signifieds that are identified by the analyst will only make sense in terms of other elements that can appear somewhere else in the narrative (we could learn elsewhere in the narrative that the female character is a gym instructor, for example). Barthes notes that folktales are heavily functional and rely on metonymy – part to part or actual relations between the functions – to deliver their meaning, while psychological novels are heavily 'indicial' (indexical) and rely on metaphor – symbolic or virtual relations – to deliver their meaning (Barthes, 1993: 265).

2. Next we have the level of action, which is concerned with the actions taken by characters, as well as events that happen naturally (i.e. without human intervention). Actions take two general types, those which are essential and present key turning points in the narrative, and actions of a second type that serve as fillers to move the story along.

3. The third level of analysis is that of narration, which operates at the level of discourse, being concerned with how the story is arranged for presentation.

As we move down the levels from function to action to narration, the significance of a level is revealed in the context of the next level below. This is very much in keeping with the ideas of structuralist linguistics: a function, as a word, has significance not only in itself, but also in the context of the action of which it is a part (as a word has meaning in the context of the sentence of which it is a part); and the actions have meaning in the context of the narration of which they are part (as sentences take on significance in the context of the discourse of which they are part). The analyst works through the levels paradigmatically while also working syntagmatically from the beginning to the end of the story. The same is arguably true for a general reader or listener, who moves from one level to another as they work through the narrative, even though they probably would not describe their reading experience in Barthes' theoretical terms.

Barthes argues that bourgeois society tends to conceal the inner working of its key narratives to make them appear as natural, when they are in fact constructions by skilled people working in often powerful institutions. The purpose of this concealment is to preserve the status quo. The main point to take from Barthes is that narrative is neither fundamentally random nor the product of individual genius. Every narrative, in so much as it is a discourse, draws on pre-existing structures and forms, just as every sentence draws on pre-existing structures and relations. The strength of Barthes' approach is in its power to describe the forms that narratives take and also describe how the different elements work together. He applied his scheme to written texts, still images, bodily practices such as sport, as well as film. His work on narrative is part of a large body of work on ideology and myth, under a broad umbrella of semiotics.

Labov

Linguist William Labov's approach to analysing narrative originated out of work on the oral narratives. In a classic paper (Waletzky & Labov, 1967) Labov and his colleague Waletsky looked at narrative strategies in the oral narratives of Black American adolescents in inner city neighbourhoods. This work was part of a broader movement to counter a view that was widespread in the 1960s and 1970s, that black Americans had inferior language skills to their white counterparts, as part of a cultural deficit model (Riessman, 2008: 78–9).

Labov's approach is at the core of the structural approach in narrative methods, where the concern is with the organisation of the narrative, with an emphasis on how the material is conveyed in a narrative discourse. Labov defines narrative as 'one way of recounting past events, in which the order of narrative clauses matches the order of events as they occurred' (2008: 4). The 'narrative clause' is made up of a temporal connection between two independent clauses; we can test for the existence of a narrative clause by checking if a change in the order of the two independent clauses will lead to a change in how we interpret the events referred to in the clauses.

Box 3.3   Labov and Waletzky's framework for analysis of narrative

Labov and Waletsky developed a now widely-used scheme comprising functional sections into which the narrative text is divided, with each section providing a potential answer to particular kinds of questions that might be posed by the narrative's listener (or reader). These sections are:

Abstract: a summary of the subject matter of the narrative.

Orientation: This section gives information about the setting – time, place, situation and the participants; it sets the scene by providing answers to who, when, and where questions.

Complicating action: what actually happened; what happened next.

Evaluation: This section yields insight into what the events that are narrated mean to the narrator. The account of the events that happened will be interwoven with a presentation of events that either did not happen or that might have happened; these 'non-factual' events serve to open a space for the narrator to make claims and support claims for the value of the story, and for the investment of time on the part of the listener.

Resolution: This section brings the narrated events to a close.

Coda: Returns to the present, and addresses the question of what happened then.

In order to apply this analytical scheme, we begin by numbering the lines of the text in order to facilitate the close referencing of text down to the level of the individual clause and even word. Then, clauses are assigned to sections depending on the function they are seen to serve. The narrative clause is the most basic unit: it is a clause that cannot be moved to any other point in the text without a change in semantic interpretation. The 'displacement range' of a clause is the range of possible repositioning of that clause, *without* changing the interpretation of the temporal link between clauses. The analysis proceeds by testing each clause: a clause which cannot be moved without the change specified above is the simplest kind of narrative clause.

Not all elements are present in all narratives, and the sequence of the elements is not strict. Moreover there can be some iterations/repetition of elements within the narrative. The elements relate to codes and these codes indicate the function of the various causes in the narrative. Riessman (2008: 81–2) notes that the sequencing of the narrative elements is important.

Labov's scheme focuses on the internal structure of the narrative, and is effective in looking for recurrent elements across a range of narratives; it is a categorising approach. It is usually applied to a large number of relatively short and strictly defined textual segments. The major functional sections such as abstract and coda provide a starting set of top-level codes or categories, which we apply across a range of texts. As with categorising approaches in general the narrative text is the object on which we work, and our analysis entails breaking up the text object into smaller chunks that are compared and contrasted with chunks from other narrative texts, because our aim is to make claims about narration that have implications beyond a single narrative text.

As Patterson (2008) notes, a key advantage of Labov's approach is that it allows the analyst to compare narratives and directs our attention to the perspective of the narrator. On the other hand, one problem with Labov's approach is that it works with a strict conception of narrative as two or more clauses that are temporally related in that they are about events; the problem for Patterson is that not all texts that we would reasonably treat as narrative fall under this definition. Labov's scheme is based on an 'objective' event sequence, and to use it we have to be certain about what should count as an event. This is not always clear-cut. And we have the ever present problem of cross-cultural comparison: what would count as narrative in different cultures may not fit with Labov's model, and so while the model does facilitate a comparison of narratives, such a comparison can be difficult to justify in many situations.

Thematic Analysis

Another established way of analysing narrative is in terms of themes (McLean & Fournier, 2008), where a researcher brings from her research questions a set of thematic issues to the narrative being analysed. These issues would then constitute a conceptual framework against which the narrative is read. A contrasting way of doing thematic analysis sees the researcher employing a bottom-up strategy, in which she keeps a relatively open mind on relevant themes and builds up to a set of thematic issues from close reading of the narrative (this approach is related to grounded theory but not limited to it). In this way themes may be seen to emerge from the narrative.

In the various forms of structural analysis of narrative that we have discussed so far, the emphasis has been more on the form of a narrative text, on the way in which different elements in narrative are organised so as to underpin the overall narrative conveyed in the text. In thematic analysis, by contrast, we focus more on the content of the narrative; on *what* is being conveyed more than on *how* it is being conveyed. Riessman (2008) notes that thematic analysis is the most common approach to analysing narrative and that it is also most accessible to persons not trained in linguistics or literary analysis. She cautions that thematic analysis should not be confused with grounded theory (2008: 53); thematic analysis, as with grounded theory, relies on close and repeated reading of the text from which words and passages are identified as significant. The difference for Riessman is that grounded theory works across a range of cases (Corbin, 2008) while thematic analysis of narrative seeks to work within a case taken as a whole. Narrative theme analysts seek to keep the story intact while grounded theory analysts treat themes as categories that are to be used to analyse a range of texts. In grounded theory analysts working on a range of narrative texts would break these up in order to isolate coded categories that run across them, and then these coded categories are used to inform the analyst's findings from the body of texts under consideration. The thematic narrative analyst would work closely on a narrative as a whole, endeavouring to base their findings on the reading of narrative texts treated as more or less whole objects.

But how do we come up with themes around which we can organise our analysis of the narratives? Frequently these themes will come from prior research and theory, or from the particular political or policy aims of the researcher. Bold (2011: 143] writes that thematic analysis is most effective if the researcher starts with a clear set of research questions, but also notes that, as with grounded theory, themes can also emerge from the narratives themselves. Here Bold differs from Riessman, who, as we saw earlier, makes a strict separation of thematic analysis from grounded theory, insisting that a thematic analysis of narrative works with the case as a whole. Whether driven by prior theory or by a close reading of the narrative, thematic analysis works on the assumption that there is social significance in what is being said in the narrative. Thematic analysis is useful for exploring social processes and cultural practices because narrative is one of the fundamental means whereby we make sense of our lives and of the world in which we live. Narratives are canvases on which people go about making sense of their lives and world by recounting and assessing thoughts, feelings, actions and experiences. Thematic analysis decides on an 'angle' from which to read the contents of these narratives.

Thematic analysis seeks to uncover 'concrete practices' in the text through focusing on what is said in the narrative rather than how it is said or by whom or for what purpose. What is 'told' covers the events and ideas and objects that are referenced in the narrative text, and this seems to direct our attention more toward the story than to the 'vehicle' through which the story is conveyed. Thematic analysis is quite varied and has no central theoretical or epistemological positions. Riessman suggests that the most effective way to learn to do thematic analysis is by studying examples of this kind of research.

The structures and processes that shape our lives are presented and even enacted in the stories we tell:

> Narrative is the means by which we, both as participants and as researchers, shape our understandings and make sense of them ... The truths inherent in personal narrative issue form real positions in the world—the passions, desires, ideas, and conceptual systems that underlie life as lived. People's personal narratives are efforts to grapple with the confusion and complexity of the human condition. (Josselson et al., 1995: 32)

Focusing on the content of narratives yields a different kind of information from participant observation, in that thematic analysis goes inside the stories our informants tell rather than recording what they do. Of course analysis of narrative is often used in conjunction with observational methods, and has long been part of both the sociological and anthropological ethnographic traditions.

Thematic analysis of narrative is quite flexible in the theoretical and methodological tools it employs. Phenomenology and symbolic interactionism are obvious approaches for such analysis, but so too is psychoanalysis or critical theory. Any area of social or cultural theory can be adapted to a thematic analysis, because the practices and experiences that people narrate may be analysed from many different theoretical perspectives. Thematic analysis of narrative has been used in most substantive areas of social research in sociology and anthropology.

Let us consider two interrelated areas of social research in which a thematic analysis of narratives has been often used: studies of political activism and women's personal narratives. Narratives have been used to identify and to study themes based on the histories and operation of activist projects, motivations for political activism, and the identities of activists (Alleyne, 2002; Andrews, 2007; Mostern, 1999; Polletta, 2006). The narratives in these works are derived from various sources: fieldwork interviews, informants' personal narratives, published works, and project documentation, among others. These narratives are treated as vehicles through which activists articulate identities, word-views, political strategies, and justifications for their political work. The themes employed in these studies are generally broad ones (such as motivation, world-view, and justifications for political choices, as we pointed out above), and researchers often derive these themes initially from prior research findings, though in some cases themes were refined in the process of the work. The narratives in these studies appear in many different lengths, from book-length project histories, biographies and autobiographies, to shorter stories told in the course of an interview or more informal conversation. Different media have been employed: text, audio recording, film and video, photographs, and blog postings. Thematic researchers tend to use a very broad definition of narrative. Often the thematic analysis of the narrative is part of a research text that may be presented as an ethnography, an individual or collective life history, a history, a case study, a journalistic report or an essay. Researchers employing thematic analysis often do not engage with narratology and semiotics, and as I pointed out earlier, are less concerned with the form of the narrative and more with its content (thematic analysis can of course be used alongside structuralist analysis). Having settled on one or more themes, researchers working in the thematic mode will then work on individual narrative texts in order to illustrate, verify and/or challenge the theme(s). The narrative text here is a means to other analytical ends that often do not have much to say about narrative itself. The theme, however arrived at, is mainly what matters in a thematic analysis of narrative.

Narrative has become a core method and product of feminist work (Personal Narratives Group, 1989). Starting from the fundamental feminist insight that historical and autobiographical narratives, as other non-fiction narratives that inform social science, have been largely constructed from the perspective of dominant men in society, researchers such as bell hooks (1994) and Liz Stanley (1995; 1996) have set out a challenging agenda for feminist use of narrative. Feminist narrative research begins with the assumption that the events and entities of the story should be based around the experiences of women in a patriarchal society, and more generally, on the lived experiences of those who are relatively less powerful. This focus on the lived experiences of ordinary people is one shared with social history from a Left perspective, and with work informed by the black and gay rights movements. Indeed, narratives by and about women, whether black, white, gay, straight, middle or working class, have come to constitute a vast body of work. As Stanley (1995) notes, the recognition of the marginalisation of women's lived experienced has led many feminists to question the assumptions of objectivity that underpinned much biographical and autobiographical work. For Stanley, feminist narrative employs women's experiences in terms of events that may or may not be of significance for anyone apart from the subject of the narrative in question. Narrative here is a set of textual practices that have political consequences because such narratives promote an understanding of lives that have not conventionally been seen as worthy of scholarly investigation; at the same time, no claim is made for these narratives in terms of objectivity, and no epistemological privilege is seen, for Stanley, to follow on from the production and reception of these narratives.

Discourse Approaches

On discourse

While there is some overlap between 'narrative' and 'discourse', it is important to distinguish the two. 'Narrative', as we saw earlier, is held to be encompassing story and narrative discourse, or discourse. 'Discourse' is itself a term with varied usages in different disciplines. In many works on narrative, discourse is taken to refer to the story as presented, or rather *re*presented, because of the assumption that a narrative is a presentation of a story entailing events that have already happened. The term 'discourse', like 'narrative', is used differently in different disciplinary contexts. Bax (2001: 34) discussed discourse in terms emerging from working linguistics and looked at in two ways: 'texts that are authentic' and 'texts of any size, spoken or written'. In their editors' introduction to *The Discourse Reader,* Jaworski and Coupland write:

> ... discourse is language use relative to social, political and cultural formations – it is language reflecting social order but also language shaping social order, and shaping individuals' interaction with society. (Jaworski & Coupland, 2005: 3).

Mills (2004) points out, following Foucault, that discourse in part constitutes the objects of which it speaks, which does not mean that reality is entirely constructed in language, but that how we conceive, represent and communicate our understanding of the world is largely through discourse. She notes also that 'discourses structure both our sense of reality and our notion of our own identity' (2004: 13). Our knowledge of the world comes from our senses, from experience and from discourse. In a densely mediated culture, in a globalising network society, the greater part of our knowledge comes from discourse; despite homespun assertions that 'seeing is believing' or that 'experience is the best teacher', neither direct observation nor personal experience can account for more than a fraction of what a typical adult now knows. The greater part of our knowledge comes from discourse, and much of that discourse is in the form of narrative, so the study of narrative entails at some level the study of discourse. Mills asserts that 'Discourse does not simply construct material objects . . . [it also] constructs certain events and sequences of events into narratives which are recognised by a particular culture as real or important events' (2004: 48). This notion of discourse as constituting narrative takes us back to how I earlier set out my own usage of narrative. From this statement by Mills we can see that the sense of discourse, as concerning the presentation of story events in a narrative, is in part involved in constituting a kind of object, that object being the overall narrative. Discourse analysis and critical discourse analysis are both relevant as they provide a set of tools to analyse texts, some of which are narratives. Given that discourse is a constituent element of narrative, then discourse analysis overlaps with the analysis of narrative.

In narrative research the wider linguistic and for that matter Foucauldian (Foucault, 1977, 1979) uses of the term can be useful, though in keeping with accepted usage in narratology and narrative analysis, this book will usually use discourse to mean a particular representation of story events, and therefore as one of the key constituents of narrative. When discourse is used in the broader sense of the social and political uses and effects of language, as in the usage in critical discourse analysis, then I will indicate this.

Basic textual analysis

Before plunging into discourse analysis and exploring how and where it overlaps with analysis of narrative, I will present some fundamental tools of textual analysis that have been developed in linguistics. Narratives are texts and discourses are texts, so it makes sense to look at textual analysis at a general level. I have based this section on Richardson's (2007, see Chapter 3) excellent discussion, which I would recommend to the reader.

We analyse a text on two different levels. The first micro level is that concerned with words, clauses and sentences; the second looks at how the objects of the first level are combined to persuade and narrate. The micro-level analysis addresses: lexis – regarding the choice and meaning of words used in the text; transivity – people and their actions as described in the text; and modality – the judgments and opinions of the author or narrator of the text.

Let us perform a basic textual analysis of an article about WikiLeaks that was published on BBC online on 2 September 2011, which I summarise in part in Box 3.4.

Box 3.4   On the Wikileaks controversy

In late 2010 hacker politics came to global media prominence with the web publishing of classified US State Department documents by Wikileaks. A furious controversy ensued, with some on the conservative Right in the USA even going so far as to call for the execution of founder Julian Assange endangering US citizens' lives, while on the other side, many libertarians and radicals took up Assange's cause, seeing the Australian hacker as a persecuted freedom fighter. Wikileaks was at the centre of a transnational storm. Apparently under pressure from the US government, VISA and Paypal blocked donations to Wikileaks, and Wikileaks' bank accounts were frozen. Hacktivists in support of Wikileaks responded by launching cyber-attacks against the online operations VISA and Paypal. To many commentators it appeared that the world was witnessing a full-blown cyber-war. The transnationally dispersed hackers who responded to what they saw as the persecution of Assange (and related on-going attempts to silence Wikileaks) employed various techniques, such as flooding target websites with millions of requests in a short period of time in order to overload the servers, and altering or defacing 'enemy' websites.

In September 2011, a number of major newspapers in the US, Germany and Britain, that had previously published material leaked by Wikileaks, distanced themselves from Wikileaks' decision to mass-publish these hundreds of thousands of classified US documents. Up until that late 2011 leak, Wikileaks' exposures had had the support of The Guardian, The New York Times, and several other major newspapers. These media organizations argued that the information published so far by Wikileaks was on balance weighted toward a public interest in disclosure; indeed these newspapers expended considerable resources, including legal resources, to defend their decision to publish material provided by Wikileaks. But the prospect of an enormous mass leak of the US cables led to tension between these news organisations and Wikileaks, with Assange and his close colleagues favouring full and immediate disclosure, while the media organisations wished to edit and to limit the quantity of material to be published. Wikileaks would choose to go for immediate publication. After several attempts to avoid extradition from the UK to Sweden to face charges of sexual assault, Assange was granted political asylum by Ecuador in 2012, and has since been resident at the Ecuadorean embassy in London. He faces immediate arrest by British authorities should he ever leave the building.

The BBC published an article on its website covering the controversy on 2 September, 2011. The full text of the article can be found online at http://www.bbc.co.uk/news/world-us-canada-14765837. We will use this article as the basis to explore some issues in textual analysis.

As is normal in journalism, the structure of this news story is that of the 'inverted pyramid', with the crucial facts at the beginning, followed by a body with important but not crucial facts, and with less important facts towards the end (and in the side panel). In a sense the news story opens with the climax (classical Act 3), and then fills in the background to the story. In lexical terms, as is typical for the online outlet of a major global news organisation, the vocabulary is non-technical, with a few exceptions that we shall come to next; the piece is carefully copyedited, with no spelling errors. The reader of the piece will need to have some basic knowledge of the Web and of social media: 'Twitter' and 'online' are used without explanation and therefore the reader is presumed to understand the difference between a print and online publication. The presumptions behind the use of these terms are sound when applied to a person who would be reading this piece on the BBC's website. There is one term that is somewhat specialised – 'redact' which in this context means to obscure text in a document by covering the text in a solid block of colour, usually black. With respect to transitivity, we can identify the participants, processes and circumstances as follows: the key participants are WikiLeaks and its leading figure, Julian Assange (the main human participant); newspapers; and the US government, in particular the State Department. These are the human and institutional actors in the story.

Modality, according to Richardson (2007: 59–62) is usually indicated by use of modal verbs such as *may, would, will,* and *must,* and by their negations. Adverbs are another indication of modality (certainly, probably). For Richardson 'modal choices . . . are an indication of the attitudes, judgements or political beliefs of the writer/speaker' (2007: 63). The position of the article towards WikiLeaks is mildly critical as indicated by their 'steadily releasing cables' despite many of the files being marked 'Strictly protect'. The article accepts the position of the US government, whose officials 'thought sources could be endangered if identified'. In contrast, the joint statement of the *Guardian, El Pais, New York Times* and *Der Spiegel* is reported and linked in the article without judgment. The BBC's modal stance in this article is aligned with the major international newspapers with which WikiLeaks originally worked to publish some of the controversial material, and is implicitly critical of the decision by WikiLeaks and Assange to publish materials irrespective of their US government classification.

In everyday speech we often adopt the term 'rhetorical' to mean a use of language that is intended to score a point in a debate. But rhetoric is more fundamentally an art and discipline of using language to persuade others. It is neither inherently good nor evil. Various rhetorical figures have been identified, of which some are *synecdoche, metaphor, metonymy,* in addition to which we have *rhyme, alliteration, exemplification* and *encomium* (where we praise a thing by making reference to its characteristics). As Laurel Richardson (1990) reminds us, rhetorical devices such as metaphor are mainstays of scientific writing, despite the claims that scientists write in an objective manner, with the implication that objectivity is the opposite of rhetoric. Indeed, as Sword (2012) has shown from a study based on a survey of hundreds of academic papers in a range of scientific, social science and humanities disciplines, the academic works most admired by other academics are those which exploit a range of rhetorical and stylistic devices to the full. So it seems that academics may not be as wary of rhetoric as many claim to be.

Discourse analysis

A discourse is an instance of language use in a social context. The spoken or written text is brought into being by a human agent, and the analyst is concerned to study that instance of language in use within the full social context. That context, at the barest minimum, would comprise the speaker/author and a listener/reader. These two need not be present in the same place and time, but the act of bringing language into social being requires at least one other party to fulfil the social requirement.

For Gee (2005, see Chapter 2), discourse (with a small d) is about 'language in use' and 'building things through language.' Language is used to say, to do, and to express being. Gee identifies seven aspects of discourse, of which I will highlight three:

1. Significance: we use language to give meaning to the world
2. Activities: we use language to draw attention to our engaging in certain activities – we use language to be recognised as engaging in certain activities.
3. Identities: we use language to express and to assert identities.

For Bax (2011) discourse analysis approaches a text with three key questions: what is the text achieving or seeking to achieve? How does the text achieve or seek to achieve this? And why does the text seek to do this? These questions are clearly analogous to asking what a text is doing or attempting to do, or to an examination of the use of language to signify, or to draw attention to action, or to express identity. Further combining questions from Bax and Gee, we could ask what, why and how identities are being expressed in a text. Bax's questions for discourse analysis, like Gee's, are addressed to language in use.

Critical discourse analysis

The 'critical' in critical discourse analysis indicates the standpoint adopted by practitioners in the field (Blommaert & Bulcaen, 2000). They have given a critical tone to discourse analysis by taking the position of the weak, and focusing on how domination and power shape and are shaped in and through discourse. It is worth noting that some practitioners of discourse analysis, such as Bax, hold the view that all discourse analysis is critical in the sense that to analyse a text we have to take a critical stance and go beyond what is obvious or manifest in that text, to ask about how and why it has the features that it does.

Critical discourse analysis (or CDA as it is often termed) is distinguished by a generally sceptical and questioning perspective that draws on some elements of Marxist and neo-Marxist thought, especially the ideas of the

Frankfurt School on critical theory and Antonio Gramsci's work. The concepts of ideology, domination and hegemony play a major role in this type of work. Raymond Williams (1977, see Chapters 6, 7) wrote that there are three general usages of the term' ideology':

(i) A system of beliefs characteristic of a particular class or group.
(ii) A system of illusory beliefs—false ideas or false consciousness – which can be contrasted with true or scientific knowledge.
(iii) The general process of the production of meanings and ideas.

Critical discourse analysis is informed by all these conceptions of ideology. Another key concept for critical discourse analysis is that of hegemony, which entails domination but is not tyranny. Hegemony is in some ways quite subtle: the ruled, to some extent, support the right of the rulers to govern; they lend some legitimacy to the status quo. The skilled manipulation, by the ruling bloc, of ideas and practices of legitimisation is more important than force in the maintenance of hegemony. For critical discourse analysts, discourse is an important site where elites develop and deploy symbolic resource and practices through which they legitimise their status; hegemony is constructed and enacted as much in discourse as in the material world.

The ideas of the Frankfurt School on critical theory have had a considerable influence on the development of critical discourse analysis. The origins of this body of thought are seen to go back the 1920s and the founding of the Institute for Social Research in Frankfurt, Germany (Wiggershaus, 1994). Critical theory is critical of all established structures and practices, asking in whose interest do these exist? This is a question that is raised repeatedly in the work of leading critical discourse analysts such as Ruth Wodak (2009), Norman Fairclough (2010), and Teun van Dijk (2011).

Identifying Discourse

Narrativity

So what makes a text a narrative? Is it a question of kind – i.e. a text is categorically a narrative or it is not – or is it a matter of degree – i.e. to what extent is a text a narrative? These questions lead us to consider the *narrativity* or the *narrativehood* of a text, which entails a consideration of the qualities and characteristics of a text that would have us treat it as narrative. We will first examine the linguistic concept of discourse modes as a way of identifying narrative, and then we will look at how narrative theorists have conceived narrativity.

From a linguistic perspective Bax identifies different discourse modes, which are ways of using language that can be 'characterised and distinguished in terms of their relation to the world, and also by their internal linguistic features' (2011: 64). Discourse modes treat space and time in different ways. The following is a brief summary (see Bax, 2011, Chapter 4, for a full discussion).

- The **interacting** discourse mode is characterised by turn-taking and turn giving, and by a high incidence of question forms (2011: 87). It is fundamentally conversational.
- The **describing** discourse mode is characterised by frequent use of verbs such as 'be' and 'become', by the verb 'have', and also by use of present and simple past tenses, and by frequent use of descriptive adjectives and adverbs of frequency such as 'constantly' (2011: 90).
- The **reporting** discourse mode is characterised by frequent use of the deictic present tense, such as ' the board has decided' (the term 'deictic' means the use of terms to refer to the time or place of the person speaking, e.g. 'this man', 'today'), and deictic adverbs of place such as 'here' and 'there' (2011: 91).
- The **instructing** discourse mode is characterised by frequent use of imperative verbs ('heat the water'), use of adjectives to specify the items to be used ('chopped carrots'), and adverbs of sequence to specify the order of events ('first', 'next') (2011: 94). A recipe or instructions on how to use a gadget are typical texts in this mode.
- The **narrating** discourse mode is characterised by the presentation of a sequence of events within a recognisable narrative structure (2011: 77).

By now we will be familiar with some of the structural features of narrative, so we can see how the notion of discourse mode can help us to identify the narrative elements of a text and also identify a text as being a narrative. These discourse modes are not mutually exclusive, and can and do appear simultaneously across different types of text. A text that may be seen as primarily of one type will often have elements of one or more of the others. Narratives of any length beyond a few sentences or short paragraphs will have descriptive passages for instance. Discourse modes are well suited for identifying and classifying shorter texts and text segments, but as social researchers we need additional tools, given that narrative texts have been shown to be enormously varied, ranging from simple sentences, to short folktales and accounts of everyday activities, to book-length biographies and life histories, and on to the complex narratives that found in the novels of Charles Dickens or Henry James, where we find narratives within narratives and complex relations among narratives at different levels. In narrative theory the term 'narrativehood' is often used to refer to the characteristics of a text that make it a good candidate for classification under the narrative discourse mode. As I have described them here discourse nodes are text types and may be usefully viewed in terms of social science ideal types that can assist us in identifying and delineating what it is we intend to study but will not define exactly each and every relevant instance.

Let us turn now to the narrativity of a text, which requires judgment as to the text's quality of being narrative. This entails a different approach from the classifying of discourse modes or text types, in part because different discourse modes as defined above can add to the narrative quality of a text, and as we work with larger and more complex texts it becomes more difficult to make clear-cut classifications of texts into discourse modes or text types. Assessing the narrativity of a text involves paying attention to features of that text which are characteristic of narrative in general but may be optional for a particular narrative. One such feature for some narrative theorists is the presence of dual temporality in the narrative text: there is a passage of time in the discourse (discourse time) which is time taken to read or view the narrative, and another presentation of time in the events themselves (story time). Another feature of narrativity is a representation of experience.

Narratives themselves display distinct modes, ranging from the simple narrativity of a folktale to the complex narrativity of a novel with multiple plot lines and multi-layered narratives. The narrativity of historical writing or ethnography could be seen as a narrative mode that is distinct from the fictional narratives in the sense that the events and persons represented in historical or ethnographic narratives are assumed to be based in fact and not in the author's imagination, and as such narrative in history or ethnography will employ techniques to persuade the reader of the truth of events represented in the text. Historians will support their narratives by citing primary and secondary sources, while many ethnographers will rely on techniques adapted from social realist fiction, such as detailed descriptions of objects and places, characterisation, and direct quotation, as well as citing relevant research in support of their claims.

As a first step in analysing narrative we must consider the narrativity of the text before us. To what extent does this text have the quality of being a narrative? Drawing on the above discussion of narrativity, we can take a strict classifying approach where we identify in advance a set of criteria that a text must meet in order to count as a narrative for the purposes of our research. This categorical approach works well with shorter texts in which it is relatively straightforward to identify the linguistic features of the narrating mode of discourse as we set them out above, and if we come to the view that these features are prominent in the text then we can take that text to be a narrative. For long texts we will often find that many different discourse modes coexist within the same text, and so we have to use broader and more 'fuzzy' criteria to judge the narrativity of a text. For a longer text we would most likely be working well above the level of the individual sentence, and as such syntactical analysis would not help us much. We might seek to identify passages of text of whatever length that display more general characteristics of narrative: are there events in the form of action and happenings, and are there human and non-human agents? Is there transformation taking place? Is experience represented in the text? These more 'literary' criteria, when applied to a longer text, enable us to make a judgment as to the narrativity of that text.

While discourse mode or text-type analyses lend themselves more readily to a top-down or theory-driven approach, a more 'literary' as opposed to linguistic approach to narrativity can be employed in a top-down fashion, using the structuralist frameworks of Todorov for example, or can be used in an exploratory manner more akin to grounded theory. But as an analyst of narrative in social research, you will likely never be working without *some* kind of prior theoretical or conceptual framework. The difference in emphasis is between a purely theory-driven approach where you have a detailed set of criteria that you will use to assess the narrativity of a text, and a more open approach where you have some set of starting theoretical concepts and as you work through your texts you add to and refine these.

Narrativisation

To narrativise is to render a discourse in narrative form in order to enable an understanding of the characters, events and experiences that are the subject of the discourse. Narrativisation is the process that we earlier discussed as a connecting strategy. Historians narrativise events by shaping them into a story, by plotting them (White, 1987: chapter 2). Ethnographers narrativise by organising their materials into stories that aim to present a coherent account of the social and cultural setting that the ethnographer studied during their fieldwork (Atkinson, 1990; Van Maanen, 2011). Narrativisation here is a writing strategy. But it is also a reading strategy, where the reader reads a text as a narrative by interpreting the events represented in that text in a storied frame. We make sense of experience by narrativisation, as we saw in the earlier discussion of Bruner's notion of the narrative mode of understanding in Chapter 2. For Bruner, narrativisation is a fundamental and universal human capability that is exercised both consciously and unconsciously.

Box 3.5   How narrativisation works

To narrativise is to create a discourse in narrative form:

- In order to enable an understanding of characters, events, and experience.
- It is a connecting strategy – meaning is in the connection.

(Continued)

> *(Continued)*
>
> ### Ethnographers
>
> - Narrativise by creating storied accounts of a social/cultural set-ting based on events the ethnographer actually witnessed.
> - The aim is to present a true account.
>
> ### Historians
>
> - Narrativise by plotting events that actually happened.
>
> ### Novelists
>
> - Narrativise by plotting events that they wish the reader to believe could have happened.
> - The fictional account can be intended to seem as if it could have happened by having the fictional world work according to the same laws as our own world.
> - The account can be fantastical in that the fictional world works according to different laws from our own; these laws must still make sense to us though!

Narrativisation works differently in fictional and non-fictional texts. In fictional texts, emplotment creates coherence and gives shape to experience and emotion; in realist novels the emplotment facilitates a sense of verisi-militude. In non-fictional texts the emplotment facilitates the truth effect of the text by the selection and presentation of events and actors in a text that has a supporting infrastructure of description, reference to other works, referencing and citation of sources. We can see how this works in the creation of historical writing. In discussing the use of narrative in writing history, Polkinghorne (1988: 61–2) writes that historical narrative comprises two kinds of referents, those of the first order – the events that make up the story—and those of the second order – the plot. The information content of these narratives exists at both the level of the sentence and at the level of the discourse where a higher level of coherence is created by ordering the sentences. He notes that historical texts, as other kinds of non-fiction texts, do not only depend on emplotment to create coherence: such texts will also draw upon logical structures of argument and on paradigmatic discourse, which presents knowledge in terms of discrete hierarchies of categories. In historical writing a key paradigmatic device is the chronicle: a listing of events in which each event is located in a specific time period. The key point to grasp here is that the chronicle does not make any causal connections between the events it records; in other words, a chronicle is a listing of events with no plot. Polkinghorne asserts that 'historical narratives

are expansions of the type of paradigmatic discourse called the chronicle'
(1988: 61). The meaning of the chronicle derives from the location of
events in objective or real time. When these events are emplotted in narrative form, the author renders the chronicled events in a different time
frame, one which she determines; this emplotted time frame, which is discourse time, is for Polkinghorne (1988: 61) 'historical or recollective time':
'As narrative discourse, historical writing does not use formal logic as its
protocol for patterning events into a unified plot; but neither does it use
patterns of sound and meter of formal poetry. Its concern is with the patterns of events as they contribute to a story's plot' (1988: 62). The meaning
in historical narrative, as in literature, is produced by means of plotting. The
difference between literature and non-fiction narrative is that the events in
non-fiction are supposed to be real, while those in literature are fictional.

In summary then, plotting (i.e. selecting) which events are to be represented, and in what order, is a key element of the process of narrativisation.

Analysing a Fantasy Narrative: *The Lord of the Rings*

Let us put some of these ideas to work. J.R.R. Tolkien (1892–1973) wrote
the fantasy novel *The Lord of the Rings,* a work which is on some estimates
the most popular work of fiction published in the twentieth century (Shippey,
2005). The Peter Jackson film adaptions are among the highest grossing films
ever produced. Tolkien is credited with establishing an entire genre of epic
fantasy. Certainly his narratives are justly famed for their richness. He was a
philologist who invented completely new languages and mythologies, histories and geographies, in which he set human and non-human characters. He
built entire imaginary worlds, and then stories, songs, poetry, and different
kinds of historical text in order to bring his story to life. Let us apply some
of the analytical tools we discussed in this chapter to this work of fiction.

Box 3.6   Narrative overview of Tolkien's *The Lord of the Rings*

Genres

- Epic.
- Quest.
- Helped to define a subgenre of fantasy literature.

(Continued)

(Continued)

Discourse modes

- Narration is dominant.
- Supported by description.

Narrativity of the text: fictional in the main, but supported by extensive extracts from and allusions and cross references to 'historical' narratives (these 'histories' appear in full in other texts that Tolkien wrote, some of which were published after his death).

Narrativisation: Tolkien narrativises by emplotting events and rendering characters so as to persuade the reader that the events of the story could have happened. In addition, in appendices to the novel and in multiple other texts to which the novel refers, he uses narrative techniques of the historian, setting out and then drawing on chronologies and genealogies. Throughout the novel, Tolkien makes reference to a long prior history. Though he would not have used the term, I would argue that Tolkien also employed ethnographic techniques in his work, in the preface and appendices to *Lord of the Rings,* as well as in other texts, in which he emplots events and characters in accounts of social and cultural settings, drawing on detailed 'data' of 'races', kinship systems, belief systems, and systems of governance. *The Lord of the Rings* is a complex multi-layered narrative.

We can usefully apply some basic concepts of structuralist analysis to the *The Lord of the Rings.* As an example, let us apply Todorov's framework, which we discussed earlier in this chapter, to examine Tolkien's novel as story structure. This exercise is largely a syntagmatic analysis: in following the sequence of events as structured by the author, we can consider what Levi-Strauss referred to as the 'manifest' or the 'overt' content of the story.

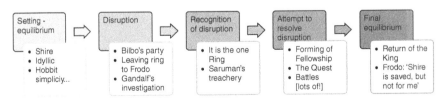

Figure 3.2   Narrative structure of *The Lord of the Rings*

Staying with the structuralist tradition, we can turn to a paradigmatic analysis of Tolkien's novel in which we examine the main structural oppositions in the work. These oppositions give us insight into the moral world-view and the motivations for the actions of the human and human like characters in the story. This is for Levi-Strauss the latent aspects of a narrative, where we can analyse *why* the events that are emplotted along the syntagmatic access took place. The syntagmatic analysis tells us what happened, but the paradigmatic tells us why events happened in the way that they did, and why agents acted in the way they did, given the possibilities of the world in which the narrative is set.

Table 3.1   Paradigmatic analysis of *The Lord of the Rings*

Paradigmatic analysis: key structural oppositions in LOTR			
		Manifest [denotation]	Latent [connotation] – myth is at work here
West	East	Geography	Culture, morality
Fair (Elf)	Dark (orc)	Luminescence	Morality, good vs evil
Fair Speech	Orc Speech	Linguistic difference	Moral hierarchy; a beautiful language implies a beautiful people /culture etc.
White	Black	Colour spectrum	Moral distinction
Light (Elf)	Dark (Elf)	Variation within a group	Measure of enlightenment
Cold	Hot	Temperature	Climate indicates/determines character

Analytical Templates

In order to apply the various analytical approaches we've discussed so far, it is useful to think of these as templates that you bring to bear on the material you wish to analyse. These templates need not be overly complicated, in fact you can get started by using a simple table that sets out on the left the issues and criteria that you wish to deal with, with empty space to the right which you can fill in by typing or copy/paste from the source texts, or summarise those parts of the text you are studying. In Chapter 6 I give advice on how to implement some of these analytical frameworks in both general and specialised software, but here I will take a more generic approach that requires no special software; a word processor, or pencil and paper, and some time to think are all that you need to get started on analysing narrative. I have not presented templates here for the structuralist approaches, because by their very nature an explanation of how they work is also a presentation of their structure; I have, however, included templates for all of these on the book's website (www.narrativenetworks.net). Here I offer a description of the templates; you will find them most useful if you download them from the website.

All of the templates presented here are available on that companion website, in three formats:

1. Microsoft Word template.
2. OPML (a generic format that can be imported into many outlining and mind map packages on both PC and Mac).
3. NVivo template projects (for both PC and Mac).

The templates comprise either a table or a hierarchical set of analytical concepts and codes, with each concept and code having an accompanying descriptive text. Each template also contains a list of references to works from which the template was derived.

In using the templates, you should note the following:

- Social research and social theory will determine how you employ the analytical approaches I outlined in this chapter: this book is addressed to sociologists and anthropologists who want to work with narrative material, not to narratologists or linguists.
- These templates are guides to start you thinking analytically; they are not mechanical aids to be rigidly applied. The templates are in a sense concept maps, and not all of the concepts will be equally applicable, or applicable at all, to every narrative text with which you work. You should be prepared to modify these templates/maps as the needs of your own work suggest.
- Labov's structural approach is of general use; applicable to both written and oral narrative (after transcription) of various lengths.
- It is essential to bear in mind that narrative operates at several levels, at the sentence level, and also at the discourse level. A narrative sentence connects two or more story events; a narrative discourse also connects story events, some of which may themselves be made of smaller combined narrative units. Discourse analysis (and critical discourse analysis) are important for the analysis of narrative because a narrative is a type of discourse, and in order to work with narratives, we must have some understanding of the tools that have been developed to analyse discourse (and discourses) in general.
- At times you will have to determine the narrativity of a text, which can be done either categorically by discourse mode or text-type analysis, or more flexibly and for longer and more complex texts, by using the concepts of narrativity and narrativisation.
- At other times you will be certain that you have narrative material at the very start of your analysis, and your main early task is to decide on the best analytical strategy.

- In some situations you might want to generate narrative from various kinds of event data: understanding how narratives work in structural and thematic terms is clearly of use to you in creating narratives of your own. In a later chapter I look at the creation of narrative from the point of view of a social researcher.

Semiotics template

This is a generic template. Berger suggests that this scheme be used for analysis of all texts. You should find it useful for making notes on the range of semiotic features that can be found in a text.

Table 3.2   Semiotics template

Syntagmatic elements
Event sequences
Causal links
Real connections among people, places and things
Overt meaning
Paradigmatic elements
Structural oppositions
Virtual connections among people, places and things
Latent meaning
Other Semiotic features
Icons
Indexes
Symbols
Synecdoche: part-whole relations of various types
Metaphor
Metonymy

Discourse analysis templates

For the analyst of narrative, these templates are useful for the analysis of any kind of text, not just narratives: you might find them especially useful for thematic analysis, where you want to investigate what the narrative is seeking to say and why.

Bax's heuristic for discourse analysis

Bax (2011; based on the framework he set out in Chapter 5) suggests that we pose three fundamental questions: What does the text achieve? How does it achieve its aims? Why does it seek to do what it does?

What does the text achieve (or not)?   The analyst first considers each text in context, so as to identify its impact or effect in broad terms:

• Impacts on readers or listeners – cognitively, socially.
• Function of text.
• Wider impact – beyond individual reader or listener.
• Any other impacts.

How does the text achieve this?   The analyst can then consider how each text achieves that impact or effect. In essence, the analyst seeks to identify the ways in which particular features of the text relate to their function(s).

What are the core features of the texts, and how do they relate to the overall function(s)?   These features might include reference to the following:

• Aspects of the text structure.
• Main discourse modes (narrative is our main interest here).
• Layout and AV resources.
• Significant intertextual links.
• Grammatical, lexical and phonological elements.

Why does the text seek to do this?   At this point the analyst could consider why the texts do what they do, including the following questions as relevant.

What other resources do these texts employ in order to achieve their effects?   Socio-political and ideological underpinnings.

• What does it foreground, and why?
• What does it obscure or 'background' and why?

Gee's schema

As with the Bax, this scheme from Gee is for general discourse analysis, and may be useful to you in thematic analysis. For Gee (2005, see Chapter 2) discourse (with a small d) is about 'language in use' and 'building things through language', which involves the following:

1. Significance – language is used to give things meaning or value.
2. Activities – we use language to be recognised as engaging in certain activities.
3. Identities – taking on/asserting an identity or role.
4. Relationships – to signal having or wanting to have certain kinds of relationships with others.
5. Politics – convey a perspective on the nature and distribution of social goods.

6. Connection – to render things connected or relevant (or not).
7. Signed systems and knowledge – everyday language, standardised technical, and/or specialised.

Templates for analysing narrative

As a first step in conducting any analysis of a narrative text, we can apply a widely accepted definitional framework. According to Chatman (1978: 26) a narrative text comprises a Story (content) and Discourse (expression). A Story is made up of Events and Existents. Events in turn are of two types: Actions, which are events caused by a character (she opened the window); and Happenings, which are events that have no human cause (the rain fell, or the sun set). Existents comprise Characters, and are human, animate or human-like, so people, animals, robots or even aliens can cause events to happen. Setting comprises the background to the story. The Events and Existents together make up the content of the Story. For Chatman, the Events and Existents are the form of the content, while the actual named people, objects and places are the substance of the content. You can think of the Events and Existents as abstract place holders (form) for the people and places (substance or content) of the Story. The Discourse of the narrative will have a structure (the most basic of which is the three part structure of equilibrium, disruption, and new equilibrium, as first set out by Aristotle as we saw earlier in the chapter). In addition the Discourse will be manifested as a substantive object such as a novel, a film or a comic strip. These points are illustrated in Figure 3.3.

The three-act structure

This is the most basic template, moving from *Equilibrium* (Act 1), to *Disruption* (Act 2), to *Restoration of (New) Equilibrium* (Act 3). Bear in mind that a narrative need not follow this strict sequence and that it is quite common to open a narrative in the Disruption stage and use flashbacks to present the Equilibrium; moreover, a narrative can use flash forward to present elements of a later stage. We are all familiar with these variations on the three-act narrative from film, television and fiction. You job as an analyst using this simple scheme is to tag or code events and sequences of events in the story as belonging to the relevant stages/acts. The actual ordering of the narrative is a matter of the narrative discourse through which the author of the narrative chose to present the story. *You* must make the analytical distinction between the story and the narrative discourse.

Masterplot

It can be useful to think about whether the narrative to be analysed is derived from any kind of generic story form. The concept of the masterplot might be helpful here. Abbott (2008: 236) defines masterplots as:

Recurrent skeletal stories, belonging to cultures and individuals that play a powerful role in questions of identity, value, and the understanding of life. Masterplots can also exert an influence on the way we take in new information, causing us to overread or underread narratives in an often unconscious effort to bring them into conformity with a masterplot.

You should note the following:

- Overreading: when we import into a text material that is not signified in it.
- Underreading: when we ignore material that is signified in a text.
- The term is 'masterplot' and *not* 'masternarrative'; for Abbott the skeletal story is a guide as to how to arrange actual events into an actual story, to apply the skeletal story is to plot these events. All of this takes place below the level of the narrative.

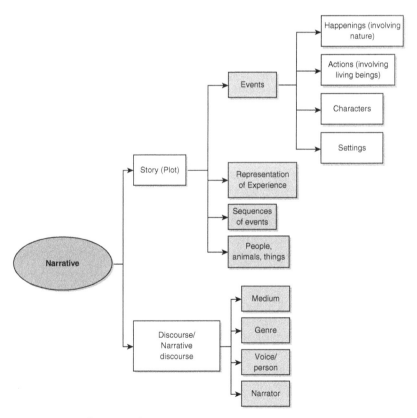

Figure 3.3   Basic features of narrative

Thematic analysis

In working with thematic analysis of narrative text, you should bear the following in mind:

- Work, at least initially, with a broad definition of 'narrative'.
- Focus on what is said.
- Remember that themes frequently come from prior research and are often refined and supplemented by work on the selected materials.
- Remember also that the narrative materials are often used to confirm, exemplify, illustrate, and explore these prior themes.
- Focus on the individual text as a whole. Even if you are working with multiple narratives/cases, you should work on each text as a whole – *after* close reading of the individual text, you can then move on to explore themes across texts.

You might want to use a template structured as a table (in many instances you will be working with just one narrative text/case). For example:

		Theme	Theme	Theme
Narrative text	(case)			
Narrative text	(case)			
Narrative text	(case)			

Analysis of Digital Narratives

The theory and methods for analysis of narrative have been tried and tested in print, graphics, film and television. We should not however assume that these methods of analysis will adapt unproblematically to digital media. In the following chapter we will look at a number of exemplar works in which narrative approaches were employed to work in various kinds of digital media, but I will foreshadow that survey here by highlighting some characteristics of digital media that must be borne in mind by a researcher wanting to work narratively with them.

Hypertext stories

We live in a world saturated by digital media and much of the text we consume is in digital form. Taking the World Wide Web as the definitive example of digital textual communication, we can see immediately that one of its key properties – the hyperlink – means that our analysis and construction of narrative must be adjusted to take into account this new aspect of textual openness (Dicks, 2005; Dicks and Mason, 2011). Texts have always been open to some extent, but hypermedia bring a new degree of openness. In one sense, the chunks of text that are linked in a hypertext network (often referred to as *lexia*) can be treated as any other text. For relatively short texts we can apply discourse mode or text-type tests to determine if the text is narrative. More generally we can examine longer texts for narrativity using the concepts we discussed earlier in this chapter. Yet in another sense there is a fundamental property of hypertext which makes a network of hyperlink lexia extremely problematic as an object for analysis of narrative. The fundamental issue here is that however defined, narrative text is characterised by a coherence that links human and non-human agents, their actions, experiences and other happenings, into a temporal chain – the following of which leads us to some kind of conclusion. The problem here for thinking about 'hypertext narrative' lies in the very nature of hypermedia: unless the author of a hypertext network deliberately imposes a narrative structure on that collection of texts, the collection will have a degree of openness which militates against narrative coherence. Put another way, the greater the openness of a set of hyperlink texts then the lesser the narrativity of that collection of texts. So hypertext reality and narrativity exist in an inverse relationship. When working with hypertext stories there is additional work involved in establishing narrative coherence above the level of the lexia.

We can see this illustrated in one variation on hypertext narrative that became a distinct sub-genre of interactive fiction. Among the best known examples are the classic text-based adventure games of the 1980s such as *Zork* and *The Hitchhiker's Guide to the Galaxy*. These are hybrids of hypertext narratives and games, in which the player is presented with narrative sequences followed by a prompt where the player may type in a set of actions that will determine where the story goes next. In this type of hypermedia there is an underlying narrative structure that is revealed in chunks to the player. The system's designer will have programmed a multi-threaded narrative that allows players to branch off, but which ultimately limits what they can do, and so they remain within the confines of the story world. Interactive fiction therefore sacrifices the open-ended possibilities of hypertext in order to maintain some degree of narrative coherence.

Videogames

Videogames are now a larger industry than film, but scholarly attention has been somewhat slow to engage with the expansion of the medium. In *Games of Empire* (2009), Dyer-Witherford and de Peuter write that for most of the first two decades after they were first developed in the 1960s there was no critical scholarly engagement with the products or their users. Then came a wave a negative commentary that saw videogames as simplistic and anti-social forms of entertainment, that too often glorified violence. The 1990s witnessed a reaction to this in the form of a new wave of critical commentary and academic studies that argued videogames were as deserving of serious study as literature or film. Computer games began to be taken seriously by scholars and by journalists. Researchers brought approaches from semiotics, film criticism, visual arts and design to the study of such games, and social scientists applied tools for survey and ethnography to the people who played those games and the communities that began to emerge on a rapidly expanding Internet. In the second decade of the twenty-first century the global value of videogames rivals that of the global cinema industry, and with close to two billion mobile phone users on the planet, most of whom game to some degree on their phones, the videogame is a core part of entertainment across the planet.

Among the critical tools applied to the study of videogames, narratology was adopted by many researchers. It is beyond doubt that we can discern narrative elements in such games. Cut scenes, i.e. mini cinematic sequences used to introduce many kinds of games and within those games to introduce players to new levels, are clearly amenable to analysis using established narrative approaches to film. Adventure and role-playing games display many story elements that frame the environment and experiences through which the player must proceed, but proceed to what? We read a narrative toward an ending that is an essential property of the discourse itself: all narrative discourses have a beginning, middle section and ending. But some game scholars argue that playing a game is not the same as reading a narrative, for the obvious reason that to play a game means to act in a system governed by rules, make choices, and aim to achieve a goal – winning the game (Dovey, 2006: Chapter 5). These 'ludologists' (from the Latin term meaning 'to play') further point out that the progression of events in a narrative is fixed in advance by the way its author plotted the story, whereas the progression of a game cannot, *by definition of what it means to play a game,* be determined in advance of the player making the next move, save that the rules of the game will set some limit on the range of possible moves a player is able to make. For the ludologists, a narratological approach can be useful in illuminating *some* aspects of games, but cannot properly deal with the experience of playing a game as against reading a narrative. Most game scholars would agree that while videogames are not narratives, they all possess narrative elements to some degree. With that caveat in mind, it is the case that narratological methods have been used to analyse game narratives (Ip, 2010a). The narrative properties of games have also been analysed from a thematic perspective, paying attention to what is being narrated in the game rather than how the narrative is constructed. Thematic analysis focuses on the settings, social and political relations, and the relationships between character types and real world identities. We will discuss how these approaches illuminate narrative in real videogames in the next chapter.

Analysing Social Networks and Social Media

One of the most notable features of social media and social networking sites is that they present us with a vast stock of spontaneous or ready-made discourse, some of which can be argued to be in narrative form. I will use Facebook as the example here, as it is the most widely used such site with more than one billion active users. How we understand narrative is important here, because it is not enough just to declare that Facebook postings or profiles are narratives and leave the matter at that. It is obviously the case that Facebook posts are a kind of event data, in that they are about something and the time of a post's creation and modification are attached to the post itself. But what do people do when they create entries in a social networking site? Are they engaged in a form of storytelling? And what of the narrativity of social media?

Let us start by considering the formal properties of social networking sites, using Facebook as an example (Boyd, 2011; Dijck, 2012). The main structural features of Facebook are as follows:

- The user profile, where biographical information and a wide range of preference and tastes can be presented.
- The friend list, which can be organised into subgroups that enable control over which friends see which posts.
- The public board, which is a reverse chronological stream of the user's own posts/status updates, those of their friends, updates from Facebook pages to which the user subscribed (apart of friends), and posts from advertisers. Facebook now organises the public board in terms of a timeline, allowing the user greater control over the time periods that are displayed and which items appear.
- Messaging – a private channel that enables the exchange of text messages.
- A chat window, in which the user can have real time chats with one or more friends using text mode, audio, or video chat.
- Photo album.
- Advertising sidebar.

Facebook combines the elements of scrapbook and journal (two traditional forms of storytelling) with newer possibilities for instant sharing/publishing. The personal scrapbook is a well-established practice and form for assembling stories. It combines text, drawings, and as technology allowes, photographs, clippings from print media, and even physical objects. More recently digital technology has expanded the media that can be collected within a scrapbook. Whatever the underlying technology, it is a collection of words, images and objects that are invested with meaning by the scrapbook's creator (Good, 2012). Items may be arranged chronologically or thematically. We may analyse someone's scrapbook and seek to understand

the logic of the contents: are there themes, is there a story? What is significant about the place and events and people represented in the scrapbook?
How do the different media used tell us something interesting about the
preceding questions?

Through its timeline, Facebook facilitates assemblages of text and audio
visual media that have story properties. Postings on a timelime, like those in
a blog or a personal diary/journal, are pre-packaged event data, but the significance of these events has to be established by drawing on one or more
of the approaches to analysing narrative that we discussed earlier in the
chapter. Like any other body of discourse, social media data can be analysed
by a narrative researcher through narratology, semiotics, discourse analysis, or
biographical analysis. As a preliminary step, we have to define what are event
data, and we also have to work out what would constitute a proper connection between events. Having defined narrative sequences, we can then
extract textual 'chunks' from the social media stream that we want to analyse,
and from there we can apply semiotics and discourse analysis to those texts.

One current buzzword in the already feverish development of social
media is that of 'personal analytics'. Analytics on social networks and social
media are potentially a rich source of data analysis of social media, provided
that we establish what would count as narrative from the base collection of
discourse in these media. Wolfram alpha (www.wolframalpha.com) offers a
'personal analytics' that can be applied to a Facebook account to which we
have full access. This is web-based tool that allows you to explore your
Facebook social network, in terms of how your friends cluster, where they
are located in the world, and how often you communicate with them. In
addition, you can analyse those friends' profiles and activity, as well as where
they are situated in a generic life course. You can also view the summaries
and frequency of your Facebook activity over time.

These 'personal analytics' can be useful to you as a narrative researcher
working with Facebook because it automates the processing of large
amounts of data into a form that is more manageable. The results are by no
means analysis of narrative, but they can be useful as input into a wider project. Let us look at how this can be useful. Wolfram alpha's Facebook report
displays the terms the user has employed most often in the form of a word
cloud: you then have options to display 'significant words', 'significant words
and pronouns', 'pronouns', and 'all words'. The 'significant words' is immediately useful as it gives insight into the lexis of the analysed postings which
could help with discourse analysis. Another useful analytic output includes
the most commented-on posts and photos and the most frequent comment-
ers on these, which can be helpful in exploring posts and comments as event
data as stories in the interaction between/among two or more persons.

Most of these analytics, and especially the social network analysis of a
person's Facebook friends, are not directly relevant to analysis of Facebook
material as narrative. Rather, depending on your research questions, these

analytics can yield useful contextual information that can inform your project. Should you decide to use these analytics, it is vital that you find out what the assumptions are on which these are based: Wolfram alpha's founder has several posts on the site's blog where he explains the thinking behind personal analytics.

Having decided on what will count as narrative for your analysis of Facebook data, and whether analytics of the type produced by Wolfram alpha might be of use to your work, you next need to choose a suitable narratological approach for the identified elements. We will discuss work that analysed social networks as narrative in the next chapter; for now I suggest lines of investigation that you should consider in planning for analysing these kinds of data as narrative. From an initial examination of the semiotic properties of a user profile, we can move on to working with individual posts as event data for a connecting analysis. Extracting the posts is not technically difficult – this can be done manually using copy/paste and then imported into a qualitative data analysis package such as NVivo 10 or 'scraped' using a script that you can write yourself if you have that skill. What is difficult is accessing the profiles. If the users you want to study are unwilling to give the passwords (very likely to be the case), you might be able to get them to copy and paste the parts of their timelines in which you are interested. Alternatively, they could grant you temporary access to their pages so that you could run a script on those pages to extract what you need, and then they could inspect the result to assure themselves as to the content of the material they are sharing with you. Users can export the contents of their Facebook pages to an html file, and then pass that over to you for analysis.

Having surmounted the access and permission issues, getting hold of the data is relatively easy. Assuming you have reached the stage where you have gathered the Facebook data you require, then you have manage these as event data, i.e. as data with a time stamp attached. Once you have full access to the timeline data either directly or through import and then reconstruction in some kind of analytical software package, you can begin to generate the time sequences you want. NVivo's (from version 10 onwards) dataset presents Facebook data that it imports in a tabular format, which makes sorting and searching easier.

Structural approaches can shed light on how events are organised into stories and conveyed, and this applies to Facebook. A single post recalling an event is well suited to being read using Labov's scheme. Connecting a series of posts and comments can be the start of exploring how a person has structured a life story in social media. User profiles can be read in terms of a story about the self. The structural properties of Facebook lend themselves to creating autobiographical narrative discourses, but what about other types? Thematic analysis offers possibilities as well for addressing what is being told in Facebook posts and profiles. Messages and chat lend themselves to analysis in terms of the how narrative is constructed in interaction.

Summary

In this chapter we discussed some of the main approaches to the analysis of narrative. The survey was a partial and necessarily tight discussion of a vast field that spans several disciplines. My purpose was not to teach you how to become a narratologist, but to introduce some narratological theories and methods that are of use to the social researcher. The list of further reading that follows will direct you to some of the main works on narrative theory and method.

We now have a guide as to how to structure a project of narrative analysis in social research. The steps that follow are not in a fixed order, and note that not all of these are necessary for every kind of project and the list is not exhaustive:

1. Identification of the narrative text is necessary to ensure the validity of your project: this can be done for relatively short texts by using discourse mode analysis (Bax, 2011); for longer and more complex texts you should assess the extent to which key concepts of narrativity and narrativisation are present in your text. You should do this even if you are certain that your text is narrative from the outset, as it is always useful to reflect on the narratvitity of your materials in order to decide on the best strategy for analysis.
2. You should explore the core narrative features of your texts. What are the events, agents, characters, and experiences in the text? Who is the author? What is the stance of the narrator (e.g. first or third person, partial or all-seeing, embedded or 'objective')? What are the structural features – story, plot, narrative genre (fiction, ethnography, history, and biography)? How is the story being told – the narrative discourse?
3. You should explore the textual features of your material: syntax, lexis, and rhetoric. Are there ideological positions being made explicit, or do they remain implicit? Are there visual materials (handling visual materials is not addressed in this book, but see Becker, 2007, Chapters 10, 11; McClean, 2008; Riessman, 2008, Chapter 6) and/or multimedia? Tools from discourse analysis and critical discourse analysis can be useful here.
4. What emerges from structural analysis? A set of categories that describe the internal structure of narratives, and which can be applied to any number of narrative texts for purposes of comparison and classification.
5. What is the narrative about? What is being told? Even if you are not aiming to undertake a full thematic analysis, you must give consideration to this. While content and form are interrelated, it is useful to anaylse these as distinct properties of a narrative text, using the most appropriate tools.
6. Being social scientists, we always come back to the social and cultural setting. A key question for us is this: what is the social and cultural context for the creation and reception of the narrative on which we are working?

7. The analytical templates I presented in the chapter are intended to support you as you work though these issues and as such they are general guides, not rigid recipes. You can download these in different formats from the book's website.

Questions to consider

1. For analysis of narrative
    a. Outline the key points of structuralist analysis of narrative.
    b. Outline key points of thematic analysis of narrative.
    c. Think about why you would use either of the two above in your own narrative research project, or, why you might want to draw on both types of analysis in the same project.
2. Why is discourse analysis important for a narrative researcher?
3. What are the special features of videogames and hypertexts that make them potentially problematic for analysis as narratives?
    a. What are the narrative elements of videogames?
    b. Think about now narrativity and interactivity relate to each other
4. What must you consider before engaging in an analysis of social networking sites as sources of narrative?
    a. How would you identify narrative in social networking and social media?
    b. What methods would you use to analyse social media narrative?

Further reading

Bax, D. S. (2011) *Discourse and Genre: Using Language in Context* (1st edn). Basingstoke: Palgrave Macmillan.

Berger, A.A. (1997) *Narratives in Popular Culture, Media, and Everyday Life.* Thousand Oaks, CA: Sage.

Chatman, S. (1978) *Story and Discourse: Narrative Structure in Fiction and Film.* Ithaca, NY: Cornell University Press.

Clandinin, D.J. (ed.) (2007) *Handbook of Narrative: Inquiry Mapping a Methodology.* Thousand Oaks, Calif. ; London: SAGE, Available from: http://srmo. sagepub.com/view/handbook-of-narrative-inquiry/SAGE.xml.

Elliott, J. (2005) *Using Narrative in Social Research: Qualitative and Quantitative Approaches.* London: Sage.

Franzosi, R. (2004) *From Words to Numbers: Narrative, Data, and Social Science.* Cambridge: Cambridge University Press.

Riessman, C.K. (2008) *Narrative Methods for the Human Sciences.* Thousand Oaks, CA: Sage.

4

NARRATIVE AT WORK IN
THE WORLD

OVERVIEW

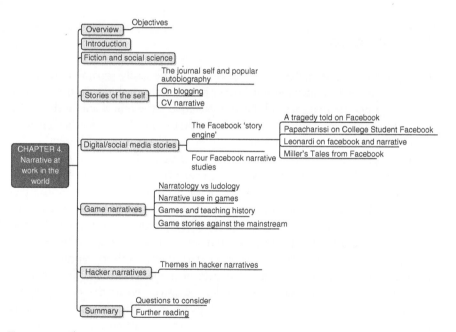

Figure 4.1   Chapter map

Key learning objectives

- To distinguish between a first and second order narrative.
- To apply our knowledge of theories of narrative to examine how narratives are used in stories about the self.
- To discuss narrative aspects of social media, using several studies of Facebook.
- To discuss research on narrative in videogames.
- To discuss how narratives have been used by hackers to represent themselves, and by others on hackers and hacker culture.
- To apply the analytical frameworks discussed in the previous chapter to the discussion of cases and exemplar work.
- To develop the ability to read narrative research.

Introduction

Using narrative and analysing narrative cannot be easily separated; however as social scientists concerned with narrative we must do both. In this chapter we look at people making and sharing narrative – the tellers and authors, the listeners and readers, the relations between them, and the media they employ. Note that here is one distinction that you *must* bear in mind here: the difference between first and second order narrative. First order narrative is narrative produced by people as part of everyday activity, 'everyday activity' here referring to whatever people do apart from social research (and especially social research involving narrative!). Second order narrative is narrative produced by social researchers as part of their work to understand some aspect of social life. In narrative research some second order narrative refers to the form and substance of first order narrative: an ethnographic text is a good example of this – the subject matter of such an ethnography could be narratives told by informants (first order narrative), while the ethnographic account (second order narrative) will display some narrative elements in its presentation and analysis of the narrative materials gathered in the field.

Fiction and Social Science

While narratology and literary criticism are huge domains in their own right, sociologists and anthropologists have taken fictional narratives as objects of analysis (Rapport, 1994; Ruggiero, 2003; Swingewood, 1975). The sociology of literature applies existing sociological theory and methods to literary works, most often works of fiction. As Swingewood notes (1975: 14), 'Literature is not a passive reflection of determinate interests – class, race environment – or merely the personal biography of the writer; rather, literature emerges as both an interrogation and a questioning of reality, the complex response of specific men [sic], who live out their lives within specific social groups, to the dominating human, social and political problems of their time.' Berger (1977) argued that the novel and social science have long had similar aims: both sought to address the situation of the individual in the context of emergent modern industrial society. As anthropologist Nigel Rapport (1997: 25) sees it 'the actual nature of the human world is of individuals in action . . . moreover, knowledge of these personal relations is individual knowledge. There is nothing else for it to be.' Individuals in action and their relations are at the core of the myriad stories we create and share for Rapport, who has applied ethnographic methods to the fictional worlds created by E.M. Forster.

In *Drinkers, Drummers and Decent Folk* (1989), cultural anthropologist John Stewart brings into question the distinction between social scientific (in this case ethnographic) and fictional texts. He argues that what the ethnographer does when writing ethnography is similar to what the novelist does when writing a novel. On this view ethnographers need to be aware of how literary devices like metaphor, plot, characterisation and symbolism work to construct texts, including and especially, their own ethnographic texts. Stewart's book weaves life history, short story and more conventional ethnography into an account of village life in Trinidad. In arguing for a 'literary ethnographic' approach he suggests that science and communication are distinct categories, and that the results of ethnographic enquiry may be communicated in different ways and need not be restricted only to scientific terms. This is very much in keeping with Bruner's fundamental distinction between classifying and narrating modes of knowing.

The events, characters and experiences inscribed in realist novels have referents in our everyday world – this is true almost by definition of what social realism is and is why fiction can bring forth emotional responses in us as readers: our own experience and knowledge and ideology serve to affirm or deny or distance us from the characters and situations in the realist novel. But the relationship, such as it is, between the world of the realist novel and our own world, is not a direct one. Reading fiction is more than checking off characters and situations in the text against our own reality, it is creative act that draws upon our fundamental capacity to shape our sense of being in the world in narrative terms. As we read a fictional narrative, something new is created in our imagination out of an interplay between the world of the text and our own world.

When trying to come to terms with a world as inscribed in an ethno-graphy or a personal narrative such as a biography or autobiography, we might be able to corroborate or challenge the ethnographic or biographical data by drawing on other ethnographic or biographical data or on wider social science or historical literature. But we may still be left with a feeling of distance from the world in the ethnographic or biographical text, per-haps because the stories narrated in an ethnography or a biography ask us to enter into a contract with the author, whom we accept, at least provi-sionally, to be telling the truth. All narrative social researchers should be aware of what work has been done on the sociology and anthropology of fictional narrative, but in this chapter I am concerned with the non-fiction uses of narrative.

Stories of the Self

People narrate stories in the course of their everyday lives for all kinds of reasons. Often they will do so to make sense of their own lives and the world around them. The focus of this section is on how social researchers can use such stories to gain insight into some of the fundamental concerns of sociology and anthropology, such as social and cultural identities, social processes, and cultural representations.

Brian Fay asked 'do we live stories or just tell stories?' (1996, see chapter 9). This question is quite appropriate for a consideration of how narrative is used by people in their everyday lives, *and* how social scientists use narra-tives. If we live stories it implies that our lives follow a kind of script or perhaps a plot, and that being socialised into a given society and culture involves learning to recognise and follow fundamental stories by means of which we can act our lives. If, on the other hand, we just tell stories, the implication is that those stories are the means whereby we give meaning to and justify the actions that we take throughout the course of living our lives. The difference here, to put it another way, is between following a script or plot on the one hand, and on the other hand, using a script or plot to make retrospective sense of our actions.

We rely on narrative modes of understating in order to make sense of our lives and decide on how to act. Giddens (1991) asserted that there are three existential questions that are characteristic of late modernity: What to do? How to act? Who to be? I would like to suggest that our answers to these questions are framed in terms of masterplots and realised as narratives. For Giddens we respond to the challenges posed by these questions through authoring narrative projects that connect our past to our imagined and desired future. This construction is in constant interaction with the social and cultural contexts in which the individual life is lived. In working on ourselves and our identities we engage in practices that connect habits to bodily appearance and practices of eating, exercise, sex and more. The self is a work constantly in progress, and we constantly monitor and adjust that work. Giddens draws attention to the vast array of self-help manuals, diets, fitness programmes, and therapies of all kinds that promise to enable us to become the person we want to be. He notes that self-help is a reflexive project that places on the individual the responsibility for implementing desired changes. Lifestyle (worked out through the life plan), as he sees it, is not only about consumption but also about work; it implies choice, agency, and information. A lifestyle is a cluster of characteristics. In all this Giddens sees the individual crafting and revising a personal narrative that connects the autobiographical past to the desired future, and from which that individual can judge opportunities and risks so as to decide what is the best course of action to pursue in order to live the desired life.

So, who we are and how we should act are questions that we seek to answer by drawing on sets of personal stories combined into an autobio-graphical narrative that explains our present in terms of a biographical trajectory. We then project from this present into a future in which we hope to become who we want to be. In shaping our desired selves, we draw upon a range of techniques for self-improvement, and we use a diverse range of technologies and media, including social networking and social media, in order to connect the past and present. We both live *and* tell our lives as stories. Let us turn to journaling, popular biography and auto-biography, and the crafting of the CV, in order to see how this works in practice.

The journal self and popular autobiography

The personal journal is a very private document, a place where the author records and reflects on life's events. Knowledge of the self in the personal journal is retrospective knowledge and therefore potentially narrative self-knowledge. The contents of a personal journal are a chronicle of the author's life. This is all we can know for certain about another person's personal journal: a collection of journal entries do not of themselves possess much by way of narrativity. If the author were to recast the personal journal into turning points where key life choices were made, and to think about events in terms of causes and consequences, then we are looking at the emergence of a narrative self-knowledge. One noticeable feature of the expansion of self-help therapies is that of journaling as a way to mental and physical well-being. In various fields of psychotherapy there has been an increase in the use of journaling as a form of or a supplement to therapy

(Thompson, 2009) alongside an expansion of non-specialist books and online resources on journaling aimed at the general reader. The International Association for Journal Writing (http://iajw.org/) brings together people from a range of different disciplines, all with a focus on the creative and therapeutic potential of journal writing. The IAJW offers its members a wide range of articles, online classes and 'telechats', and discussion forums. The organisation's website asserts that journal writing is a cycle during which you spend some of your time creating the journal contents, and some of your time 'harvesting' from your journal; the harvest comprises self-knowledge, which I would add is framed as personal narrative by the very journaling processes of writing and reflection.

The growth in resources and workshops for journal writing must be set in the context of the expansion of self-help, life-coaching, and personal development practices that we saw in the earlier discussion of Giddens's work on self and identity in late modernity. The spread of the web-connected portable computing devices enables these developments, with myriad software tools and apps that facilitate the creation, editing and sharing of life event data. Indeed the Web has given a huge boost to popular autobiography and biography, with apps and websites making it easy for anyone to assemble a life story and even to present it in the form of a printed book using print on demand technology. A great deal of the research work required to gather genealogical data is now made easier by websites such as Ancestry.com, and templates and interactive prompts mean that a person can simply fill in the details of a life story and the software can produce a well-formatted personal narrative text, including pictures and multimedia elements. It is no longer mainly the rich, powerful and famous who enjoy the privilege of having their lives rendered in biographical narratives. Just as digital photography brought to the masses tools and techniques that used to be the preserve of professional photography, so too have the means to produce personal narratives been made widely accessible through digital information technologies (King, 2010; Roorbach & Keckler, 2008).

On blogging

Blogging took off in the 1990s. Its impact is explicable in terms of its continuities with already existing journaling and diaristic practice, and through its facilitation of easy publishing due to its being web-based. Clearly any literate person has the skill necessary to keep a diary/journal, and people have been doing so for centuries. The personal journal on paper was private: those of us who kept one will recall our anxiety/horror at the prospect of another person reading it without our consent. We construct a sense of who we were and are through reflection on the entries in our personal journal. Journaling is in this case a private and introspective affair. Blogging shares with the keeping of a journal the formal property of being organised into dated entries, but is different in that the blogger has an audience in mind. I would treat the *private* blog as a digital version of the personal diary/journal, as it is part of the character of blogging that there is at least one other reader apart from the author. Comparing the personal journal to the blog is akin to comparing private retrospection to public retrospection. The blogger constructs a storied self in public, and readers' comments become part of the retrospection on the contents of the posted entries. For many bloggers, their blogs are a means whereby they can be themselves in public; many bloggers see their blogs as a textual public version of themselves (Reed, 2005). Technology has moved on since the early days of blogging, leading data scientist Stephen Wolfram to reflect on 'life analytics' (http://blog.stephenwolfram.com/2012/03/the-personal-analytics-of-my-life/). Wearable technology now offers new possibilities for digital recording of a person's entire audio-visual environment. This is an area to watch.

CV narrative

The CV is a kind of late modern autobiographical narrative. The Latin term 'Curriculum Vitae' renders as 'course of life' in English; and the course ('curriculum') is a kind of story. A CV is an instance of using narrative to construct a specific kind of self-presentation, one intended for an audience with specific expectations regarding the characteristics of the applicant for the post which is being applied for. In a CV we weave selected events and experiences from our own life into a narration of the suitable candidate.

Topics highlighted in a CV are connected by explicit narrative sequences (short texts or sentences such as where a job and its requirements are described, where an applicant states how they acted in such a way that indicates that they already possessed the skills required for that job, or developed them in the course of doing that job). Initiative, creativity, discipline, and flexibility are all characteristics that are demonstrated on the CV by making explicit or implicit narrative sequences that connect those experiences you choose to write about and qualities, the characteristics you wish to demonstrate, and to show that your experiences and qualifications led to your being the right person for that job.

You choose which experiences to highlight, you assign significance, you construct periods, gaps have to be managed. The basic structural features of a CV are sections that address the various aspects of your personal and professional development. The main sections include secondary schooling, university, technical training, work experience, other skills, languages spoken etc. The temporal ordering of events produces effects. Strict chronology renders a straightforward biographical development, while the reverse chronological order works backwards from the present to the earliest stages. On reflection it becomes clear that both orderings possess narrativity: as pointed out at several places in this book, we live our lives prospectively but tell our lives retrospectively. The functional CV stresses our skills and achievements over chronology; it is generally seen as best for professional persons, while the strict chronological ordering is used more for a younger person just out of school or college. Whichever temporal ordering we choose for our CV, we are ordering our development based on our retrospective self-knowledge and with a view to communicating a certain view of who we are to the reader. The chronological and functional structures are different narrative discourses, i.e. different ways of telling our professional life story. The underlying story of our educational and professional progress is fundamentally a sequence of events and experiences that we recall for rendering in CV form. We emplot a CV not only by ordering events but also by our initial selection of which events to include; we also emplot by choosing what to highlight in each section and by deciding which start and end dates to include. Descriptive passages help the reader by supplying details on the events in the CV. We employ rhetorical devices to convey to the reader our suitability for the post we are applying for: we use *comparison; exemplification,* as in the kinds of tasks we successfully completed in previous employment, or subjects or authors we studied in education; and *encomium* (to praise a thing by reference to its characteristics), as for example when we refer to the characteristics of an employer or school so as to cast these, and by extension ourselves, in a positive light through our association with that employer or school.

The CV generally uses the simple past tense ('studied', 'worked') and most often employs the first person ('I worked', 'I trained') or may omit any personal pronoun altogether, in which case the reader would take the author and the subject of the CV to be the same person. In the case of a third person CV the third person pronoun or the subject's name would be used: third person CVs are frequently used in promotional materials by PR firms and publishers and on corporate communications regarding key personnel in an organisation or on project reports and proposals. A key lexical feature of the CV is the use of adjectives that contribute to the overall positive tone of 'selling' oneself as the best candidate for the post. You are advised to find one or more 'unique selling points' that are supposed to make you stand out from a field of other qualified candidates. As a life story the CV is very selective in that it omits virtually all negative events and experiences, and if you must include a negative event, such as failing an examination or being dismissed from a post, you are advised to make as little of it as possible without being dishonest. Guides to writing an effective CV advise using keywords from the job description in order to craft your own personal summary; these keywords then become core elements in the lexis of the final CV. The thematic contents of the CV, i.e.which particular events and experiences and characteristics to include, are determined by the requirements of the post being applied for. There is a substantial industry of books, seminars and online resources that give guidance on how to write a CV as well as offer examples and templates. In addition, many colleges and universities and other 'training providers' (to use the currently fashionable term that captures the growing private sector in adult education) as well as state employment agencies offer these.

Miller and Morgan (1993), in a paper on the professional and specifically the academic CV, locate the CV in a set of 'auto/biographical' practices that come into play when we are called upon to make a presentation of our professional self. Drawing on Goffman's (1959) ideas of the presentation of the self, these two authors claim that the circumstances and audience expectations for the CV presentation are illuminated by the practices that form that CV. They write that the appraisal meeting is part confessional and part psychoanalytical session in which the person being appraised articulates an account of how they came to occupy the particular present set of circumstances in their professional life.

Digital/Social Media Stories

The Facebook 'story engine'

Facebook provides a vast collection of spontaneous material which is already organised as time-based data. For the first time in our history as a species, hundreds of millions of us are keeping what amount to diaries and scrapbooks in a digital form that is instantly searchable and sharable. This offers a potential goldmine for the narrative researcher (here I focus on Facebook as it is the most widely used social networking application, but what I discuss applies to other social network sites such as LinkedIn, the virtually now-defunct MySpace and a growing Google+, as well as the myriad other social networking sites). In the previous chapter we looked at the structural characteristics of Facebook and discussed some of the issues that arise in using this as a source of narrative material. In the previous chapter, we made note of the importance of thinking about the narrativity of user profiles, postings and comments, and the need to establish this rather than assume it to be the case. Here I want to return to the question of the narrativity of social networking sites and then discuss several exemplar works that addressed different aspects of Facebook in terms of the stories and narratives that users made on the site.

Facebook, as with other social networking sites, encourages and enables some activities and relationships, while constraining others (Papacharissi, 2009). A useful way to think about what users can and cannot do on a social networking site is in terms of *affordances:* the features/qualities of a material or digital technological object that allow or enable a person to do something. An affordance includes but covers more than usability. The creator of the technology will have designed certain features that users are expected to use: such features are affordances, but users may discover or invent other uses for a technological object that are outside the design of that object. Whatever we can do with an object is an affordance of that object, whether designed or intended. The personal computer is now known to provide affordances well beyond those of its original creators (Collins, 2010, see Chapter 2). As the technology evolved, so did the range of affordance expand in tandem. The same is true of Facebook, as of social networking sites more generally (Boyd, 2011), which was originally designed and built for use by students at an elite US university, and is now used by more than a billion people of every background and in every national state on the planet. As the social anthropologist Daniel Miller (whose work on Facebook I will discuss shortly) notes, Facebook is what people do on Facebook. So what *are* its narrative affordances?

Facebook has potential narrativity with respect to the journaling functions it affords, in part because journals (and scrapbooks and blogs) possess narrativity to some degree. Of the various features of Facebook, two stand out as being directly of relevance to thinking about it as a tool for narrative construction: the ability to jump to stories from your past, and the ability to represent and engage with the user's community. A key issue that a narrative researcher must consider when working with social network/media data has to do with what kind of persona is constructed in these media. As we shall shortly see in the discussion of several of our exemplar studies of Facebook that used narrative in various ways, the persona that we put to work in a social networking site is a construction and projection of our self that attempts to bridge the gap among our personal sense of self, our desire to be seen in certain ways by others, and our sense of how others see us. Work on the self and persona in social media owes much to the pioneering work on virtual identities carried out by Sherry Turkle (1985, 1995).

Facebook is a tool for reimagining community (Dijck, 2012; Parks, 2011). It has the potential to reverse the trend identified by classical sociologists such as Weber and Durkheim, who argued that modernity promoted the breakdown of ascriptive, 'traditional' identities, of belonging to close knit community. The shift from small-scale community to large-scale impersonal society offered greater possibilities for social mobility and cultural change, as well as different possibilities for identity construction. While these possibilities have often been seen and experienced as empowering for some, they come with increased anxiety about who one is and how one is to be in regard to others. Social networking sites offer a way to reimagine oneself as belonging to a close community, though that community is close in a virtual sense and not necessarily a physical community. Communities are partly symbolic constructions and can be distinguished by a shared set of narratives; belonging to a community is knowing and sharing that community's stories. Facebook, as with any other SNS, enables a kind of personal community; it affords a combination of intimacy and distance. When we look at the exemplar studies to follow, we will see how Facebook is implicated in the making and communicating of stories in and about communities.

Four Facebook narrative studies

A tragedy told on Facebook

On 9 December 2010 the *Washington Post* published 'A Facebook story: A mother's joy and a family's sorrow', based on events in the pregnancy, giving birth, and then death of 35 year old Shana Greatman Swers (Shapira, 2010). This piece is an example of building a narrative from Facebook event data. Ian Shapira, a *Washington Post* journalist, with the permission of Swers's family, transformed Facebook posts and comments into a narrative about the tragic death of this new mother. In an interview, the story's editor, Marc Fisher, explained how he and his team constructed the narrative (the interview is online at: www.niemanstoryboard.org/2010/12/10/facebook-as-narrative-the-washington-post-tries-it-out-online-and-in-print/). Fisher discussed the work of selection and structuring – in short, the emplotment of the events leading to the birth of Swers's baby, her subsequent severe illness, and death. The story as published in the newspaper presents a sequence of posts by Swers, interspersed with passages which give the reader background information on key characters (Swers, her husband and others). In the final story we see all the fundamental elements of a narrative: sequences of events that are causally linked, human characters and their experiences, and happenings. The narrative concludes with Swers's death from medical complications following her giving birth and her funeral. The very last posting is that of Swers's husband expressing his loss and love for his deceased spouse.

The raw material for a story originated in the events that Swers wrote about in her postings, events that chronicle her pregnancy and childbirth, with authorship passing from Swers on her death to her husband, who posted the news of her death and continued the chronicle to her funeral. This chronicle would have had narrative coherence for Swers and for her family, friends and doctors, but in order to have narrative coherence for people who did not know her, it had to be narrativised by Fisher, the journalist. The chronicle became for Swers and her intimates a first order narrative, because they had the background and contextual knowledge to frame the events in narrative terms. For the general reader, these events had to be transformed into a second order narrative by Fisher's emplotment, which made narrative sense of the events for those not part of the circle of family and friends.

In Facebook posts may or not be fully emplotted. Unless the poster is intentionally making a narrative, Facebook accounts of events are loosely structured. Individual posts may display the characteristics of mini narratives, especially if we apply a basic three-act structure of narrative as normal situation, challenge, and resolution, or if we use Labov's scheme. But in general Facebook posts are not explicitly written as emplotted. They may however be *read* as emplotted, which brings us to narrativisation as a reading activity: the comments and questions posted by Swers's Facebook friends suggest that they were 'following the plot', that plot being the unfolding events of her childbirth and illness. They could have made of these events a first order narrative. A second order narrative was constructed by the *Washington Post* editor. The case demonstrates the work required to generate a narrative from a set of postings that may have been storied for those persons closest to the events, but need to be plotted and contextualised for a general reader. If there is narrativity in Facebook, then we must work to reveal it, or perhaps we have to work to narrativise the social network.

Narcissism on college students' Facebook

Papacharissi's (2011) analysis of US college students' Facebook profiles employed visual anthropology and semiotics to study a sample of 333 college students, all of whom were interviewed about their use of the social networking site, and of these, 89 agreed to have their Facebook photographs examined further. The starting point for this study was the photograph as visual narrative: as Papacharissi notes, 'photographs have long served a significant function of preserving biographical memories [and they serve as] mnemonic devices for moments that bind us together' (2011: 251), and 'tagging of others and self-portrayal on Facebook is a contemporary means introducing the self and performing one's identity'. In this study narrativity was identified and analysed by bringing theories of visual storytelling to bear on the photographs. Paparchissi found that most of the photographs posted and tagged by the students were images that constructed scenes of college life, and persons of a different sex were generally presented in platonic poses. A large part of the visual narratives was of students having fun and often being silly together ('hanging out'), encompassing the fun side of being a college student. When the poster got a significant other, the content of the posted photos changed and the relationship now became the main focus of the narrative. Paparchissi sees a form of narcissism at work in the students' emphasis on self, but argues that this is a collectively performed narcissism through posting, tagging, retagging and commenting. It constructs a shared college life sociality and performs a college student identity:'the narcissism is not motivated by selfish desire, but by [a] desire to better connect the self to society'.

In this study we can see that the students used photos and comments on photos to assemble a representation of being a college student that would fit into a widely accepted set of practices and images about college life. There was a high degree of conformity in the events that were portrayed in the photos, and we can see also that the comments from other students on those photos served to reinforce a shared way of representing student life and to reaffirm that the posters and commentators were all engaged in similar activities. For this group, the stories that were being narrated on their Facebook pages were stories about college life that showed little variation in terms of class, gendered and ethnic identities. The students narrated activities that showed their being part of a shared college student culture. These Facebook college student pages story the lives of the students in terms of a set of narrative templates about a middle-class, North American, ideal type of student life. The photos display a similarity of themes, settings, poses, activities, tags and comments, which tells us there is a collective work of construction taking place in which all the participants are playing an agreed and shared role, with few exceptions. So Facebook afforded the means to make and share stories about the student self.

Facebook and narratives of identity

Leonardi (2010) addresses Facebook and communication as a rhetorical narrative performance in a study that focuses on 'narratives of self-presentation'. The work was based on a rhetorical analysis of 100 Facebook profiles of college students and was informed by interpretive, phenomenological, and symbolic interactionist ideas. The profile analysis was supplemented by focus group discussions. Leornardi worked with a notion of the self drawn from the work of Mead, which sees communication as central to the construction of the self. For Leonardi, online identities are continuous with off-line selves. The research questions that informed the study were:

1. What features are used in the narrative performance of identities on Facebook?
2. What types of identities result from the narrative performances on Facebook profiles?
3. What role does cultural capital play in the narrative performance of self (2010: 18)?

For Leonardi, online presentation of the self is a kind of textual performance that can be understand in terms of rhetoric. Users want to be seen by their friends in terms of particular arrangements of who they know (social capital), what they know, and what kinds of symbolic practices they want to be seen as having command over (cultural capital), and to be associated with certain kinds of symbols. Users know what they want to construct as their identity, but they are also aware that they do not exercise full control over this process for a number of reasons, including the limitations imposed by the structure of Facebook itself, and the difference between their own sense of self and how others respond to them. In order to achieve the desired online identity users draw on a range of rhetorical devices in building their user profiles. One such strategy is to seek to control the amount and type of information they disclose on their profiles. They make choices about what they will reveal about their tastes in film or music, and aim to have these revelations support the kind of self they want to project through their profile. Facebook users are not entirely free to construct a self in their profiles for another reason, which has to do with what Leornardi sees as the inevitable link between the online and offline self: at least *some* of the user's friends on Facebook are also friends in (physical as opposed to virtual) reality who, through face-to-face contact, might spot what appear to be dissonant elements of a user profile, that is, items that do not fit the person.

The narrativity of the profiles is partly the result of other Facebook users filling in 'the gaps created by the narrative fragments in order to create a theme for the fragments and make sense of the story'. The narratives in personal profiles, then, are the result of choices made by the creators of those profiles, within the constraints of the social networking site. Users construct their profiles with reference to others in their group of friends, as suggested by shared elements of taste displayed through cultural capital in profile sections for books read, music listened to, and favourite films. Some individuals choose to go against the grain of shared cultural capital, but even then the deviation is in terms of broader shared sets of preferences, against which their choices are contrasted.

Leornardi identifies five aspects to the self that users aim to construct in their profiles:

The five categories of narrative fragments of identity are: (1) The Essential Self, which is a primary category by which the profile's creator articulates an idealized self through personal descriptors; (2) The Desired Self is a secondary category in which the profile's creator expresses desires for the future; (3) The Preferential Self is the tertiary category in which the profile's creator offers personal valuations through one-sided arguments; (4) The Dynamic Self is the quaternary category in which the profiler narrates a self through affiliations with certain activities; and (5) The Demanding Self is the final category in which the profile's creator invites readers to participate in the narrative through certain language choices. (2010: 94)

The narrative properties of the profiles are the result of a joint constitution of the user's textual construction of these five selves, and of their friends' stories being told through the profiles. Leornardi conceives narrative in this study in terms of a 'Narrative Performance Model', which is a construct that she created to identify the process where by readers of profiles connected 'narrative fragments' and created coherent narratives of identity. These narrative fragments were the result of 'the rhetorical choices of form, style, and content found in the 'Personal Information,' 'Say Something' and 'Photo Album' sections of the profiles'. Leonardi is clear that the narratives identified in the study are the result of theoretical construction on the part of the researcher, as well as the work of stitching together that other users perform in order to make the fragments come together into a narrative; a combination of analysing the profiles *and* focus group interviews was required to demonstrate the narrative construction. So Facebook in this case is a technology that enabled performance of identities through the joint construction of narrative fragments in the profile of the individual user, and by her Facebook friends reading the profile and connecting the fragments. It was the audience of Facebook friends who finished the work of narrativisation.

Miller's Tales from Facebook

Tales from Facebook (Miller, 2011) is a book about Facebook use in the Caribbean island of Trinidad. A British social anthropologist, Miller has previously published studies of capitalism, modernity, and Internet use based on fieldwork in the same location. He notes that he chose Trinidad in order to dislodge the assumption that US and British usage of Facebook *is* Facebook. For Miller the origins of Facebook in elite US university student circles need not and in fact do not dictate its current usage or its future. This is the kind of dislocation of ethnocentric assumptions that is characteristic of social/cultural anthropology, and indeed, of much sociology. Miller is at his most provocative with:

> ... I am hoping that, given the time lag it takes for publishing a book, some of the already apparent trends described here for Trinidad may well match those starting to become evident in slower-moving places such as London or Los Angeles. We shall see. (2011: xiv)

Miller, through this challenge, is in effect asking his (presumably) North Atlantic readers to exercise their sociological imagination. Indeed, reading this book was a refreshing break from the studies on Facebook which were mostly based on US research, and often with college students (as in two of the studies on Facebook we discussed earlier). As Miller rightly points out, most Facebook users do not live in the USA, and the social network has grown well beyond its college student beginnings.

Miller's study features both first and second order narrative. In the main part of the text he uses stories to communicate his findings. The 12 core stories, which he terms 'Portraits', are mostly based on composite individuals, combining elements from different individual stories. Each is structured around one person and that person's use of Facebook and experience of the site. Each of these is a joint narrative about Facebook and its use, with Miller sharing the narrative stage with the informant. He sets the scene in terms of the portrait subject's everyday world, and characterises the person by sharing with us details of their appearance, everyday home or work environment, and style of speech, as well as information that is conveyed through direct quotation. Miller's is the narrator's voice in each story, and that narrator is the classical ethnographer. Each story is a multi-threaded weaving of his own account and observations as the ethnographer who offers up reflections on Trinidadian society and culture that set the context and background for the story, and these interweave with narrative passages about the person at the centre of the portrait, on that person's use and experience of Facebook.

The stories are structured around an anonymised main character. Miller informs us that the characters, with one exception, are composite, combining information from several informants. I find that this insight into the construction of the text serves to bring the crafting of ethnographic work into sharp focus, but without requiring the reader to wade through the specialised literature on the history of ethnographic writing. Straddling the divide between academic and general non-fiction writing, he tells us that his style of writing the 12 portraits is 'taken more from short story composition them from academic genre' (2011: xi). Miller develops several key themes regarding Trinidadian society and culture into threads that run throughout the book: negotiating the public and private in the context of an island society of just over one million people; ideas of the self as well as community. These themes were all explored in Miller's prior ethnographic work in Trinidad (Miller, 1994), and the Facebook user stories are in a sense additional ethnographic 'sites' that deepen the reflection on these themes.

One interesting twist on Facebook use in Trinidad is that the verb 'to friend' has been in use in Trinidadian English for over a century. As Miller explains, 'friending: To ask someone to be a facebook friend. But (my emphasis) traditionally in Trinidad to be having sex with, or to be in a visiting, i.e. noncohabiting, relationship with' (2011: xviii). Coincidence yes, but intriguing when set alongside his claim that Facebook use in Trinidad is high when viewed from an international comparison. Trinidadians have in fact renamed Facebook in terms of two important folk categories, as the 'Fasbook' and the 'Macobook'. 'Fas' and 'Maco' Miller defines as:

Fas – Trying to find out about another person's business with inappropriate speed (2011: xviii).

Maco – To be nosy or to spend time finding out about other people's private business. So also a 'macotious' person (2011: xviii).

So we see that for Trinis (Trinidadians, i.e. natives of Trinidad) Facebook is a virtual space where the private and the public come into tension. Miller suggest in *Tales*, and in his earlier work, that for Trinis the self, unlike 'western' notions of the self as something deep and usually hidden, is a set of surface assemblages, for which one metaphor is carnival. If we are persuaded by Miller on this point then we can see just why Facebook becomes the 'Fasbook' or the 'Macobook', the latter two being a local reconfiguration of Facebook into a tool used by Trinis to perform acts of creative self-fashioning that follow on from the Trini cosmology. For many Trini Facebookers, the self as portrayed on Facebook is the true self. Facebook's use by Trinis reveals new affordances.

Miller's account of Facebook use in Trinidad suggests that the thesis of decline of community under modernity, as set out most famously by Putnam in *Bowling Alone* (2000), may be based on too narrow a definition of community. While social media may be read as supplanting some forms of face to face communication, e.g. Trinis say that interaction with their friends on Facebook is a way to resolve the problem of high levels of crime that make it difficult to leave the home to visit these friends, many of the stories Miller presents suggest that Trinis use Facebook to supplement and indeed to deepen personal relationships, and one aspect of that deepening is an intensification of face-to-face relationships. In another vein, the book documents how Trinis use Facebook to record and comment upon face-to-face sociality: Miller notes the prevalence of Trinis posting photos of themselves and their friends at parties, weddings etc., with extensive commentary on how the people in the photos were able to carry off a choice of apparel, or hold a theatrical or just plain silly pose. This last use of Facebook is clearly not a supplanting of face to face, but is instead a way to engage in conversation after the fact of a face-to-face encounter. This compares with the findings in Papacharissi's study where, as we saw earlier, the college students in that study were engaged in a narcissistic performance on the Facebook pages, but with a social rather than a selfish aim.

And this takes us back to Miller's account of Trini cosmology, and more specifically, what he sees as the Trini construction of the 'true self' as an assemblage of public presentations of the self. In his previous research Miller engaged with established work on the idea that a key dualism in Caribbean society is that which contrasts reputation and respectability, which may in turn be rendered as an opposition of home and street. This duality is gendered, with the respectable space of the home being the ideal domain of the female while the street is the ideal domain of the male, and also classed and 'raced', but – and this is significant – for Trinis the key event of the carnival is when the barriers between reputation and respectability are shattered, and this shattering crosses class, 'race', and gender boundaries, often inverting settled notions of respectability and reputation, home and street. For Trinis there is an unveiling and a revelation in the carnival, when in a sense one can come to know some truths about a person through that person's performance of a 'carnival self'. 'Vishala', one of Miller's informants, believed that there was often more revealed of the truth of a person in their Facebook profile than in meeting them face to face.

For Miller, Facebook is a public medium where we express the private and the intimate. He sees it as changing our relationship to time and revitalising old relationships. I would argue that all of these different aspects of Facebook as a social networking site should be understood in terms in its narrative affordances: it enables us to reconfigure relationships without the constraints of the present and the face to face.

Miller renders his findings partly in narrative, the forms of short story and travelogue, as complementing the related yet distinct form of ethnography. He embraces forms of narrative that foreground empathetic explanation and rich description. In doing thus he acknowledges the centrality of narrative to what anthropologists do. His book is a particularly apt example of a social science narrative research report. He states at the very beginning of the text that he has deliberately employed narrative forms, i.e. a short story in travelogue, in order to make the book accessible to an audience outside the academy. Instead of having narration work backstage, Miller propels it to the centre of the performance.

Game Narratives

Narratology *vs* ludology

Even the one billion plus Facebook user total is dwarfed by the numbers of people who play video/computer games. The videogame is the most widely used form of digital entertainment, given that even in the poorest parts of the world, with relatively slow internet access which makes it impossible to stream video, people can play casual games on their mobile phones. It is impossible to say exactly how many people play videogames on computers, tablets or mobile phones, but it is a safe guess that of the three billion people who have access to the Web in one form or another, the majority have played a videogame at least once. While videogames display narrative features they cannot be fully analysed as narratives. This is a medium worthy of narrative researchers' attention, but we cannot simply apply narrative theories and methods developed for print and TV/film to videogames. There nonetheless remains scope for analysing videogames using structural narrative approaches, and narratology has been part of the videogame designer's toolkit from the start (Crawford, 2003; Rollings & Adams, 2003; Ryan, 2001; Salen & Zimmerman, 2010). Many computer games are based on the three-act narrative structure of situation, conflict and resolution, with that same structure being repeated as the player moves through the game. Propp's approach has been effective in describing the structure and workings of role playing and adventure games (Ip, 2010a, 2010b). The classic fantasy type of quest videogame (*Neverwinter Nights, World of Warcraft, Morrowwind*) is based on characters with defined roles and capabilities; the narrative form is that of a quest in which the player-character must confront and overcome a series of challenges. The game is won when the player-character succeeds in achieving the quest's goal.

Narrative use in games

The narrative aspects of videogames are manifest in different ways. First there is the story world. i.e. the world in which the game is set: as a player progresses through the game, they come to know more of the story world. Narrations will be built into the game that present the player with elements of its backstory (a background, contextualising story). All videogames have a storyworld and backstory. These are based in either pre-existing fictional or film narratives (Tolkien's *Lord of the Rings* trilogy provides a story world and backstory for various videogame adaptations of that novel; the *Star Wars* films provide the story world for the various *Star Wars* game adaptations. For some other games, such as *Morrowwind* or *Portal* an entire story world is built from scratch). If the game backstory is based on a film or novel, then there is an already existing underlying narrative that can be analysed using the many established techniques for the analysis of narrative in these media. For videogames with backstories that come from adaptations of novels and films, the existing body of critique around the original narratives should inform your own analysis of the narratives in the derivative games. Narrative is also present in videogames in cut scenes – prerendered video sequences that are used to open games and frequently to set the scene for the coming gameplay when a player moves from one level to the next. These narrative elements provide vital information for the player. Cut scenes sometimes combine the presentation of a backstory with a tutorial on the mechanics of gameplay.

Juul (2001) assesses the arguments for and against games as narrative. In favour are: 1) We use narratives for everything; 2) Most games feature narrative introductions and backstories; 3) Games share some traits with narratives. Juul then discusses three reasons for refuting the proposition that games are narratives: 1) Games are not part of the narrative media ecology formed by movies, novels, and theatre; 2) Time in games works differently from that in narratives; 3) The relation between the reader/viewer and the storyworld is different from that between the player and the gameworld. We have already looked at arguments in favour of games as narrative, so here we'll look more closely at Juul's points against. One of the first points against is that we can see that videogame production and consumption have developed around them particular techniques and technologies, working practices, corporate structures, criticism and producer/consumer relations (Dyer-Witheford & Peuter, 2009), and these ideas and practices are in some ways distinct from those of the print, television, and film industries. The best example is contemporary ludology (the study of gameplay) which is unique to the videogame world. On the second point we can see that time in a narrative is unilinear over the course of the narrative discourse; even in a narrative with multiple plot lines, the flow of time along that plot line moves inexorably from event to event and on toward the conclusion. The reader of a novel or the viewer of a video can jump forward to a later point, but in doing so they risk losing the plot, literally. Stories organise events and experience toward a preordained conclusion, and the reader follows the narration toward that conclusion along the path set by the author of that narrative. But games are played prospectively towards a point in the future that is not fully determined by a plot. Videogames present an environment which must be constantly manipulated; the player is always confronted with choices of actions and there are various paths through which a game proceeds. It is only *after* playing a game through to its end that a player can look back and construct the experience in narrative form. The third point I see as related to the second: we read and view novels and films, while we play games. And playing is about acting and making choices within a set of rules.

In order to do a structuralist analysis of the narrative elements or characteristics of videogames, you will have to position your project in terms of whether you will take a strong stance on games as narratives, or employ a more nuanced analysis of one or more specified elements of a game. Having identified the narrative elements, and after that the narrativity of these elements, you will have to decide on a suitable structuralist framework. Many of the tools of structural analysis can be employed in this regard: variations on the Hero's Journey, for example have proved popular with game designers

(Rollings & Adams, 2003), and have been employed in the analysis of narrative in games (Ip, 2010a).

When considering thematic analysis of videogame narrative, we might well ask; if it is only a game, then why bother with the themes? The simple answer is that as cultural products, games carry ideological messages that we can analyse to learn something about the makers and consumers of the product (Cassar, 2013). The most popular videogame subgenre is that of the action game, which is characterised by the recurrence of a small set of themes. Without adopting *a priori* either a condemnatory or celebratory standpoint, as social researchers we would probably want to give some consideration to why so many videogames have narrative content that is focused on warfare, or we might ask why is it that heroic characters are mostly racialised as white, or why the cultures most valued and defended are recognisably western, and why is it that evil characters are frequently recognisably Middle Eastern or Oriental. When the narrative content of videogames is based in a fantasy world, the settings and characters are invariably medievalist and recognisably of European and specifically Northern European provenance. The plots for mainstream games are also shaped around fighting an evil Other that is frequently Orientalised. Thematic studies of game narratives have thus highlighted frequent and recurrent themes of sexism, racism, homophobia and xenophobia. Conquest and colonisation are other recurrent themes, as are variations of the Second World War, the Cold War, and the 'war against terror'. The content of mainstream videogames would seem to mirror the world and articulate the world view of a white western 'mainstream' (Japanese gaming cultures are a study in their own right).

Games and teaching history

Historical simulation games are among the most popular, with Sid Meier's *Civilization* series selling many millions on each release. Can historical simulation games be useful for teaching history? This question emerges out of wider considerations of the pedagogical value of computer games (Crookall, 2010; Roos et al., 2004) and there are arguments for and against. The main argument in favour is that historical simulation games can bring events and people to life in a medium that is as familiar to people under the age of 30 as the book or magazine was to their parents: people born in the last twenty years are 'digital natives' – at least in the most industrialised part of the world – for whom computers and the Web are integral aspects of normal life. Since digital media have already captured the attention of digital natives as their preferred way of accessing information, the same media could be used to deliver learning content effectively, historical understanding in this case. The main point against using historical simulation games as teaching tools turns on the narrative content of these types of games. In order to make these games worth playing narrativity has to be balanced with playability, which means departing from the tight emplotment of historical events that is at the core of historical narrative. For Rob MacDougall (www.robmacdougall.org/blog/2009/03/technology-grows-on-trees), writing on the problems of using games to teach history (play *vs* narrative), the openness of games makes them poor tools for fostering the narrative understanding that is the aim of studying history.

Game stories against the mainstream

Alternatives to mainstream games that present more radical and less ethnocentric worldviews, plots and characters have always been part of gaming culture (Dyer-Witheford & Peuter, 2009, see Chapter 7). Such alternative games draw on different masterplots, and display a set of different thematic narrative concerns. Instead of having the payer take on the character of a US (or less frequently a British or Israeli) soldier in a military conflict, a radical alternative such as the Syrian-made *Under Ash* has you play as a Palestinian fighter engaged in combat against the Israeli army (Galloway, 2004). *Under Ash* sticks closely to the mechanics and gameplay of the first shooter. What is different is that the storyworld is set in the occupied territories, and is thus built on a set of themes that are very different from those of mainstream western shooters. Molleindustria is a collective of radical game makers who state that their mission is to recapture the medium of videogames, to tell stories that, as they say, 'challenge the conscience' (http://molleindustria.org/). For them the videogame medium is a vital space for expressing alternative political visions, precisely because of the popularity of gaming worldwide, and because the technology for production and distribution has lowered the barriers for entry.

In addition to games made by independent radical game producers, there is the politically radical variant of the game modification scene. Modding is where the content, rules, or gameplay are modified, which usually requires access to the source code and original digital assets of the game in order to be modded (Hong & Chen, 2013). Radical modding occurs when modders do not acknowledge the ownership and control of a game's producers/owners, and develop mods that are intentionally subversive. Such mods are designed and built by programmers, artists, testers, and users in the game industry who have developed techniques to resist corporate control, finding ways to circumvent that industry's systems for intellectual property protection (Dyer-Witheford & Peuter 2009). Radical modders repurpose digital art assets and remix established game narratives and characters through political frames that are different from those of the games' original creators. Radical mods can take a game's resources and storylines and recast these into a radicalised narrative discourse, where the relations between characters, gameplay and game outcomes are changed to suit an anti-establishment agenda.

The thematic narrative content of radical games is distinguished by story-worlds built on different ideological and cultural assumptions from the western (especially the US mainstream) ethnocentrism of mainstream games. What is also relevant to analysis of radical games as narrative is that the characters in many such games are derived from 'unusual' settings, e.g. African migrants as heroes in an adventure game, or non-European fantasy heroes.

Hacker Narratives

For the final set of cases of narrative use, I will look at hacker stories. But first we must ask, what is hacking? Hacking covers a broad range of activity, from building and sharing software, to repurposing source code and manufactured objects, to breaking into secure computer systems (Jordan, 2008). Hacking combines technical skill with inventiveness and experimentation. Sometimes, but not always, it has an overt political motivation and/or message. That message can be anarchist, anti-authoritarian, or broadly communitarian. It is often, but not always, anti-capitalist, in that it can take on an extreme individualistic form of liberalism that is not incompatible with some types of capitalist ideology. It is always opposed to established notions of intellectual property. One point on which all hackers agree is that information should be free.

William Gibson is often credited with introducing the term 'cyberspace' into popular culture; his (1984) novel *Neuromancer* was a runaway best-seller that in many ways invented much of the imagery and terminology used to represent high technology focused on computer hackers in fiction, film and videogames. In *Neuromancer* we have virtually all the elements that have come to shape fictional representations of hacking: 'cyberspace', a 'matrix' of networked computer systems and databases, high value digital data that become the target of criminal activity, and the hacker (as a young male from the industrialised part of the world system) whose skill is co-opted by sinister forces. In widely read novels such as Gibson's *Neuromancer*, Stephenson's *Snow Crash* (2002), and Larsson's *Girl with the Dragon Tattoo* (2008), hackers are portrayed as extreme individualists – social misfits with overdeveloped technical skills and often with underdeveloped interpersonal skills. It is worth noting that Larsson's hacker is a young woman: in Lisbeth Salander, Larsson presents one of the most complex figures in the genre. Her gender aside, Lisbeth in fact fits the established mould of the clandestine hacker: she is a recluse, socially awkward and emotionally inarticulate, and many of her hacking exploits take place on the dark side of legality.

These representations of hackers draw on themes from a body of science fiction film and literature collectively referred to as Cyberpunk. Two pioneering works that helped to set the literary and visual style of Cyberpunk are Gibson's already mentioned *Neuromancer* (1984) and Ridley Scott's film *Bladerunner* (released in 1982, adapted from Phillip K. Dick's novel, *Do Androids Dream of Electric Sheep?*). Cyperpunk narratives follow a masterplot of decline and social decay in a dystopian world ruled by giant corporations that rival nation states in their power and influence, while Cyberpunk society is characterised by rampant individualism and extremes of wealth and poverty. Everything looks grimy and everyone seems depressed. While the classic masterplot of science fiction was one of progress through technology, Cyberpunk plots depart from mainstream science fiction in one crucial regard: they reject classic science fiction's modernist faith in progress through science and technology. Cyberpunk's politics combine cynicism, individualism, and some elements of anarchism ('high-tech and low life').

So that is hacker fiction. Another set of narratives about hackers that we find in the news media and in popular culture is based on stories of hackers turned 'Stock Market Hero' or 'Dot Com Millionaire'. A (very) few individuals have indeed earned enormous wealth through turning their hacking skills into products or services. These individuals are almost mythical figures, especially in the USA from where most of them have come; there are literally dozens of popular biographies in print, some hagiographies, and a few documentaries and feature films about computer whizz-kids who went on to become rich and famous, of which the late Steve Jobs is the most famous. Found in this genre are works on the Google founders Sergey Brin and Larry Page (McPherson, 2010), on Microsoft founder Bill Gates (Cheongbi, 2009; Wallace & Erickson, 2005), and more recently books and a feature film on the Facebook founder Mark Zuckerberg (Kirkpatrick, 2010; Mezrich, 2009). These works are shaped in terms of masterplots based on admiration for the self-made person, and they all draw upon well-established tropes and masterplots that construct contemporary mythologies of celebrity.

In contrast to hagiographies of hackers turned billionaires, there is a smaller body of narratives about hackers as corporate dupes, in which commentators take a sceptical view of intellectual labour in the capitalist software industry. There is an interesting 'backstory' here: as computing spread and became an ever more important element in the infrastructure of business and public administration, it spawned its own kinds of knowledge worker, who came to greater visibility from the 1980s: these knowledge workers were the computer programmers, hardware engineers, technicians, systems analysts, and system administrators, who built, designed and ran the ever expanding computer infrastructure. All of these job functions existed from the earliest days of computing, but by the 1980s these jobs had increased in number by orders of magnitude (Campbell-Kelly, 2004). The (stereo)typical geek/hacker as corporate dupe works in a large corporate machine or government organisation; s/he is a cog, following orders given by the 'pointy-headed boss' who is a political animal but technically ignorant (as seen in the Dilbert cartoons and comic strip: www.dilbert.com). The corporate dupe is derided by many other hackers, but is undeniably part of hacker culture broadly conceived. The figure of the corporate dupe is most famously fictionally represented in Douglas Coupland's best-selling (1995) novel *Microserfs*. We can also track this figure through two popular television series in which geeks/hackers are central characters: *The IT Crowd* and *Chuck*. In both series we have central characters who are smart and skilled in computing but lacking in social graces, and in both the (male) geek/hacker is both a sympathetic figure and a figure of fun. We are invited to laugh at their social ineptitude while admiring their technical skill.

There are recurrent forms employed in narratives by and about hackers. The many popular non-fiction and journalistic accounts use variations on the classic three-act structure, with the action usually opening at some point of crisis in the life of the hacker, and working backward to the early development of the hacker (Mitnick, 2011; Torvalds & Diamond, 2002; Williams, 2002). These texts draw on standard masterplots that are recognisably versions of the Hero's Journey, the voyage of discovery, the coming of age story, the confessional, and the conversion story. A widely-read biography of Richard Stallman, the founder of the Free Software Foundation (www.fsf. org), opens with a malfunctioning printer.

Box 4.1   Stallman and the printer

Richard Stallman is one of the world's most famous free software hackers. Of the many stories in circulation about Stallman, there is one about how a malfunctioning printer spurred Stallman to become a free software hacker and activist. In 1980 Stallman was working as a programmer in the artificial intelligence laboratories at the Massachusetts Institute of Technology. In those days there were not really any personal computers or printers. You had to share computer time and join printer queues. As the story is recounted in a biographical work on Stallman's life and work (Williams 2002), Stallman one day discovered that his printout had gone astray in the shared laser printer's queue. We are told in the overall text that Stallman was from early childhood gifted in mathematics and science and that he was keen to understand how things worked. On this occasion his curiosity was thwarted: he had no access to the source code of the

(Continued)

> *(Continued)*
>
> software that controlled the laser printer, and therefore he could not diagnose, and fix, the fault that had mislaid his printout. This incident may be read as an epiphany - a moment in a biographical account that for the subject of the biography is a turning point and moment of revelation, after which life runs on a different course and the world takes on a different appearance. Later in life Stallman would look back at the malfunctioning printer for which there was no available source code as a stimulus to what would become decades of writing and promoting free software and radical information politics.

In this passage, and in the opening chapter of which it is a part, we can see several of the narrative techniques of creative non-fiction at work: the setting of the computer laboratory tells us that we are about to meet people who are immersed in advanced science and technology; the presentation of the technical challenges of computer programming and how Stallman confronted these tell us something about his character, namely that he is bright, a loner, and likes to get inside complex systems to figure out how they work. The second chapter presents the mature Stallman explaining and advocating for the politics of free software. Then in the third chapter we are taken back to his childhood where the structure is that of the much-used tale of the child prodigy who was misunderstood by his early teachers, was a social misfit, and then eventually came to have his genius recognised at university. The structure of *Free as in Freedom* has elements of the coming of age story and the struggle of a brilliant but misunderstood genius to be accepted for who he is.

Themes in hacker narratives

In his ethnographic account of free software culture, Kelty (2008) found that many hackers narrated accounts in which they represented their work as analogous to the Protestant Reformation. The hackers saw themselves as Protestant reformers up against the centralised authority of the Catholic Church/State, which they refigured as the capitalist software industry and its state supporters and guarantors. This is a recurrent theme in much writing by and about hackers coming out of the USA (Coleman, 2012), the country from which most hacker literature originates. The theme does appear somewhat ethnocentric to me in light of the fact that hacking is a global activity. Even remaining within the confines of the US-Western

European environment from which most research on hacker culture comes, one could well ask the question why should French, Spanish, or Italian hackers identify with this image? And when we leave the confines of the North Atlantic, the Reformation metaphor seems of little use. A libertarian politics might well be apt for shaping narratives by hackers from the USA, but Western European hackers frequently articulate a collectivist radical Left politics. It would appear that while hacking is a transnational activity, hackers narrate what they do and why by drawing upon culturally specific masterplots and themes. More research needs to be done here. Let us explore these issues in narratives written by two famous hackers: Kevin Mitnick and Eric Raymond.

In *Ghost in the Wires* (2011), Mitnick presents an account of his formation and career as a hacker, detailing exploits that eventually led to him spending a period of time in prison (the text was co-written with the help of a journalist, a not uncommon practice). At the time of writing the account Mitnick was, in his own words, an ethical hacker, putting his skills to work as a consultant in order to foil the activities of other hackers. Mitnick is at pains to point out that he never deliberately caused harm or derived financial gain from his hacking activities. All he wanted to do, he says, was to get inside secure systems for the joy of the activity.

In keeping with established practice in creative non-fiction, *Ghost in the Wires* opens with a preface that drops the reader into the middle of the action: Mitnick is about to slip into a secure building using a false ID card that he had earlier fabricated. His aim is to get physical access to a computer workstation, which he will then hack into in order to get onto a secure computer network. As with the Stallman printer incident, we have here the hacker being confronted by a problem, and the setting and the action give us insight into the character of that hacker: in the case of Mitnick we immediately get a sense that he is clever and willing to take risks, two defining characteristics of hackers in stories by and about hackers.

After the action preface, Mitnick's story moves to an account of his childhood memories of a supportive mother and a series of abusive men. He describes himself as being good in school, bright, and curious; he writes of 'sharing a gene' with his salesman father and uncle that gave him the facility for persuading people. He writes of a childhood interest in magic, noting that he realised at a young age that people 'enjoyed being tricked'; he also writes of how he gained insights into his own psychology and the psychology of other people. The form of the narrative combines the confessional and coming of age tale. Working back from where he is as a famous hacker writing his life story, Mitnick recounts events and experiences from his early life, and presents these as pointing to the hacker he would eventually become. This is narrativisation at work.

Eric Raymond has described himself, and has been described by others, as an ethnographer/anthropologist of free and open source software. He is an insider and writes with critical insight and encyclopaedic knowledge. In *A Brief History of Hackerdom* (http://oreilly.com/openbook/opensources/ book/raymond.html) Raymond notes that he became the folk historian and ethnographer of hacker culture. In that paper he writes that he created the narrative in order to promote self-knowledge of hacker history; he also draws attention to his narrativisation of early hacker culture, to his active selection and ordering of events.

A Brief History of Hackerdom is structured as a tale of the emergence of hackers into self-awareness, and as such it is part voyage of discovery and part coming of age tale. The narrative presents the story in event chronological order, which Raymond divides into six major periods.

Box 4.2   The six periods of Raymond's history of hacking

1. The early hackers, which deals with the 1960s and covers the pioneering period of computer development at MIT and several other US universities.
2. The Rise of Unix, which covers the 1970s, in which a focus on sharing code and anti-corporate politics came to the fore; this was the period in which Richard Stallman came to prominence as a hacker.
3. The end of the Elder Days is significant turning point the story, when the software and systems that were developed in the early hacker culture became the objects of corporate interest and then profit seeking.
4. The 1980s were the period of intensified corporate efforts to capture the work of hackers and create closed property systems in Unix software; this attempt failed.
5. The 1990s opened with the now famous efforts of Linus Torvalds to create a completely free version of Unix (which he named Linux) which was combined with the ongoing work of Stallman and his close associates; this was wildly successful.
6. Then, with the late 1990s came the 'explosion' of the World Wide Web, and Linux would become the most used software platform for machines that served up webpages and other digital resources. The triumph of the hackers was now complete.

Hackers are the main characters in Raymond's account, with many rendered in heroic terms, though he makes clear that many of these were not aware

Table 4.1 Summary of selected cases

	Analytical framework	Structure	Themes	Narrativity/narrativisation
Facebook				
Papacharissi (2011)	Visual anthropology; semiotics	Semiotic relations of visual elements in photographs	College student identity; narcissism; virtual identity	Visual storytelling in photos; comments and likes on the visual stories
Leonardi (2010)	Narrative Performance Model; Goffman and Mead on the self	Architecture of profile page as enabling and constraining	Cultural capital; performance of 'taste'; presentation of the self'; virtual identity	Joint work of the Facebook user and his/her friends responding to the profile
Miller (2011)	Ethnography; creative nonfiction	Character profiles; individual story; travellers' tale	Community; sociality; identity; virtual identity; 'national' culture	Combination of ethnographer's second order narrative and first person stories of interlocutors
Swers Story Shapira (2010)	Creative non-fiction; journalism	Chronology of individual posts; editor's contextualisation and commentary	Death, tragedy, grief	Established by journalist selecting posts, emplotting them and setting the scene
Hackers				
Mitnick (2011)	Mass-market/popular assisted biography; creative non-fiction	Dramatic opening scene; flashback to early development	Development of technical skill; psychology of deception; justification for actions taken	First-person account of key events; narrator is part of the action; insider account
Raymond (1999)	Creative non-fiction; historical narrative	Chronological ordering divided into major periods; each major period defined by technology and social relations	Coming of a group to self-awareness; birth and growth of a new technical and political culture	Connects real people and real events; explicitly aiming to produce an historical account, to turn chronology into historical narrative; narrator begins as observer and then becomes part of the action

of the significance of their actions at the time they carried them out. He also notes that the main impact of Linux was sociological more than techno-logical, because of it combining free software, with an open way of working and sharing code that was facilitated by the Internet; this was one of his main insights and he stresses that it was arrived at retrospectively, by his own reflection and reconstruction of events (I would say by his emplot-ment of events). This first narrative then ends, and Raymond writes that he 'passes out of history' and into a period where he becomes a participant in the events. The second connected narrative is the 'Revenge of the hack-ers' which treats hackers as a self-aware group (culture, social movement), aware of their influence and with a distinctive culture, engineering meth-odology and politics (http://oreilly.com/openbook/opensources/book/raymond2.html).

Hacker narratives display a core set of themes that fall into two main groups: those concerning the character of the hacker, and those concerning hacker politics. The first group of themes include: an early interest in tech-nology, maths and science; being bookish, geeky or nerdy; being socially awkward, and eventually coming to be recognised as part of a cognitive elite (being bright). The second group of themes deal with politics and include: objecting to a closed technology (the story of Stallman and the printer at MIT that we saw earlier is widely circulated among hackers); commitment to a politics of individual freedom to investigate, build and share technology; and narrating a David *vs* Goliath scenario where the hacker is David and the large corporation that controls access to software is Goliath. These themes are manifest in Mitnick's narrative, as in the Stallman biography. We saw them recur as well in Eric Raymond's narrativisation of hacker history.

Summary

In this chapter we applied some ideas from the analysis of narratives that we discussed in Chapter 3 to look at narratives in use. We examined several narratives of the self, using the CV, journals, and blogs as examples. We also addressed questions of narrative in social media, paying special attention to several exemplar works on Facebook. Facebook furnishes its users with a series of affordances that enables the recording, sharing and reflection on life events. Social networking sites not only share properties with journals, scrapbooks and blogs, they also extend these in important ways and enable users to do much of what they have done with the prior forms/media while enabling new activities.

While scholars and critics have veered from dismissal to over-enthusiasm about videogames, it is now generally accepted that these games are a core element of a global media culture. As with social media and social networking sites, videogames have become embedded in everyday life and are therefore deserving of our attention. We discussed how narratives are articulated in videogames. While these are not the same as narratives, they do contain narrative elements. We saw how a thematic focus on the narrative content of videogames yields insight into masterplots and dominant cultural codes. You might find it useful, in planning how to bring a narrative approach to understanding a game, to think about 'story' in two senses: the stories in the game as a text, and the stories that the players tell about their gameplay, and for that matter, about themselves as game enthusiasts. We saw that hackers are skilled enthusiasts who work with software, and that we can obtain useful knowledge about the use of narrative by examining the stories that hackers tell about themselves and that are told about them in fiction and in mass media.

Questions to consider

1. How have digital media affected the ways we create personal stories?

    a. Investigate 'lifeblogging' as a form of personal story-making.
    b. What are the privacy implications for privacy of the widespread use of social networking/social media platforms (Facebook/Twitter)?

2. Drawing on any study that examined some aspect of narrative in Facebook, assess how the author dealt with the question of narrativity.

3. What are the main issues in debates about narrativity vs ludology in the analysis of videogame narrative?

Further reading

Coleman, E.G. (2012) *Coding Freedom: The Ethics and Aesthetics of Hacking.* Princeton: Princeton University Press.

Dovey, J. (2006) *Game Cultures: Computer Games as New Media.* Maidenhead: Open University Press. (See especially Chapter 5.)

Galloway, A. (2004) 'Social realism in gaming', *Game Studies,* 4(4). Retrieved from www.gamestudies.org/0401/galloway/

Good, K.D. (2012) 'From scrapbook to Facebook: a history of personal media assemblage and archives', *New Media & Society*.

Juul, J. (2001) 'Games telling stories? A brief note on games and narratives', *Game Studies*, *1*(1). Retrieved from www.gamestudies.org/0101/juul-gts/

Papacharissi, Z. (2009) 'The virtual geographies of social networks: a comparative analysis of Facebook, LinkedIn and ASmallWorld', *New Media & Society*, *11*(1–2): 199–220.

For an online journal, see www.gamestudies.org. More online resources are given on the book's website.

5

CONSTRUCTING NARRATIVE

OVERVIEW

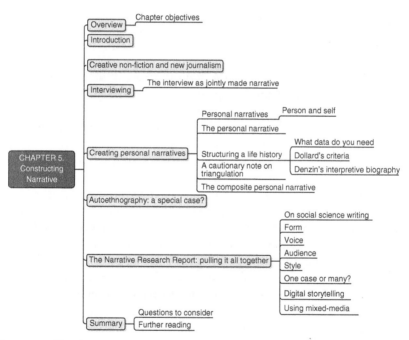

Figure 5.1   Chapter map

Key learning objectives

- To introduce the fields of new journalism and creative non-fiction.
- To examine the fieldwork interview as a process that creates narrative.
- To introduce the types and characteristics of personal narratives.
- To show how personal narratives are constructed from the perspective of a social researcher.
- To introduce the autoethnography as a hybrid of ethnography and personal narrative.
- Drawing on the above, to show how to put together a narrative research report, and to suggest how hypermedia and online sharing can enhance the report.

Introduction

In this chapter we will focus on the writing aspect of social research, specifically on the work of producing social science texts in narrative form. Here we use mainly a connecting strategy in assembling and presenting our materials, aiming to build explanation and interpretation through connecting people, places and events in terms of an account that develops over a period of time, that is, as a narrative. Here we will treat the writing of social research findings as the creation of narrative. While in quantitative and mixed methods research 'narrative' is used to refer to any text beyond that of a pre-coded response, here as elsewhere in the book we work with a more precise meaning of narrative, namely as a text that conveys a sequence of events with an obvious or implied causal connection among those events.

We begin with a discussion of what has been variously termed the 'new journalism', 'creative non-fiction', and 'creative journalism'. These three inter-related approaches to the writing of non-fiction are the mirrors, in artistic and journalistic circles, of the questioning of some of the assumptions of classic realist social science writing; this questioning has been going on since the 1960s. We discuss the interview process as an exercise in storymaking as narrative construction. The life history is the form of personal narrative most frequently employed by social researchers and our consideration of it follows naturally from a discussion of creative non-fiction and from interviewing, given that many works of creative non-fiction have been built around the life history, and also because interviewing has been central to both life history work as well as creative journalism. Of course, interviewing is a fundamental technique for those sociologists and anthropologists who work in an ethnographic tradition. Autoethnography, to which we will turn later, would seem to present somewhat of a special case, falling as it does somewhere in between ethnography and personal narrative. It would be unforgivable to write about the creation of narrative by social scientists in today's world without making reference to the fact of ubiquitous digital information and communications technologies. We consider some of the possibilities offered by digital media for the social researcher who wishes to employ narrative in the presentation of his or her work. The chapter culminates with a consideration of the narrative research report, which pulls the various strands together. We consider some generic features of social science writing and how these overlap but sometimes come into tension with the forms and conventions of presenting research in narrative form.

Creative Non-fiction and New Journalism

In Chapter 1 we saw how social realist narrative was a key element in the work of reform-minded journalists in late Victorian Britain, as well as for several of the founding figures of the Chicago School of sociology, mainly Robert Park, and for W.E.B Du Bois. In 1973 Tom Wolfe introduced his famous work, *The New Journalism*, with the declaration that non-fiction had supplanted the novel as the most important form of literature in the USA (Wolfe & Johnson, 1973). As Boynton (Introduction, 2005) sees it, Wolfe was making a partly self-serving argument in favour of journalism as the preeminent literary genre. As Wolfe saw it, the New Journalism innovated by using techniques adapted from fiction: full dialogue, character study and description, shifting points of view, carefully constructed and sequenced scenes, and speculation into the inner psychology of the people in the story. Exemplary works in the genre include Wolfe's very own *The Right Stuff* (1979), about 'heroic' figures in the US space programme, and Truman Capote's *In Cold Blood* (1965), a 'non-fiction novel' about a multiple murder which was a pioneering work of new journalism.

Box 5.1   The 'new' new journalism

Boynton's (2005) edited collection explores the 'New' New Journalism. In his introduction to the volume, he surveys the work of the three decades since Wolfe's manifesto, claiming that the 'New New Journalism builds on the social realism of nineteenth-century

(Continued)

(Continued)

reporting and the formal experiments of 1960s New Journalism. For him the newer work is more 'rigorously reported, psychologically astute, sociologically sophisticated, and politically aware' (2005: xi) than its New Journalism precursor. Boynton highlights the engagement in the later body of work with race and class, social activism, and the employment of deeply immersive periods of participant observation in several of the works.

Ted Conover, one of the writers interviewed by Boynton, has written on hobo culture, illegal immigration and prison guard work, in studies that were all built on extended periods of immersion in the milieus he studied (Conover, 1998; 2001; 2011). In fact, Conover studied cultural anthropology at university, and his works read like classic ethnographies, minus most of the scholarly trappings of footnotes and referencing. Conover is an ethnographer who writes for an audience beyond the academy: 'anthropology seemed like philosophy as lived by real people' (Conover interview in Boynton, 2005: 9). Conover, as with the other writers interviewed by Boynton, stresses the importance of narrative as a universal form that can be adapted to tell any kind of story. His 'non-fiction narratives' as he terms them are aimed at taking the reader into an unfamiliar social setting and getting them to think deeply about that setting and the forms of life that make up its everyday reality.

Widely held concerns regarding realist presumptions about the truth of representation in social science writing were captured under the 'postmodern turn' in ethnography (Clifford & Marcus, 1986), which led to a focus on the writing of ethnography as more than a supposed objective account of social life. Agar (1995), in reflecting on ethnographic writing after the 'Writing Culture' turn, worried that something was lost in the turn away from realist representation, and that the new ethnography led to researchers treating the writing of ethnography as quite separate from doing fieldwork. He wanted to reintegrate text and research process. Drawing on some of the ideas of the New Journalism, which he also referred to as creative non-fiction, he suggested that social researchers in general, and ethnographers in particular, could learn from some of the innovations made by journalists who had adopted fiction writing techniques in their work.

Agar focused on scenic method, character development, plot, and authorial presence. We will look at each of these in turn. The scenic method concerns how scenes are constructed within the text. The New Journalism advocates showing rather than telling, and stresses the creation of a sense of immediacy. The idea is to draw the reader quickly into the scene being described through a focus on vivid details and using techniques of evocation. Characters are treated in New Journalism in terms of a few carefully selected and well-rounded persons who are presented through different points of view. A well-rounded character is one whose appearance, actions and personality are all rendered in the text. The plot concerns itself with the sequencing of events, and the New Journalism uses techniques of foreshadowing as well as flashback to break up the strict linear sequence of 'this happened first and then that', in order to create a dramatic effect that draws the reader more closely into the story. On authorial presence New Journalism makes clear that there is an organising consciousness at work, and that this organising consciousness can shift points of view in order to enter into the heads of characters and speculate as to their interpretations and motivations.

There are problems in adapting techniques of New Journalism to social scientific writing, chief amongst these being that the fictional form entails a kind of writing that necessarily goes beyond the factual content (Agar, 1995: 119). While creative non-fiction authors often discuss their methods and sources in a preface, foreword, or in notes accompanying the main text, the materials used to construct a scene as plausible may not meet the strict empirical requirements of conventional social research. This blend of fiction and journalism has come at some cost to social research, from the perspective of which the New Journalism is vulnerable to questions about overall credibility and reliability.

Agar concludes that, bearing in mind the concerns which social researchers, and ethnographers in particular, should have with regard to the techniques of New Journalism, creative non-fiction can and should become part of the ethnographer's toolkit. He notes that grounded theory, especially when supported by appropriate software (see for example, Corbin 2008), makes the writing-up of research iterative and dialectic, thus allowing the opportunity for the social researcher to weigh up the gains and losses of employing creative non-fiction techniques at various stages of analysis and in the writing-up of the final presentation. He also notes that ultimately ethnographic texts are more about making a case from data than about providing entertainment, and as such, techniques of creative non-fiction must be drawn upon in a cautious fashion.

All social researchers must tackle the research report at various points in their working lives. Sometimes the requirements for such a report are explicit in requiring that it be cast in narrative form, but even when not specified, most reports informed by qualitative research will benefit from the researcher being aware of the narrative issues as highlighted by Agar, and employing at least some in writing their report. Zeller (1995) advocates paying attention to narration, and to genres in which it is central, such as ethnography, journalism in general, and specifically so-called creative non-fiction and literary journalism.

We must be mindful of how time is used and represented in the report. There is no objective recounting of events in the sense of being free of the selection and indeed the bias of the observer and recorder. As such, we must be clear that even in the initial field observations there is selection at work: there is selection when we record and revise our fieldnotes, selection when we transcribe, and selection when we produce successive drafts of what will become the final research report. The research report is an artefact. Like Agar, Zeller (1995) draws attention to the techniques developed in New Journalism. The non-fiction author must take responsibility for creating a plot, or better, for framing the events of the story that she or he is rendering in terms of a plot. In addition to narration we must also be conscious of how we use description. In the realist novel descriptive passages give texture to the text and promote verisimilitude. The same holds for the research report. You will need to make decisions about the point of view through which you will present the report. Some forms of the new ethnography employ a first person point of view in order to stress the subjectivity of the researcher, as does the autoethnography, which we shall see later in this chapter. The New Journalism developed by Wolfe and Capote favoured the third person point of view; for Wolfe that point of view should be that of specific characters, so in New Journalism the perspectives of different characters are moved on and off the textual stage. The subjective third person point of view is not one which many social researchers use, perhaps because it raises questions about ethics and validity: is it valid to make inferences about the inner mental states of a person based on documentary or interview data, and even if this is valid, is it ethical?

Interviewing

Various kinds of semi-structured and open-ended interviews, including ethnographic and narrative interviews, can be viewed in terms of a researcher eliciting responses that often take a storied form (Wengraf, 2001). In contrast to spontaneous narrative, when interviewing we are dealing with induced narrative, i.e. narrative produced in response to a researcher. We must pay particular attention to the shared story making work that takes place in an interview situation. Such interviews are frequently employed in ethnographic fieldwork broadly defined. With a living respondent, interviews will be a pivotal source of material to be used in constructing an individual or collective life history. A considerable amount of material used in narrative research is generated from interviews conducted by the researcher, or from the secondary use of interview material generated by others. Given the open-ended nature of the story text the most common kind of interview used in narrative research is semi-structured (perhaps supplemented by a questionnaire with pre-coded responses which is very useful for gathering the basic biographical characteristics of an interview subject – the kind of demographic information which you should endeavour to collect for the participants in your research).

Two types of semi-structured interview are most relevant for us here: the narrative and the ethnographic (Flick, 2009, see Chapter 13). There is considerable overlap between the two and perhaps the major distinction is in the circumstances in which each is conducted. The ethnographic interview has an element of spontaneity attached it, in that it arises in the course of a wider participant observation study. There is some degree of the opportunistic in the ethnographic interview in that it cannot be fully planned in advance and therefore it would be impossible to have a fully-fledged interview schedule ready to go. If the opportunity arises in the field to conduct an interview then you must be ready to proceed; perhaps you already have a generic or even a specific interview schedule which might form the basis of an ethnographic interview, but the key point of the ethnographic interview is that it gives you as the researcher a chance to explore issues about which you do not already know a great deal. By contrast the narrative interview is one in which you intend to invite someone either to present a fully-fledged life story in the biographical sense, or to present a story-type account of some experience or event or practice with which that person is involved. You would generally know in advance when and with whom you will carry out a narrative interview and you would normally have a set of background topics ready to prompt the interviewee if necessary as they proceed through the narration of their story. Of course a narrative interview could begin with you as a researcher asking the other person to tell you their life story, and you just sitting back to take notes or start your tape recorder, but generally you would want to have some prompts ready particularly for those situations in which the other person comes to a lengthy pause or perhaps even a halt. If you are working with some model of a life or event course then your prompts should reflect this to ensure that your interviewee has the chance to speak to the various stages across that life or event course. For example, when talking to free software programmers and hackers, I will have either in writing, or committed to memory, a list of key events and life stages that I know are significant for programmers and hackers; I know this because of previous reading and research, prior fieldwork, and my own experience of learning computer programming. Adequate preparation is essential for narrative interviewers as for all interviewers.

The interview as jointly made narrative

An interview can be viewed as a joint exercise in narrative construction, according to Mishler (1991), who aimed to present an alternative to the mainstream tradition of interview research by focusing on the interview as a form of discourse. Halliday's (1973) work on the functions of language employed a system of three distinct yet interdependent functions that together comprised for Mishler 'a framework of linguistic analysis':

1. *Textual* – how parts of the text are internally connected through various syntactic and semantic devices.
2. *Ideational* – or the referential meaning of what is said.
3. *Interpersonal* – referring to the role relationships between speakers that are realised in the talk (Mishler 1991: 77).

Mishler uses this framework to discuss three approaches to narrative in the interview situation: structural analysis of personal narratives; creation of coherence in narratives; and the interpersonal context of the interview. In Mishler's structural analysis of elicited personal narratives, he uses the work of Labov and of Propp. Their approach worked on the textual level, and as we saw in Chapter 3 where we discussed Labov and Waletsky's work, the main concern in this kind of analysis is to identify minimal units of text that work in different ways to support the overall production of a narrative text. And, as we also saw earlier with Propp's approach, we can identify a definite set of functions in terms of a full story, and these functions, together with events and actors, combine in various ways to produce different kinds of narrative. The main problem with this approach is that of generalising from the limited range of texts used – think of Propp's folk/fairy tales, and the rather constraining prescription in Labov's work that we identify and concentrate on minimal clauses as the raw material of narrative sequences.

The second area Mishler examined is concerned with how coherence is jointly created in the interview situation. Since narrative discourses are usually longer than a single clause (the smallest possible narrative would comprise at least a sentence with events and entities, such as 'the old woman died, and then her husband died of grief at her passing'), the examination of how coherence is created in a narrative is important for the researcher. Narrative analysts examine how clauses, sentences and larger linguistic units, as well as social interactions and different cultural resources are combined to achieve coherent narratives in written, spoken and audio visual texts. One problem for the analyst studying interviews as narrative is that methods for studying coherence across different social and cultural settings have yet to be developed, as coherence seems to be embedded not only in the formal properties of language and conversation but also in the cultural contexts in which each interview takes place. The third aspect of Mishler's analysis of interview narrative is to do with the interpersonal, where the focus is on the interplay between the interviewer and the interviewee. The kinds of questions that are asked, as well as how these are asked, will clearly influence the responses given by the person being interviewed. In addition, how the interviewee is socially positioned (class, gender etc.), and the micromanagement of the interview in terms of prompting, interruption, seeking clarification, encouraging explanation or seeking to control the flow of the interviewee's talk, must all be taken into account.

Creating Personal Narratives

In this section we will discuss various kinds of narratives about an individual human subject: biography, autobiography, life story and life history. These are collectively known as personal narratives. We will examine the differences among them and the kinds of data used in their making. We will then focus on how to construct a life history, which is the kind of personal narrative most widely used in the fields of sociology, anthropology, social work and various therapeutic disciplines. But before examining these types of narrative we shall consider ideas of the self and person.

Personal narratives

Person and self

Sociology established itself in the nineteenth century as a discipline that was concerned to understand social change in modern industrial societies (Craib, 1997). The collective and the social structure were the key units of analysis. It was not until the early twentieth century that a focus on the individual and on the self came to occupy a significant space in the discipline, in the wake of work by George Herbert Mead (1863–1931) and several founding figures of the early Chicago School (Bulmer, 1986). In early social and cultural anthropology the focus was on small-scale 'primitive' social and cultural settings (Eriksen, 1995; Stocking, 1992); as with sociology it was not until the early decades of the twentieth century that the individual became the focus of some fieldwork (Kluckhohn, 1947), with the early life histories of native Americans (Radin, 1925; Wong, 1987).

It was French ethnologist Marcel Mauss (1872–1950) who arguably made the major contribution in early twentieth-century anthropology by specially addressing the individual as a distinct socio-cultural category (Mauss, 1985). Mauss argued that awareness of one's own embodied being as distinct from all others is found universally. He termed this awareness 'the self'; by contrast, 'the person' – which Mauss conceived as a category of being that went beyond a name or right to assume a role to being a fact in law – was unique to western societies, having its roots in Antiquity. The person as a fact in law, the juridical persona, was seen by Mauss as a development that went beyond the self and the biological individual. The *concept* of the self, as opposed to an awareness of the self, was also uniquely western because only in the West was the abstract notion of the self used in a reflective manner.

It is not always easy to distinguish between the self and the person. I will take 'self' to mean the psychological and physiological entity of which each of us is uniquely aware. Self-awareness is a human universal that is articulated in culturally specific ways. The 'person', in contrast to the 'self', we may take as a sociological and legal entity, as an instance of the general social category of human being. It is still widely believed, as did Mauss, that 'western' notions of the person are individualist while non-western notions are collective, but more recent work in anthropology has challenged this view (Sökefeld, 1999). Carrithers (1985) notes that westerners elaborated the sociological person because they saw it as the subject of change, while Hindus and Buddhists elaborated the philosophical, part metaphysical self because they saw self-realisation as key to moving up the ladder of reincarnation, a movement determined beyond the material sensuous world. What is most important for us here is that there is no unitary western notion of 'self' or 'person' which can be contrasted to some non-western notion. The still widespread (and in my view unfortunate) tendency to make such simplistic contrasts may be accounted for by what Said (1985) termed 'Orientalism' – an organising and controlling discourse of certain Western European intellectual formations that has as its object those spaces and people over which a Euro-American ruling bloc has been dominant for three centuries, and which imagines and mobilises ideas about the cultural uniqueness, and implicit superiority, of the West. Both Western and non-Western social and intellectual histories reveal varied conceptions of 'self' and 'person', namely what is most important for the culturally-sensitive and historically-aware narrative researcher (Goody, 2006).

The personal narrative

The personal narrative is a narrative about the lived experience of an individual (Angrosino, 1989; Plummer, 2001; Roberts, 2002, chapters 3 and 4). Personal narratives often display elements of self-representation, but since not all personal narratives are self-authored not all personal narratives are self-representations. A personal narrative is inherently dialogical in the sense that the author of the narrative is 'speaking to' a real or implied audience. In this the personal narrative is subtly different from a self-representation, which may be private as well as communicated. Think about your own sense of self: no doubt you make efforts to communicate aspects of this to others through how you dress and groom yourself, how you speak to other people and such, but there are aspects of your self-representation that remain private to you, depending on the circumstances in which you find yourself – your own sense of yourself as a political person has both public and private aspects. Self-representations may be expressed in a social field, but they may also remain private. I would argue that the private self-representation is the special concern of philosophers and psychoanalysts, and it is therefore not central to the narrative work I discuss here, which is concerned with self-representations in a social field to the extent that these are part of personal narratives. Personal narratives can take on various forms and draw on varied sources (Maynes et al., 2008); here I divide them into four main types: autobiography, biography, life story and life history (I will discuss the autoethnography later in the present chapter).

Box 5.2   The personal narrative

I. Autobiography

- Self/co-authored

II. Life story

- Researcher-authored

III. Biography

- Researcher-authored

IV. Life history

- Self/co-authored

V. Autoethnography

- Researcher/self-authored

Categorising and connecting in the personal narrative

- We can analyse a range of personal narratives where we code elements for categorising. For example, we can use the category of 'becoming a political activist' to organise and analyse a series of personal narratives about political lives. That category is based around a key event in the activist life and one which prior research tells us that people see as significant in their careers as activists. We can, to take just three aspects of this category of 'becoming a political activist', read across a series of activist narratives to: a) compare how people recount becoming politically aware; b) examine at what stage in life they became activists; c) study the reasons people gave for becoming activists (Alleyne, 2002; Andrews, 1991; Poletta, 2006).
- We can explore an individual personal narrative in terms of how events are storied, i.e. connected in a temporal sequence that is seen, by the person for whose life story the personal narrative is intended, as an explanation/account for how that life proceeded (Herzfeld, 1997).

St Augustine's *Confessions* (4th century C.E.) is one of the earliest texts we can recognise as autobiography. Written as it is in the first person, with the effect of the subject narrating directly to the reader, the autobiography is perhaps the most intimate and *personal* of personal narratives. The autobiography is an account of a life, as remembered and written down by the subject: it is generally the case that the author and subject of the autobiography are the same person, but some autobiographies are the result of a collaboration between a researcher or editor and the subject, where the subject was helped in creating what is in effect an assisted autobiography. The assisted autobiography blurs the boundary between autobiography and biography. The narrative researcher must be aware of the autobiography's limitations as a research resource: until recently, an author of an autobiography was by definition literate, so that the narrative analyst would thus have to take into account the cultural, social and political significance of being literate in the author's time and place, which is especially relevant when reading autobiographies of those who have been oppressed and socially marginalised. There is one further complication caused by recent technology: using speech recognition and automatic transcription software, an illiterate person can produce a written text, and so the subject-authored autobiographical text is no longer the preserve of the literate. We may need to allow that digital technology now means that textual production no longer requires formal literacy, and that ubiquitous digital multimedia mean that it is as easy to make and share an audio autobiography as a text.

The biography is another person's account of the life of the subject in question. The biographer, not the subject of the biography, is the interpreter and creator of this type of personal narrative. Yet the biographer is more than just a recorder and editor. No one keeps a full and complete record of their own life, and even if a person were perfectly diligent in keeping a daily journal and filing all of their printed and electronic correspondence, these materials together would be only a partial account of that person's life. And in any event most people would not be so diligent. The biographer therefore has to sift through whatever material is available on the subject; if the subject or his/her contemporaries are alive then interviews might be possible. For many biographical subjects there is a great deal of forensic work required to piece together the subject's life. And when all of the basic materials are assembled, the biographer has still to determine the story that will be written and the plot that will shape that story.

The life story is a narrative of a life as related by the subject. In this instance the subject tells their own story, about who they are and how and why they came to be that way. Not only does everyone have a life story in the sense of an overall account of how what they see as the significant events in their life explain who they are, but also we each have several life stories that we articulate at different times and places. When an adult is asked 'What do you do?' he or she will offer a statement about a job/career, interest or hobby, and will have ready a story about how they came to take up this activity and why. Relating aspects of our lives in story form is a normal aspect of our social interaction. In the previous chapter we looked at the CV as a particular kind of narrative about the self, intended to account for our development of particular skills and knowledge and our experience of performing one or more jobs. The life story is a universal means by which we express who we are and how we came to be who we are. Telling a life story does not require literacy, technological aids or any kind of special training beyond the everyday expressive competence of word and gesture.

The life history is an often scholarly form of personal narrative that is based on a life story, to which it adds a superstructure of analysis and interpretation. Life histories sometimes draw upon other forms of personal narrative apart from the life story: autobiography, biography and oral history have all been used to inform life histories. The life history narrates the course of the subject's life and seeks to account for the course that that life followed in terms of some explicit theory or theories of individual development and interaction. Life histories have been widely used in anthropology, social work, sociology, and psychotherapy. Though it resembles a biography, a life history always has some explanatory focus, and it is therefore not surprising that this is the kind of personal narrative most favoured by social scientists. The interaction of the researcher and the subject of the life history – whether alive or accessed through documents or interviews with others – will in most life histories be itself the object of methodological reflection, covering many of the issues of epistemology, validity and reliability that we discussed in Chapter 2. Theoretical and methodological issues of interpretation are made explicit in life histories in a way that is not the case in most biographies. The life history analyses the subject's life story or autobiography in a social, cultural and historical context.

We will shortly examine in some detail the materials from which personal narratives are built. What is worth noting at this point is that oral historical research, and indeed old-fashioned face-to-face interviewing, have long provided and continue to provide important data for narrative research in non-literate communities, or in literate communities where the people of interest to the researcher have not kept significant documentation on their own lives (Thompson, 2000). Now that digital media are near universally available, and with more than one billion people regularly using social networking sites that make it easy for them to record their life events, the future of personal narrative research is promising and offers new challenges.

> ## Box 5.3   What 'data' do you need to construct a 'scholarly' life history?
>
> There are many kinds of materials and interactions from which you can construct a personal narrative (see Maynes et al., 2008, chapter 3, for a discussion of sources of personal narratives). Most readers of the present volume will be writing or assessing the personal narrative from a social research perspective, from which you should ideally have full information on the provenance of each item (e.g. the date of creation, who made it, etc.):
>
> - Interview transcripts made by you or by others.
> - Audio visual recordings.
> - Hard copy correspondence, clippings, diaries, journals.
> - Hard copy and digital photos.
> - Web material:
>
>   o Sms, email, blog postings;
>   o social media profiles and posts.
>
> - Publications by or about the subject in print or digital form.
> - Relevant official records.

Structuring a life history

Polkinghorne (1995) suggests that we use Dollard's (1935) seven criteria for constructing a life history. These are as follows:

1. Descriptions of the cultural context of the case study.
2. Embodied nature of the protagonist.
3. Significant other people.
4. Choices and actions of the central person.
5. Historical continuity of the characters.
6. Plot.
7. Plausible and understandable descriptions of the cultural context of the case study ask us to render the symbolic world of the subject of the life history.

Let us take these criteria in turn. In order to understand the cultural context of the life history, you will need to investigate the value system of the subject's ordinary world, in particular the norms of communication in that world, which would involve specific ways of using language. From this you will learn something of the implied worldview from which the subject draws in order to give meaning to their life story.

As to the embodied nature of the protagonist, a key issue here would be the age of the subject in terms of what that might mean for placing that subject within a generic life cycle and also a more specific life cycle. Of course what counts as a life cycle, and how it is to be broken up into stages and what are the features and expectations of particular stages, would vary from one social and cultural context to another, so understanding the subject of the life history as an embodied being requires us to take into account some of the issues with regard to the cultural context of the life history: the subject would have lived in particular structures with particular kinds of social relations with definite kinds of cultural practices, and as such it is the job of the social researcher to construct an account of these and to place the subject as living breathing human being within webs of structures, relations and practices. We are reminded yet again of C.W. Mills's call to integrate biography, society and history, but now the emphasis is on the body of the biographical subject. Clearly gender, ethnicity, disability, and sexuality are all relevant here and these will inform how the researcher situates the embodied subject in a life history account (see papers in collection edited by Okely and Callaway, 1992). How far to go in 'embodying' your life history's subject is matter of judgement. I must note that Dollard (1935) refers to physique and genetic propensities in a way that I do not find altogether palatable; the reader must decide how persuasive they find his ideas.

Any adequate contextualistion of a life history must include treatment of significant other people in the subject's life story: these would be family, friends, neighbours and co-workers, indeed potentially any person in whatever role provided that they were seen as important enough to be mentioned by the subject in the telling of their own life story. You should note that filling in the context by paying attention to these other people need not mean that they all have to be included in your final report, only that you must give consideration to how significant these other persons were for the subject of the personal narrative. Techniques of characterisation as discussed earlier in the chapter might be useful to you in handling people connected to the subject as you build the life history, and as you work through drafts of your text you should consider and experiment with these. There is no exact prescription which will tell you how significant other people should be presented in your life history document, you will have to rely upon your own judgments and instinct, and in cases where it is possible to discuss the unfolding life history account with the subject of that life history then the subject's own views should be taken into account (though you must retain final responsibility for the document).

The subject's choices and actions are important with regard to the question of key turning points in the life account, to which we will come shortly. Issues of intention, motivation, and working towards, achieving, or failing to achieve, goals are all vital here. The question of historical continuity as discussed by Polkinghorne would lead us to place the subject's life story, as well as those of any other significant persons in that subject's life story, into an appropriate historical context. Major historical events do impact on the lives of individuals and part of your job is to work out which of these are appropriate and relevant for the life history that you are developing. You, as the author of the life history, must take responsibility for plotting the events. While the subject would have presented their own account in terms of sequenced events as they understood them, and your life history will be informed by this person's plot of their own life story, you will need to decide if you wish to add to or change that plot in any way, and if so, you must find a way to make clear what you did and why you did it.

The question of being plausible and understandable takes us back to the issue of verisimilitude. Even if you do not see yourself as working in a realist mode of representation, you must still give some thought as to how you will convey the subject's life story in a way that facilitates your readers in making connections to it. It is not a matter of assuming some naive one-to-one correspondence between the subject's embodied being, their social position, their mode of communication, or the time or place in which they lived, and the sensibilities of your reader. What you need to address here is the question of which textual strategies would be most appropriate in order to facilitate your readers' empathetic engagement with the life history that you are going to present. The list of exemplary life histories given at the end of this chapter should stimulate your thinking on this; in reading these exemplar texts, pay close attention to how the authors employ the techniques of textual construction that we have discussed so far.

Denzin's interpretive biography

According to Denzin (1989), a biographical researcher is an interpreter of the subject's life history. Working in a humanistic mode that places the subject's narrated experience at the centre of the analysis, Denzin advocates the use of thick description and thick interpretation (for the definitive account of thick description/interpretation see Geertz, 1993). Thick description requires placing the life events into a culturally meaningful context by seeking to account for how the subject's sense of the world shaped their actions. Thick interpretation requires the researcher to seek to make sense of the subject's life stories in a holistic manner that connects action with intention and reflection.

The researcher can gain insight into the symbolic world from which the subject accounts for their actions by seeking significant turning points in the life story or epiphanies. An epiphany is located in those problematic interactions and situations where the subject of the life story confronts and experiences a crisis that is seen by the subject to have had a decisive impact on the course of their life. What counts as an epiphany is not immediately obvious: while a situation recounted as a turning point or crisis by the subject may be a good candidate for an epiphany, it is the researcher's responsibility to make the argument for the analytical value of any events presented as epiphanies in the final life history report. Epiphanies are the key pivot points around which the life story of the subject are organised, and they link events into meaningful sequences.

An interpretatively adequate biographical account is one that is well triangulated. In order to achieve this Denzin advocates collecting in-depth personal histories through extended interviewing and/or documentary research; collecting multiple personal narratives from different individuals in the same milieu as that of the main subject, but located at different points in their life processes; and ensuring that the history, structure and individuals are fully and fairly balanced. The amount of work implied in Denzin's advice is not to be underestimated: one has to allow a great deal of time to collect multiple narratives for triangulation and then do the background work to construct a wider cultural and historical context for the life history.

Alongside his work on interpretive biography Denzin has also written on 'interpretive interactionism' (Denzin, 2001) where he reiterates an affinity for Mills's *Sociological Imagination,* and presents an approach that is informed by phenomenology, where the researcher identifies and brackets out significant experiences from the overall life story, studies these in isolation in order to identify their key characteristics, and then places these back into the life story with a deeper understanding of the meaning of these experiences for the subject.

A cautionary note on triangulation

Denzin (and Polkinghorne, 1988, 1995) argue for using multiple sources of data in order to triangulate the life history as we saw in the previous section, which is in keeping with C.W. Mills's approach in *The Sociological Imagination,* and also with the methods of creative non-fiction that we also discussed earlier in the chapter. But there are risks with triangulation; as Silverman (1993: 158) warns, triangulation can decouple the linkage between text and context because a triangulated text is used outside of its originating context in order to analyse it alongside other materials. While this problem should not be lightly dismissed, Silverman's caution need not lead us to reject any attempt at triangulation. The counter-posing of contexts does not inexorably lead to ignoring the context-bound character of social interaction. Triangulation may be seen as a type of categorising strategy, but it is not the ultimate aim of the life history or any other kind of narrative research report – it is rather a means whereby we seek to make interpretive sense of a core life story or other narrative data by cross checking and cross-reading with other stories and other kinds of data. We triangulate in order to give depth to our interpretive account. Moreover, software such as NVivo and similar qualitative data analysis tools allow us to preserve the original context of text as we make new kinds of connections.

Careful data management of the research materials will preserve enough of the context of the collection of the life story data so that you can share with the reader of your report the information that would allow that reader to judge how much might have been lost in counter-posing different texts and other data, and to weigh this against the gain in understanding the life history in question as located in social settings shared by others, from which shared social settings and other lives we draw material in order to triangulate the personal narrative of our main subject. In employing triangulation as a strategy in writing and reading personal narratives, we must confront the trade-off between, on the one hand, reading the narrative before us in its unique context, and on the other, setting it in a broader context that we must demonstrate to be theoretically, socially and historically relevant to the subject's life and our research questions. We have to balance the connecting and categorising based on what we wish to accomplish.

The composite personal narrative

One variation on the life history is a composite (or synthetic) report, which is a life history of a constructed person, based on elements taken from personal narratives of several real people. Here you illustrate a life course that is characteristic of a milieu or social position or identity by drawing on accounts from different individuals (Zeller, 1995). The composite personal narrative is a compact presentation that can allow a focus on those elements that the researcher thinks are most relevant. So why would you want to do this? Suppose that a survey of a range of life histories has revealed that the subjects' narratives display stages or turning points that are significant for understating particular identities or social relations that appear significant in the stories of the lives under study. These identities or relations could be further discussed under thematic heads with exemplary text from each individual life story being quoted as illustration. In a longer report or a book this may be fine, but in a shorter paper there is less scope for discussing the full range of illustrative supporting examples: faced with a need to be concise yet broad in coverage, you might find that there is simply no scope for multiple detailed personal narratives in your paper.

One way to tackle this is to construct a composite life history, drawing on elements of various life stories to create a constructed life story that integrates all of these. You must make it clear that you are doing this. There are some methodological objections but these are by no means impossible to address.

- First, to the objection that the composite narrative combines elements that were distinct in the originating life stories (namely stories of different lives) one might answer that the composite account sits in a long line of abstraction in social research: this is often employed in ethnography, where field notes on many instances of a practice are assembled by the ethnographer into a discussion of that practice as an idealised instance.
- In creative non-fiction (and the New Journalism) particular identities are rendered as assemblages of what is known about different persons who fit under the model of the identity that is being developed and explored (Agar, 1995).
- You can respond to validity concerns by making explicit the steps through which you transformed the material of the individual narratives into the final composite.
- If possible you should also make available the individual narratives so that your readers can satisfy themselves as to the basis for your composition (an online repository is ideal for this), assuming you have the relevant permissions to publish the original source narratives. At the very least you should present, perhaps in some kind of appendix to your report, brief profiles of the individual narratives on which you drew.
- It is important in constructing a composite life history that you document the background research and analysis that underpinned your choice of which elements in the individual narratives to focus on in order to build the composite, whether your worked inductively (data-first, from a close reading of the raw materials) or concept-first (if you began with a set of concepts that guided you in selecting which parts of the individual narratives to combine into the composite report).

Box 5.4   Composite personal narrative in use

In *Coding Freedom,* Coleman (2012) utilises what I call here the composite life history in order to illustrate the 'lifeworld' of hackers by, as she put it, 'visiting the sites, practices, events, and technical architectures through which hackers make as well as remake themselves individually and collectively'. Coleman drew upon the life stories of many hackers in order to present to her readers the figure of an ideal hacker, of a generic model of a hacker. By analysing practice, events and technologies she was able to create a conceptual framework which facilitated reading across the many hacker narratives to isolate common elements. Hackers narrate their personal development in terms of personality traits, abilities, technical preferences, cognitive styles and experiences that display

(Continued)

(Continued)

their similarity across a cohort and are relatively stable over time. The Free Software hackers she studied shared an identity, and from their life stories she constructed a kind of phenomenological and biographical account that maps closely onto Denzin's approach that we discussed earlier. Coleman offers a thematic treatment of the narratives of her hacker interlocutors, employing concepts derived both from the existing literature on hackers and hacking and from hackers' own accounts in order to isolate the key experiences and perspectives that make the hacker identity distinctive. Her account is interactive in that individual experiences are shown to interact with shared experience, and in turn the shared experience influences how individual hackers narrate their own experiences. In terms I have been using throughout this book, the individual and shared experiences of becoming and being hackers are both expressed in the narrative discourses through which the stories of hackers are conveyed, *and* shape these discourses themselves.

Autoethnography: A Special Case?

Autoethnography blurs the distinction between first order narratives (i.e. those produced by people about their normal life and circumstances) and second order narratives (i.e. those produced by social researchers based on data gathered in the field or from archives). This mode of reporting research combines aspects of personal narrative in the autobiographical mode with ethnography (Atkinson, 2006; Chang, 2008; Ellis et al., 2011; Reed-Danahay, 1997). On first approaching autoethnographic writing, you might find it helpful to imagine producing an account of your field research while staying centrally focused on yourself as the subject, and more so as the *research instrument*. Your observations, actions, reactions, decisions, interactions are all at the core of an autoethnographic account. So how is this different from autobiography? One obvious answer is that the autoethnography is an account of your *engagement* with the field research, and need not (and in fact in many cases would not) include a full account of your own personal life history. It might be the case that you choose to offer the reader some insight into your own autobiography that goes outside the time and space boundaries of the ethnographic research you are reporting, but that choice would be based on your deciding which aspects of your autobiography to include in order to advance the aims of the autoethnography. Because the autoethnography is a kind of ethnography your readers would expect your text to do some of the work of ethnography: giving an account of a specified social-cultural setting based on an extended period of participant observation. How then is an autoethnographic text different from ethnography? In keeping with the conventions of autobiographical writing, autoethnographies use a first person point of view, which is a clear differentiation from classic ethnography, where the third person point of view was predominant. But there is more to the autoethnography than an autobiographical standpoint: the ethnographic findings presented in an autoethnography are centrally based in the reflective *experience* of the author (Okely and Callaway, 1992). All ethnographic texts have narrativity: that quality of 'being narrative', of a text about what happened to one or more human or non-human entities, and change of state resulting from the passage of events in the narrative (we discussed narrativity in Chapter 3). The narrativity of the autoethnography has a more personal quality than many ethnographies precisely because the autoethnography is in large measure a kind of personal narrative. So the narrativity of the autoethnography is very much a *personal* narrativity.

Autoethnography emerged in the wake of a general concern with issues of representation in ethnography in the 1980s, and today displays two main tendencies—a postmodernist or evocative tendency (which is the more established), and an analytical tendency. Ellis's (2011) work represents the evocative and postmodernist tendency, while Anderson's (2006) study represents the analytical. Carolyn Ellis's *The Ethnographic I: A Methodological Novel About Autoethnography* (2004) is a genre-crossing text. The book combines autobiographical, fictional and ethnographic modes and styles of witting. This work has set the agenda for much autoethnographic writing, albeit with some controversy. In the introduction to her book Ellis draws our attention to a fundamental distinction in narrative research: between the first order narrative of the text's subject, and the second order narrative that is produced by the social researcher from another milieu or standpoint. We saw in Chapter 2 that this distinction is seen as fundamental in abductive research strategies. Ellis shows that the autoethnography blurs and even explodes any distinction between a first and second order narrative, precisely because the subject of the autoethnographic narrative is also the author. The autoethnographer is part novelist and part ethnographer, and for Ellis blurring of the boundary between social science and humanities is to be welcomed. Her autoethographic novel casts herself as a character, uses a range of literary devices to evoke the world as experienced by the author herself, and the text is unapologetically humanistic, not holding to established notions of validity and reliability. Ellis sees the autoethnographic text as free-standing in the sense of being an account from which there is no need or indeed any point in drawing generalisations. *The Ethnographic I* displays virtually none of the conventional social scientific features of positing research questions or hypotheses, of formal conceptual analysis, or critique of the literature. The novel form of this book with its dialogue and setting reads like nothing in mainstream social science, and when we follow Ellis through her rendering of feeling, of a range of emotions, we may begin to doubt that we are reading a sociological text at all.

Anderson (2006) has argued for an analytical autoethnography that is more in keeping with realist modes of social inquiry. The differences between the two tendencies were debated in a 2006 (vol. 35 no. 4) issue of the *Journal of Contemporary Ethnography*. He termed the approach of Ellis and others who work in a similar vein as 'evocative' autoethnography, which he contrasted with 'analytic autoethnography'. The key distinction for Anderson turns on the relation between autoethnography and the social world. Anderson agrees with Ellis that autoethnography is personal and humanistic, and is based on a reflexive account of the researcher's experience, but he argues that analytical autoethnography is also aiming to reconnect its works with a world outside the text, in a more classic social science move of generalisation. In terms of a fundamental distinction I have used throughout this book, Anderson's analytical autoethnography would engage to some degree with categorising as well as connecting strategies, while Ellis's evocative autoethnography is concerned only with what knowledge could be conveyed through the connection of events in the author's/researcher's experience into an autoethnographic narrative.

The definitive 'move' in autoethnography is to render connections from the personal reflective experience of the researcher to the wider social world, to 'describe and analyze personal experience in order to understand cultural experience' (Ellis et al., 2011). This work requires the researcher to be always aware of herself as the research instrument. It is her perceptions of and interactions with the research setting that form the raw material. As we saw earlier, Denzin wrote that the epiphany is a seen as a pivotal event/ point in the life story, a moment of clarity, of emotional intensity, which is retrospectively seen by the subject as marking a turning point in their life course, even if the event was not seen as such at the time it occurred. As we saw earlier as well, taking an event to be an epiphany may be partly the result of the subject reflecting on a course of life events and reinterpreting these in light of present circumstances or future goals. The epiphany does not have some objective reality. How do you identify epiphanies in your own autoethnographic work? More than keeping a detailed field journal, you will need to find ways to tap into your affective reactions to the work. There is no set procedure to follow here, but advanced journaling techniques can help. Writing a letter to yourself in the future can stimulate deep reflection on present experience. Using different media can also help: audio or video recording can stimulate different kinds of reflections from typing on your keyboard. I have personally found that going back to pen and paper increases the amount of time I can usefully spend writing in my research journal, if only because sitting at the computer keyboard is nowadays so closely associated with work in the formal sense of producing something for assessment by others, while writing by hand can seem more personal. The autoethnographer has to rid herself of the imagined thesis supervisor or journal editor who hovers over her shoulder as she writes, which means breaking with some of the established social science conventions of research writing (Richardson, 1990). If you have ever tried your hand at writing fiction, then it can help to revisit that mode of working; if not then you might try to write up some of your fieldwork in the form of a short story or even a news report. Many people find talking into a voice recorder useful. You should try all of these. An autoethnographic field journal should not be viewed only as a place to record 'proper' fieldnotes. It crosses over into the boundary of the deeply personal and private journal. Keeping two journals is a well-established technique for ethnographers: one for the recording of 'conventional fieldnotes' and another private journal. Autoethnographies are built from both types of journal and neither is to be privileged. At all times you must be mindful that autoethnography combines methods from both autobiographical and ethnographic work, and you may have to practise autobiographical journaling until it becomes as easy as a more conventional recording of fieldnotes.

An autoethnographer needs to read outside of the social science canon. Fiction, biography and autobiography should be part of your reading routine. From autobiography and fiction you will learn much about plot, pacing, point of view. Autoethnography makes more conscious use of the literary techniques developed in biographical and creative non-fiction fields. Presenting a text as autoethnography, whether evocative or analytical, creates certain expectations on the part of readers who are knowledgeable about ethnography: an autoethnography stands in large measure on the degree to which its author makes persuasive use of the autobiographic and ethnographic registers. Doing so is a matter of technique, which can be learned by studying published work in the field.

Autoethnographies run the risk of being considered not artful enough to meet the criteria of literary autobiography, and of being too 'personalistic' to meet the standards of analytical social science (Atkinson, 2006; Denzin, 2006). With regard to the first, all narrative-based research accounts can be evaluated for their literary merit; if your work gets you the degree or publication your aim for then that is satisfaction enough. Beyond that, if your work is judged to have noteworthy literary qualities then you should feel pleased that you have developed, and have had recognised, some talent as a writer. But your work should first be intended to pass the discipline-norm and peer review. Anything else is extra. As to social science assessment: the same techniques we discussed in Chapter 2 for addressing issues of reliability, validity and generalisation for narrative research across the board will apply to autoethnographic work. If you decide to use autoethnography in your own research project, you should be aware of the widely used evocative approach developed by Ellis, and of the contrasting analytic approach as discussed by Anderson. You should choose from the range of approaches in the field based on your own interests and research goals.

The Narrative Research Report: Pulling It All Together

On social science writing

Before turning to the specific structuring of the narrative research report, let us consider some general characteristics of social science writing (for comprehensive discussions of the processes and forms of social science writing, see Becker, 2007; Richardson, 1990). There are many forms of writing that a social researcher will produce throughout her career, ranging from the first undergraduate student essays, to the graduate and doctoral theses, and then journal articles, review essays, research monographs and reports. These are all in a sense final products, pieces that you hand over for assessment, review or publication. And there are various 'intermediate' forms of writing (outlines, drafts, field notes, study notes, teaching notes and journal entries) which are not produced for public consumption as it were, but are essential to process that results in the 'final' text (Emerson et al., 2011). These intermediate forms remind us that social science texts, as with all texts, are constructed; they are artefacts, they are made by people, and they display the effects and the traces of their making to a greater or lesser degree. Moreover, social science is always written in some institutional, social, cultural and political contexts, and these contexts have impact on the written product as well as on the process of writing (Geertz, 1988). Various genres and forms of writing influenced the making of the field known as social science, which, as we saw in Chapter 1, in its nineteenth-century origins, borrowed from the textual practices of the natural sciences as well as the literary arts, though the later borrowing was little acknowledged (Richardson, 1990). In keeping with generally accepted notions of 'social science', these texts are expected to present arguments and to draw on theory and/or data in support of their 'findings'. What ought to count as argument, theory and data are matters of debate in the methodology and epistemology of social research (we discussed methodology in Chapters 2 and 3).

So who are you writing for and why are you writing? Over the course of a career or even a research project, you will address different audiences who possess different analytical skills and different expectations. You will need to employ different strategies depending on whether the target audience is academic, policy-oriented, news media, the general public, or activist-oriented. The different audiences and aims might overlap. Richardson notes that 'social scientific writing depends upon narrative structure and narrative devices, although that structure and those devices are frequently masked by a scientific frame' (1990: 10). She further reminds us that social researchers must be mindful of literary devices like plot, pacing, character sketching, and metaphor. We must all be aware that these devices enter into all forms of writing if only to a minor degree. Rhetoric, in the strict sense of consciously using language to persuade, is present in all forms of social science writing, to a greater or lesser degree.

Form

It is often the case that the narrative research report will rely upon quite considerable quotation from interview transcripts or other kinds of primary source material. This has the potential to be a problem when we consider that undergraduate and Master theses, as well as most journal articles, have quite strict word limits. And then there is the question of how the conventional social scientific research report, with its structure of introduction, literature review, methodology and methods, presentation and discussion of findings, and then conclusion, can be made to work for a narrative research report (Bold, 2011). The narrative research report is after all narrative first, which means that the overall form of the text is shaped by the need to convey a storied account. It is important to distinguish the form of your research data (notes, transcripts etc.) from the form of the narrative report. There exist conventions around narrative writing in the social sciences, coming from practice in ethnography and personal narrative research, and also from the long tradition of qualitative research in the social sciences (especially useful are: Bazeley, 2013, Part 4; Becker, 2007; Richardson 1990; Wengraf, 2001, Part VI).

Because narrative research reports have formal properties that are dictated by the need to present a linked sequence of events, the narrative researcher might have to argue for a relaxation of formal social science writing conventions and for a form of presentation that is adequate for a storied account. In *Stylish Academic Writing* Helen Sword argues that all academic writing can benefit from authors seeking to convey their findings in terms of a compelling story (Sword, 2012, see chapters 8 and 9). Her point is not that academics should seek to become novelists, but that academics should educate themselves about the techniques and conventions that have been developed in literature and journalism, and apply these in their own work in order to engage the reader. 'Stylish' academic writing is neither dumbing down nor sexing up; it is about being conscious of how choices of style and rhetoric can be used to draw a reader into a work.

Voice

There are several perspectives from which you can choose to position yourself as the author of a narrative research report (Richardson, 1990; Stanley, 1995; Van Maanen, 2011). You could take on the role of the classical objective observer, keeping yourself very much in the background and confining information about yourself and your role in the project to a methodological note in the preface (as in classic works from the early Chicago sociological life histories). While this stance has come under largely justified criticism over the last few decades, such criticism by no means is fatal to adopting a classical realist stance as a social researcher. Another authorial standpoint is that of a fully engaged researcher who brings to the foreground the co-construction of the narrative research report as a shared work between the researcher and the informants. There is some considerable scope involved even within this perspective, in that a research report based on an extended period of in-depth fieldwork and interviews with one or more informants can lend itself quite directly to presentation as a shared work, as distinct from a report based on secondary sources, and more particularly on spontaneous narrative, in which the discourse studied was not produced at the behest of the researcher. Even in this latter case it is possible to 'share' authorship with those whose discourses form the evidential basis of your report (for work in which the text is shared, see Price, 1983, 1990).

Somewhere in between these two extremes we have an authorial stance which is not that of the objective observer, because the author writes herself as a researcher into the text, yet still makes a clear distinction between the social researcher as author and the elicited stories that form the basis of the report, or the spontaneous narrative discourses (for example: Coleman, 2012; Miller, 2011). You can opt to have a lengthy discussion of your own involvement and standpoint in the underlying research project in a methodology section, which could include a reflexive note on your own subjective positioning in the research. The research report in the form of an autoethnography lies on a continuum that spans the evocative to the analytical. In fact, the evocative to analytic continuum is broadly applicable to virtually any form of narrative research report.

Audience

Laurel Richardson (1990) has discussed the different genres and styles through which social science research can be reported. As documents that lean towards the humanistic end of social science writing, narrative research reports do lend themselves to presentation to an audience outside the academy. Richardson discussed the kinds of choices that she made in order to produce different versions of her work for different audiences.

Style

The style of your narrative research report will depend to a large extent on the standpoint you adopt as author, and on the intended audience. Becker (2007) argues strongly against a formal writing style built around passive constructions, hedging clauses and technical jargon. Sword (2012) concurs, seeing a passive, impersonalised style and reliance on jargon as the enemies of stylish academic writing. It is not surprising that both Becker and Sword, though they are not concerned with narrative as such, suggest that academics can learn much from novelists regarding the craft of writing. While the paradigmatic mode of cognition uses abstraction and technical language to construct its systems of concepts and its classificatory scheme, the narrative mode would appear at first glance to be open to non-specialists because its use of language is more concrete, based in everyday experience. In other words, the style of paradigmatic discourse would tend to be more analytical, while the style of narrative discourse would tend to be more evocative. But this distinction has the potential to mislead us; if we accept the view that narrative discourse is an essential element of scientific work, then storytelling is not at one end of a continuum of stylistic complexity, with science at the other.

The medium through which you will present your report will also have its own formal and stylistic conventions. Consider the classic 6–8,000 word social science journal article, as against a 1–2,000 word magazine or newspaper feature. And even within these two types of journal different stylistic conventions will come into play. The key point here is that narrative research reports by their very nature have stories at their core, but it can be a challenge, as Richardson and Becker have both pointed out, to maintain the evocative and humanistic richness of the story form while meeting the more formal requirements of academic publishing.

One case or many?

You will have to decide what would prove more effective in conveying your findings in a narrative research report: one case or many? You will also have to decide what counts as a case. At the simplest level we treat an individual's life story as a case. Sometimes though for the very same individual we might wish to treat different periods in that person's life – or even discrete events in that life – as cases. And when our report is based on observations of places and/or activities, the places or activities of interest become good candidates for being treated as cases (for discussions of designing and using cases, see Gerring, 2004; Yin, 2003).

In a report based on material from several different people, or places, or events and experiences, we have to decide how to present this material: sequentially, comparatively, or using some form of cross tabulation. The sequential is the simplest form, and will work when we want to present a set of stories for which either the ordering is unimportant, or for which the sequence of presentation is part of what is significant about our findings. This sequence is also important in a comparative report if only because story text cannot really be presented in parallel on a printed page, and even if it were, we would probably not want to read it in that way. For a comparative treatment of several narratives you will have to present early on in your report the basis of your comparison and decide the order of the stories and where you will interject the comparative discussion. For complex comparisons some kind of tabular summary of the stories could be positioned along each row as cases, and the categories or themes of comparison/contrast would occupy the columns. This tabular summary is not a substitute for a fuller presentation of the story data, but can be a supplement to it (see Wengraf, 2001: Chapter 16).

Digital storytelling

Thus far we have looked at digital media mainly as a source of data that can be analysed using different narrative approaches. These new media offer many possibilities for the effective communication of the findings derived from our narrative research (Dicks et al., 2005; Kozinets, 2009). Near universal web access alongside affordable devices for creation and consumption of content mean that researchers have new possibilities for sharing their work (Gubrium and Nat Turner, 2011). Before you rush off to export all of your materials into html format and publish it all to your personal blog, beware that there are practical, technical, and ethical issues that you must consider when thinking about making your narrative report available online. Make sure that you fully understand the implications for privacy with regard to the data you use – consult your institution's ethical guidelines.

So what are the concrete possibilities for digital research narratives? You have to consider both creation and sharing. I will address sharing first. Most academic institutions now offer a publishing platform/repository for the work of their members. Beyond the particular institution there are platforms such as scribd (www.scribd.com) and academic.edu (www.academia.edu). Scribd is an open publishing platform that allows intuitions and individuals to publish their work in digital form; it differs from, for example, Amazon's Kindle platform in that it has a strong focus on the ethics and practice of open access. Academia.edu is rather like 'Facebook for academics', offering the facilities of social networking alongside a publishing platform that is as complete as scribd, though with an exclusive academic focus. Academia.edu makes it easy to connect with people who share your research interests – there are many active groups on narrative research – and is a great way to share drafts and work in progress. The main advantages of these two platforms are: the ease of publication and sharing – you can upload a standard .doc/.odt or .pdf file, so no specialist skills in content creation are needed; instant access to a wide audience but with the ability to exercise some control over who you share your work with; no practical limitation on document lengths and file sizes, plus you have the ability to insert hyperlinks to organise your material; the appearance and underlying infrastructure are created and maintained for you, so you can concentrate on getting your work out to readers; you can bypass the traditional academic publishing infrastructure, which might be appropriate for some kinds of work. The main disadvantage of these platforms is a direct consequence of their ease of use and free cost: apart from managing copyright, there is no editorial and referee input. Open access in academia is here to stay: an online search will get you started learning about the issues and thinking about how they will impact on your own work.

In the next section we will discuss using mixed media, in particular audio-visual media, and the hypertext linking facilities of digital media, to enhance if not altogether supplement the conventional text-based narrative research report. At the very least we should consider presenting the findings of our narrative research on the Web because for twenty-first century social scientists web publishing is a given. We should also explore the potential for deepening and widening the narrative research report using various digital media and techniques. But, as we saw in the two previous chapters, narrativity and interactivity can militate against each other.

Using mixed media

I will assume no specialist technical skills here, though in the chapter following this one I will discuss a range of software tools that can enhance the work of the narrative researcher. It is not too difficult to acquire basic multimedia authoring skills (for excellent introductions see Garrand (2006) and Miller (2014); your own institution might offer training; for the independent researcher there are many online courses, I recommend those offered by www.lynda.com). I invite you to consider building some interactivity into the narrative research report. A key reason for doing so is that interactive web-based media offer one obvious way around the problem of the conventional lengths of journal articles, or for that matter research monographs, often militating against presenting the full set of textual (and audio-visual) data at the core of narrative research-based findings. Here are some ideas to get you started planning and building a mixed media narrative report:

• At the very least we can make a web accessible and searchable resource available to our readers by posting online the complete (or near complete) narrative text derived from our research.

- Another idea is to use a mind map, at the top level of which we have the major thematic points around which we have organised and analysed our narrative findings.
- Whether we use a web page or interactive mind map, the top-level points of our report can then be hyperlinked through to the supporting textual and/or audio-visual material, thereby allowing the reader to have immediate access to the evidential base upon which we have built our narrative research report. *Having a web-based supporting resource to a conventional report is the only practical way to present a large audio-visual dataset.*
- We can go further here: through using the hyperlinking and connecting features of an interactive mind map-type structure we can make it easy for the reader to follow cross-references and thus explore our findings in a way that goes beyond the linear structure of a conventional report (for a detailed guide to creating hypermedia research reports, see Dicks et al., 2005, Chapter 8). This may well reduce the narrativity of our findings, but if an interactive report is made available in addition to a conventional text-based report, then we will have gained overall in terms of communication.

Beyond this, and assuming that you either possess the needed skills or more likely that through your institution you can access these skills, then you might want to consider bringing yourself into the frame by actually audio visually narrating some or all of your research findings. With sites such as YouTube and Vimeo, making such a presentation available to readers is actually quite easy these days. If your skills and resources are relatively limited, or if you are a bit shy about going in front of a video camera, you can still increase the multimedia impact of your narrative research report by recording an audio introduction and perhaps a short presentation on the key points of your analysis, findings and conclusion. It is not too difficult, using the recording facilities built into any modern smart phone or tablet, to do a few short takes in which you record yourself presenting a short version of your research report, and this audio recording (I'm assuming here that you do not want to go for a fully-fledged video recording) could then form part of the web-based supplementary material to your report. To show how easy this can be, I have made available on the book's website a skeleton interactive/multimedia narrative research report with links to web-based and audio-visual supporting resources.

Summary

In this chapter we discussed how social researchers can employ narrative techniques as a way of analysing and presenting research. We looked at techniques used in creative non-fiction and New Journalism. It is in these two fields that writers and researchers explored the textual strategies that are shared between fictional and non-fictional narratives. Both the New Journalism and creative non-fiction explicitly draw upon narrative techniques developed by novelists and other creative writers in order to tell more compelling stories about culture and society. Ethnographers and the wider community of social scientists, especially those concerned with narrative, should pay close attention to these developments.

We then discussed the interview as a research process which could be usefully understood as the joint creation of narrative. Interviewees and the persons interviewing them are engaged in processes of meaning making through narrative. We addressed the personal narrative discussing the various types and their characteristics, the construction of personal narratives with special reference to the life history which is the type most frequently used by social scientists, and looked at the characteristics and writing of autoethnography. We then looked at how to pull all of this together into a narrative research report, both as a traditional written report and in terms of using mixed media and hypertext to enhance that research report.

Questions to consider

1. What are the advantages of using a storytelling approach in communicating social research findings?

   a. Consider the role of stories in social science writing.
   b. What skills are required of a 'digital storyteller'?

2. Regarding the different types of personal narrative:

   a. What data are needed to construct a social scientific life history?
   b. Investigate biographies of social scientists.
   c. Investigate autobiographies by social scientists.

3. What is distinctive about the autoethnography as an approach to writing in social science?

   a. Are autoethnographies more personal narratives than they are ethnographies?

Further reading

Agar, J. (1995) 'Literary journalism as ethnography: exploring the excluded middle'. In J. Van Maanen (ed.), *Representation in Ethnography.* Thousand Oaks, CA: Sage. pp. 112–29.

Anderson, L. (2006) 'Analytic autoethnography', *Journal of Contemporary Ethnography, 35*(4): 373–95.

Becker, H.S. (2007) *Writing for Social Scientists: How to Start and Finish Your Thesis, Book, or Article* (2nd edn). Chicago: University of Chicago Press.

Dicks, B., Mason, B., Coffey, A.J., et al. (2005) *Qualitative Research and Hypermedia: Ethnography for the Digital Age.* London: Sage.

Ellis, C.S. & Bochner, A.P. (2006) 'Analyzing analytic autoethnography: an autopsy', *Journal of Contemporary Ethnography, 35*(4): 429–49.

Miller, C.H. (2014) *Digital Storytelling: A Creator's Guide to Interactive Entertainment.* 3 edition. Burlington, MA: Focal Press.

Muncey, T. (2010) *Creating Autoethnographies.* Sage Publications Ltd.

Plummer, K. (2001) *Documents of Life 2: An Invitation to a Critical Humanism* (fully revised and expanded edn). London: Sage.

Richardson, L. (1990) *Writing Strategies: Reaching Diverse Audiences.* Thousand oaks, CA: Sage.

Sword, H. (2012) *Stylish Academic Writing.* Cambridge, MA: Harvard University Press.

Zeller, N. (1995) 'Narrative strategies for case reports.' In J.A. Hatch and R. Wisniewski (eds), *Life History and Narrative.* London: Falmer.

Exemplar works using narrative methods:

Alleyne, B.W. (2002) *Radicals against Race: Black Activism and Cultural Politics.* Oxford, UK; New York: Berg. (My own ethnographic and biographical study of a group of radical antiracist cultural activists.)

Herzfeld, M. (1997) *Portrait of a Greek Imagination: An Ethnographic Biography of Andreas Nenedakis.* Chicago: University of Chicago Press. (This work draws on history, ethnography, fiction and personal narrative.)

Mintz, S. (1960) *Worker in the Cane: A Puerto Rican Life History.* New Haven: Yale University Press. (A classic anthropological life history.)

Passerini, L. (1996) *Autobiography of a Generation.* 1 edition. Middletown, Conn.: Wesleyan University Press. (Blends autobiography and life history in an account of the revolutionary politics of 1968.)

6

TECHNIQUES AND TOOLS FOR THE NARRATIVE RESEARCHER

OVERVIEW

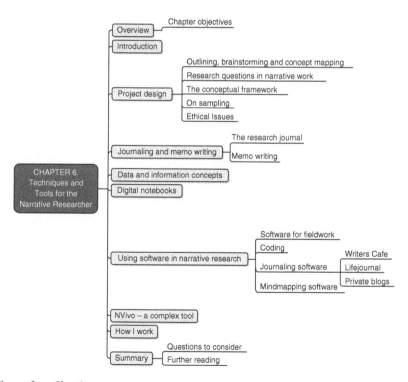

Figure 6.1   Chapter map

Key learning objectives

- To discuss issues of project design for a project using narrative approaches, including brainstorming, formulating research questions, ethical issues, and sampling strategies.

- To introduce techniques of journaling and memo writing.

- To introduce key concepts of data and information management that are relevant to narrative research.

- To discuss a range of general purpose and specialised software tools that can aid the narrative researcher in data organisation, analysis and reporting.

Introduction

In this chapter we will discuss the design and management of projects that employ narrative approaches. We will look at outlining and brainstorming the initial ideas, and then we will discuss the formulation of research questions. We will also highlight ethical issues and sampling strategies as these are relevant to the narrative researcher. Whether using fieldwork, textual analysis or archival work, you should develop the habits of keeping a research journal and writing memos. In keeping with this book's emphasis on the digital, I will introduce some key concepts of data and information management, and I will discuss a range of general purpose and specialised software tools that aid the narrative researcher in data organisation, analysis and reporting. I will refer to software that I myself used and any recommendations are solely based on my judgement of the fitness of the software for the academic purposes addressed in this book. Software is updated more frequently than printed books, so I have given general advice/instructions on how to use the packages; the reader should consult this book's website (www.narrativenetworks.net) where I have up-to-date references to software with short tutorials and supporting materials.

Project Design

Let us begin with project design. In Chapter 2 we discussed the methodological issues that are most relevant for narrative approaches in social research. Here we will bring these issues to bear on the conception and implementation of an effective research design for a narrative project (for a discussion that includes narrative among other kinds of project design, see Creswell, 2012: chapter 3).

Outlining, brainstorming and concept mapping

The importance of outlining cannot be stressed enough in the early stages of a narrative as indeed with any research project. By 'outlining' I mean organising all of your ideas into a coherent form and making explicit the connections between the various parts of your research project. Before going into detail on the tools and techniques for outlining and laying out your ideas on a project, let me just state an important rule of research: get the ideas out of your head and onto paper. An unrecorded idea is of little use to yourself or for that matter to anyone else. This is why I will emphasise the importance of keeping a journal, the form of which is not as important as the ease with which you can access it and the security with which you can ensure its contents. It is in your journal that you will jot down your initial ideas on your research project, which given that you have invested time in reading this book will be concerned with one or more aspects of narrative inquiry. So, if you have not already done so, *start a project journal:* don't worry if you are not familiar with journaling software because we will come to that. For now, it is enough to get out a sheet of paper or start a new word processor file on your computer. *You do not have to be engaged in ethnographic fieldwork to keep a project journal: all students and researchers in the social sciences should keep journals.*

A key question to ask yourself is: Why do you want to work with narrative materials and/or write a narrative research report? Your answer(s) here will do nicely as a way of starting your project journal, so write them down. At the planning stages of your work, and then throughout the project, it can be useful to sketch out a rough diagram that captures your thoughts as to what might be happening and what your initial expectations are. For a narrative project that sketch should include the people, places, events and processes in the setting or document(s) on which you will work. You can capture these thoughts in words, but why not do both? Most people find that they think more clearly when they express their thoughts in a combination of words and images. Quite a lot has been written on brainstorming; in my own work and in my undergraduate and postgraduate teaching I have found graphical mind mapping to be extremely useful. I will refer to brainstorming and mind mapping as virtually interchangeable. One of your first brainstorming sessions should involve getting your key concepts down on paper. So where do you get these key concepts from? I would suggest that you begin by imagining yourself having to explain your proposed research project to a non-specialist and having only a minute or so in which to make that explanation. Do the following:

1. So get out a bit of paper or turn on your computer and write out a few sentences or draw a simple diagram to sum up your proposed research project.
2. If you make a sketch, then add labels for people, places and events.

3. Then look at what you have written/drawn and circle all of the naming terms, the nouns (perhaps you might want to highlight these in one colour, either with a highlighter pen if working on paper, or using your word processor's highlighting feature).Your naming phrases are the objects or entities (the 'things', i.e. the people, places, objects) in which you are interested; these are the basic elements of any story.
4. Next, look at your sketch/outline and highlight using another colour the verbs in your statement of the draft research project: these verbs indicate what is happening and to whom, or who is doing what to whom or what in your project, and they can give you some insight into the processes in which you might be interested.

Repeat any of above the steps as necessary. This exercise will help you in establishing the narrativity of your research object. In formal narrative theory there is a distinction between events involving people and happenings that do not involve people, but don't worry about this at this early stage because brainstorming is all about getting thoughts out of your head and objectifying these on paper in a textural or graphical form. As you do so you will begin to get more insight into your thought processes. Early insights lead eventually to greater clarity. The templates/schemas that we saw in Chapter 3 might be useful in framing your thoughts, but remember that these are not recipes to be followed mechanically.

Keep in mind that these outlining/brainstorming steps are actually iterative and you can expect to go through them more than once and to dip in and out of the cycle as often as you feel it necessary to do so (Maxwell 2012a). I would advise that you archive all of your diagrams and outlines in your project journal: whether working on paper or on a computer, attach a date to each outline, drawing or mind map, and file it away in your research journal. It is very important that you keep a record over time of your changing thoughts about your project design.

Box 6.1   Preliminary design for (brainstorming) a narrative research project

You might find it useful to organise your early planning work around these four headings:

- Keywords.
- Questions.
- Data.
- Expectation/'working hypothesis'.

Keywords: look at a recent article based on narrative research that was published in an academic journal in your disciplinary area. Most journal articles begin with an abstract followed by a list of five to seven keywords. You might want to think about your developing research project outline as developing an account of your research which you can imagine to be a very rough draft of an abstract, and the terms that you earlier extracted from your short project description could be seen as draft keywords. This draft list of keywords should include entities and events. Expect to go over this list of key terms repeatedly and refine it as necessary.

Questions: a research project has to pose one or more questions. We will be looking at the formation of research questions in greater detail in the section following this one. For now however what you should bear in mind as you do the initial brainstorming of your project is that you must express your project in terms of a problem and/or question involving narrative materials and/or methods which the project will set out, not so much to solve, but to investigate in a way that makes sense in social science.

Data: how will you answer your research question or questions? You will need some kind of data to do so; what kind will depend on whether you are intending to do analysis of narratives or narrative analysis. Data can come from observation, ethnography, web materials, archival work, and more. At the early stages of brainstorming your research project you will need to record your thoughts on possible sources of relevant data for addressing your research question. Think about and write down any ideas that come to mind on how you will give empirical support to your proposed research. Closely related to what kinds of data might be useful is the question of how you will collect or generate those data. This will get you started thinking about your research methods, that is to say the techniques whereby you will source, collect, organise and analyse data. Whether you are engaged in analysis of narrative or narrative analysis, you will need to make clear the justification for the methods of data gathering and analysis that you chose (on data planning, see Bazeley 2013: chapter 2).

Expectation/'working hypothesis': though it might seem counterintuitive to a new researcher, it is actually quite a good idea in the early stages of planning a research project to document your expectations as to what you will find out in the course of pursuing the proposed research; this can take the form of a simple statement of what you expect to find and why, a tentative informal

(Continued)

(Continued)

hypothesis. It is rather old-fashioned to think that by reflecting at the start about your expectations as to what your eventual findings will be you thereby introduce bias into the research project. Against this somewhat quaint view I want to suggest that we all have expectations, whether vague or quite detailed, as to what we will learn in the course of pursuing a social science research project. These expectations will come from prior experience, reviewing other research, our political and theoretical standpoints, or simply our intuition. It makes sense to be honest about having these prior expectations, and by capturing them in your journal, you can ensure that you are constantly testing your expanding knowledge against your initial (and changing) expectations.

Research questions in narrative work

Research questions, as we saw in Chapter 2, take the basic form of 'what' type questions, which call for descriptive answers, and 'why' and 'how' type questions, which call for an explanation in terms of social processes or structures (Blaikie, 2009). The narrative research approaches discussed in this book can be used to address any of these types of questions. Narrative approaches tend to be mainly informed by some version of the abductive research strategy, where the symbolic world of informants is seen as having its own ordering principles which it is our job to translate into the language of social science. In analysis of narrative we frame our research questions around approaches from narratology if doing structuralist analysis, or around themes if doing thematic analysis. In narrative analysis, research questions are framed in such a way that we explore them through data about people and events that we emplot into story form, and we aim to present our findings in the form of narrative. So research questions in narrative research will be framed mainly if not entirely in terms of interpreting the lived reality of people through the stories they tell about themselves and their worlds.

The conceptual framework

What is your project about? What do you think is happening? From your reflections on these questions you can begin to construct your conceptual framework (Maxwell, 2012a: chapter 2). The concepts included in the conceptual framework should be coherent and consistent, and drawn from one or more models about the social world from which your narrative material comes. Most often the starting point for a conceptual framework will be a review of the research literature on your research topic. In narrative research, conceptual frameworks are built up from ideas that are fundamental to the various types of analysis of narrative and narrative analysis that we discussed in previous chapters. For analysis of narrative, if we are working inductively, as with some form of grounded theory, our concepts will emerge from our initial exploration of our narrative materials, and will be refined as we go over that material iteratively. If we are doing analysis of narrative from a concept-first starting point, then our initial concepts will come from one of the established approaches for analysing narrative, such as Barthes' or Todorov's structural approaches. For narrative analysis, our fundamental concepts are those to do with constructing narratives, such as story, plot, point of view, and character. I agree with Maxwell's advice to sketch out your conceptual framework in diagram form. Having decided on what kind of narrative research you are doing and being equipped with some starting concepts, you should then move to build one or more concept maps or hierarchical outlines (you can do this by hand or with any of the software tools discussed in the present chapter).

Box 6.2   Building a concept map

1. Start with a key idea.
2. Add linked ideas freely around it.
3. Think of how these ideas should be placed into a hierarchy or web.
4. Place the other concepts as appropriate.
5. Connect these and label the connections.
6. Revise and redraft as necessary.

I would advise keeping older versions of the concept maps in your field journal. On the book's website (www.narrativenetworks.net) I present a sample conceptual map.

On sampling

In narrative research we are either collecting texts that are themselves narratives or which contain narrative elements, and/or collecting observational data that we will organise into a sequence and shape into narrative. Whichever type of narrative research we intend to do, we have to consider how many texts or observations to collect, which involves sampling. There are established sampling procedures and which ones we select will depend on the questions we are seeking to explore and the kind of design we have thought up for the research project (Creswell 2012: chapter 7). As social researchers we will often want to make generalisations from our findings. We may want to move from the particular case or set of cases (a case here being a narrative text or interviewee or observation) to making more general statements about a population, i.e. the large grouping of people in which we are interested. For most populations of interest it would be prohibitively expensive to contact every member in order to pursue our research aims. A more realistic approach would be to investigate a sample of that population. This sample will be a subset of the overall population in which we are interested. Sampling falls under two main heads, probability and non-probability, and which type we choose will depend on our research design.

In **probability sampling**, each member of the population must have a non-zero chance of being part of the sample. In order to ensure this we need to have a sample frame (i.e. a data set containing some information on every member of our population of interest) as a starting point. There are many techniques for probability sampling, and here I will present no more than an overview (I refer below to people as cases, but many of these issues are relevant for selecting texts as well):

- The *simple random sample* is one in which each member of the population has the same chance of being selected for the sample. There are different methods for drawing a simple random sample: use a random number generator and match each random number to a case in the sample frame; or employ a systematic sample, where we select every nth member of the sample frame. It is important that the sample frame is not grouped in any way apart from a simple sequence, as this would lend bias to our sample.
- In the *stratified sample*, we break up the sample according to groupings that are relevant for our research, e.g. by gender or by degree subject for students, and then we use one of the above techniques to draw a simple random sample.
- In the *cluster sample*, we address issues of geographical spread: we could begin with a sample frame of geographical areas; draw some from this; then draw neighbourhoods and streets. This makes the actual legwork of surveying much easier.

With **non-probability sampling**, each member of the population does not have a specific chance of being chosen. This implies that we have no sample frame. As with probability sampling, there are many techniques for non-probability sampling, of which I present three here that should be most useful to a narrative researcher:

- With *quota sampling* we decide about desirable characteristics in our sample and then seek out cases that fit these characteristics.
- With *snowball sampling* we know little about how to locate people from the population in which we are interested, and we are in contact with

just one or two people; having contacted at least one person who fits the profile we want to study, we then ask them to put us into contact with other people in a similar situation.

- The *convenience sample* is one where the cases selected are entirely at the convenience of the researcher. It is worth repeating that we cannot draw statistical inferences from non-probability samples, but this does not mean that we are not doing proper social research.

Mason (2002) discusses strategic, illustrative, and representative sampling. In strategic sampling, the sample should capture a relevant range in relation to the universe but not represent it directly (2002: 123–4). In an illustrative or evocative sample, we intend the sample to be illustrative or evocative of some aspect of the overall population in which we are interested; it maps to the theoretical sample we discussed above. With representational sampling, we must know about the relevant characteristics or attributes of the overall population (variables), which means that the parameters of the total population must be known (it therefore maps unto probability sampling as we discussed earlier). Mason notes that this is the least commonly used in qualitative research.

Ethical issues

There are formal procedures and review processes regarding ethics for any social research project (Hammersley, 2012; Heider and Massanari, 2012). What these are in your own case will depend on your own institution and disciplinary area; you must navigate these in order to have your research project approved. It is your responsibility to find out about these and to meet all of the requirements. Here I want to consider briefly the question of ethics from a more personal perspective. It would be a good idea at the beginning and at various stages throughout your project to write a few memos about ethics in your research journal from a purely personal standpoint. The value of such an exercise is to engage reflexively with yourself as a research instrument. Your ethics memos should include something on your own prior experience, your political standpoint (which can be that of an objective observer in the sense that you may not feel you have any stake in the politics of your research setting), and your motivations for pursuing the research. Objectify this, by writing down, your own social position in terms of social class, gender etc.

Next, obtain and review the relevant codes of professional practice for your discipline and institution, and make your own annotations on these in your ethics memos/journal. Do this in addition to any formal documentation you must prepare as part of an ethical clearance procedure. Give some consideration to how you will regulate yourself in the research, because it is you ultimately who must be your own ethical monitor. How will you use others' time and materials? What will happen to your final report? Who will read/assess/use it, and how and why might they do this? Make note of the answers to all of these questions.

With the ease of accessing electronic information in today's world comes a host of new issues for the ethics of social research, around privacy, intellectual property and copyright. It is fashionable in some circles to claim that digital media mean that intellectual property and copyright are largely obsolete. I would reject any such claim. Whatever your personal and political views on these subjects, you should be guided by the established procedures on use of data as set out by your discipline and institution. If you are an independent (as in non-affiliated) researcher, then I would advise you to consult the ethics guidelines, which are freely available online, of one of the national social science associations (the American or the British Sociological or Anthropological Associations, or their equivalents in your own country) or ask for advice at a local library. Always assume that you have to attribute a source for any digital data, and that in all but the most obvious cases, you will be subject to restrictions of some sort on the use of digital data. If you do want to pursue a radical politics that rejects all forms of intellectual property and copyright then you are on your own, but you have been warned.

Journaling and Memo Writing

The research journal

You do not have to be an ethnographer to keep a journal; indeed, anyone involved in research of any kind should keep one. On this there is no better advice than that of Mills in his appendix on craft in *The Sociological Imagination*. Your journal is a tool for reflection, discovery, experimentation, and self-discovery. In keeping a journal you are in effect producing some of the raw materials that will allow you to think narratively about your research project (narratively in the sense of making a story). The point here is to think of your research project as a kind of unfolding narrative, quite apart from whether or not you intend that research to result in a narrative document (Clandinin and Connelly, 2000: chapters 6 and 7) .

You should aim to be self-aware in terms of how your ongoing research can be thought about in narrative terms, and to record these reflections in your journal. You need not of course show that journal to anyone else. There is always a story unfolding as you proceed through a research project, whether that project be qualitative, mixed methods, or even quantitative. Your research journal, understood as a narrative, is a way to reflect on your own intellectual development through organising your activities and thoughts into stories. A very fruitful exercise is to review that journal at various points in the project and write a memo/journal entry that renders your progress up to that point in the form of a story. Pay particular attention to insights or breakthroughs, which will be better understood when you can trace the steps through your research that led to and followed on from the insight/breakthrough; this story memo should then be added to your journal.

How you make entries in your journal is largely a personal matter, but in keeping with the theme of working digitally, I would recommend that you keep your journal in a digital form and later in the chapter I will review several software applications that will facilitate this. Maintaining a digital journal does not mean that you have to type up all of your journal entries on a computer. You could decide to use the 'old-school' approach of writing in a notebook, which does have the advantage of being exceptionally portable and also less likely to draw the attention of people around you, which can be important in some fieldwork situations. In such a case you should aim to type up or scan your handwritten pages and sketches on a regular basis. This is also a useful backup, especially if you copy the scanned materials to some kind of cloud-based storage (make sure that you understand the privacy and security implications of using cloud storage). There are no fully reliable means of converting handwritten text into digital form unless you invest in specialist software. Many people opt for voice memos. Any recent smart phone or tablet will have the facility to record voice notes, and some may even offer speech recognition and transcription though the results are not perfect. Dedicated digital voice recorders capable of recording 100 hours of sound are now affordable commodity items. So, with all of these options available, you have different modes of making regular entries in your journal. Choose a method and stick with it.

When to make journal entries will vary according to the individual and the circumstances of the project. In classic ethnographic fieldwork in anthropology and sociology, it is standard practice to make entries in a field journal several times a day and to have a daily review session in which the day's jottings are assembled to create a more complete entry (Emerson et al., 2011). Outside of ethnography, a social researcher using narrative approaches should aim to write at least one weekly journal entry, no matter how brief.

Memo writing is usually associated with grounded theory, but is in fact generally applicable to all forms of social research (Layder, 1998; Maxwell, 2012a). In the broader sense in which Maxwell uses the term, a memo is a particular kind of journal entry: the identity memo is where you record thoughts about your identity and standpoint; developing views on theory are recorded in theoretical memos; and your ongoing views on what you are learning through your research are recorded in analytical memos. You don't have to use this terminology, you can simply record entries in your journal on theory, identity and analysis as you work. The key point is to make the entries, date them, and then review them on a regular basis. You can use the memo facilities of a specialist package such as NVivo for this, you can use a generic journal keeping software as discussed below, or you can make dated entries in a digital notebook such as Evernote (www.evernote.com) or Onenote (www.onenote.com), or in a (private) blog, also discussed below. Whichever form of digital entry you opt for it should allow you to tag your entries with keywords. Even if you do not intend to do any in-depth coding and retrieval on your materials, it is vital that you tag your journal entries (and primary narrative data) to indicate at the very least places, people, events, and ideas about themes. No matter which methods you employ, you will need to have some minimal set of narrative concepts and themes that will frame you work. These are the basic tags/keywords which you will use in your memos and to which you will add as the work proceeds.

Data and Information Concepts

In order to take an objectifying look at data management from the perspective of a narrative researcher, we must step back to consider the very idea of data (data is the plural of 'datum', though in computing and increasingly in popular culture, data is used as a collective noun. I mostly use data as a collective noun, in keeping with the wider general usage). As a working definition we can take data to refer to facts about the world. On its own, data has no intrinsic meaning: for example, the observation that there is a large suitcase in the middle of my sitting room is data, but what does it mean? Humans give meaning to data by placing it in some kind of interpretive framework. We combine the raw data with other knowledge and so make it meaningful; sometimes that meaning comes from our knowledge of prior events that we connect to the data before us, thus creating some kind of story to make sense of the new data. In social research our theories, research questions, and knowledge of related research, all allow us to give meaning to data. When we have applied some kind of meaning-making framework to data we have created information (Hartley et al., 2008: chapters 1 and 2). Thus, information = data + meaning. When I add to my observation of that large suitcase in my sitting room my recollection that I am expecting a visit from my aunt who lives overseas, and I recall that I gave her a spare set of keys on her last visit and that she sent me a text from the airport, I have a meaning-making context, i.e. a story, by means of which the observed data, i.e. the suitcase, is combined with contextual or interpretive knowledge to transform the initial data into information.

If information is the next level up from data, then knowledge is at a higher level yet, and may be viewed as information organised in such a way as to be useful for a given purpose. As we saw in Chapter 1, organising information into storied form is one of the two main modes of human understanding of the world around us; the other is organising information into categories. Both these modes of cognition can be seen to work by transforming raw data into information and then information into useful knowledge. When information is timely, appropriate and accurate it becomes knowledge. In narrative research a great part of the data you will work with will be stories in text, graphic or audio-visual form, and recorded events from which you will build stories. As a narrative researcher your job will be to then transform these materials into social science findings, into knowledge.

The materials collected and generated by a narrative researcher will take the form of textual or audio/visual materials that have different structures and can be seen to have the status of knowledge in the formal working definitions given earlier. But it is normal to talk of 'research data' in the social societies. There is no conclusion here, just a recognition that the 'raw materials' in narrative research come in forms that already have meaning attached as it were, which it is our job to tease out and recast in social science terms. So our data will in a sense always be information, and our job will be to produce knowledge in the fields of social sciences from that material.

A *database* is an organised collection of related information that facilitates storage and retrieval. This can be a collection of index cards, interview transcripts, or texts or recordings stored on a local computer or as cloud. Nowadays most researchers will manage their data in digital form, so I will focus on digital databases, which can be divided into two basic types, table-based and freeform. In order to manage the range of data produced in narrative research we will often need both kinds of database.

The most common type of database will store information in tables, consisting of fields organised in rows and columns. A field is a single piece of information about a subject. A record is a complete set of fields relating to the same subject. Each record occupies one row in the table. A column consists of the fields on a single piece of information for all the records in your table. While you may be thinking here of vast commercial or government databases, what I have in mind is more personal in scope. You probably have already used tables to store and organise data: a simple list of persons you interviewed, with the name of the person, their date of birth and gender, and the time and place of the interview, is a database. A full transcript of an interview, with a column for the time code and another for text that runs from that time code to the next, is also a database. A list of time-stamped observations in a field diary is also a database.

What about data that do not fit into tables? In narrative research we most commonly work with textual materials that are free-form or unstructured (indeed, as we saw in Chapter 3, analysis of narrative involves applying one or more narrative theories to text as data in order to 'transform' that text into narrative, or to 'retrieve' narrative from the text). Such data can also be stored and managed in a type of database that we can term a 'freeform database'. Let us now consider the characteristics of freeform databases (Richards, 2009; chapter 2). In a freeform database your data do not conform to the table-based arrangement of rows and columns in a conventional database. In a freeform database, each record can have a different structure. This is important precisely because much of the data we need to store and retrieve in narrative research does not come in a format that can be easily mapped onto tables with fixed records (rows) and fields (columns) of the same size. Typical freeform, unstructured, or loosely structured data we use in narrative work take the form of (this is not a complete list, of course):

- letters;
- web pages;
- emails;
- handwritten notes;
- sketches;
- transcripts;
- audiovisual materials.

Digital Notebooks

I have recommended converting all of your materials to digital form. Even if you do some drafting and diagramming by hand, as I often do, you should still get into the habit of making a daily or at least several times weekly task in which you will move these items into digital form, either by scanning them or by entering them using the appropriate text or graphic-based software. The extra work involved is more than compensated for by the benefits of computer-assisted search and retrieval, backup, and information sharing on the Web. In our digital age all researchers should use some form of digital notebook and I want to discuss some of these now.

If you've decided to use journaling software such as LifeJournal (www.lifejournal.com), Writer's Cafe (www.writerscafe.co.uk), MacJournal (www.marinersoftware.com/products/macjournal) or WinJournal (www.marinersoftware.com/products/winjournal) to maintain your research journal, then you can simply keep all of your materials in your chosen application (I have provided walkthroughs for using these software packages on the book's website). But at the risk of adding an additional layer of complexity, you might want to consider whether you wish to have online access to your journal and other research materials. If you do, then note that Writer's Cafe runs only on your local computer (you should check if this is the case when you actually read this, as the software in constant development). By contrast LifeJournal, Winjournal and MacJournal offer the possibility of moving your journal online through the option to post one or more general entries to a blog. *You must be absolutely certain that you are aware of the privacy and data protection issues involved in posting research materials to a blog:* if your aim is to have an automatic back-up, and a web-based version that normally you or other people on your research team can access, then you must first set up the target blog with the appropriate security settings *before* beginning to post entries from your journaling software (consult the help pages of your blog provider and/or your institution's information technology support help). What you absolutely do not want to have happen is that you accidentally post sensitive or confidential information to a publicly accessible blog. LifeJournal offers a web-based version that obviates the need to post from a local software package to a blog; the online LifeJournal application is in effect a private blog, with all of the tagging and timeline organisation features of the local LifeJournal package. You will have to make up your own mind as to how comfortable you are with managing your data entirely in the cloud. I am not, and I prefer to have all of my data on properly secured computers that I manage and then to copy it to the cloud, which allows me to have both a back-up and web access to my research materials while I'm on the move.

Another approach is to dispense entirely with specialist journaling software and simply keep your journal and all of your other materials in a hybrid digital notebook, of which the two best-known examples are Evernote (www.evernote.com) and Onenote (onenote.com). Both Evernote and Onenote are free and run on PCs and Macs, tablets and smartphones, and both have web-based versions that are accessible from any computer with a web browser, with the ability to synchronise all of your materials with cloud storage. Both of these packages allow you to store any kind of digital data (text, photographs, audio and video recordings, and captured web pages, have all of these automatically indexed for quick search and retrieval). Because Evernote and Onenote were not specially designed with journaling in mind, you will need to have some means of allowing date-based storage and retrieval of your journal entries. Both software packages have diary templates as add-ins. Adapting either package to journal use is not too difficult as both allow you to create as many subnotebooks or subsections of notebooks as you need. So you might create in either of these packages a notebook called something like 'My research journal', within which you can store your date-based journal entries. You can either create a template page or simply begin each journal entry with the date in the year-month-date (which maintains the proper chronological order), and if necessary a time entry, below which you will enter whatever you require for the content of the journal entry.

In sum, the features of Onenote and Evernote that are most relevant for a narrative researcher are:

- tags can be applied to documents though not phrases or words;
- you can have several tags on a document;
- you can create your own tags;
- you can search for tags within notebooks and sections of notebooks and the tag display can be grouped in various ways;
- You can then create a summary page from your search, and that summary page has links back to the source pages.

I have provided walkthroughs for using all of these packages on the book's website.

Using Software in Narrative Research

A key question facing the qualitative researcher in today's world is not whether to use software but what software to use for which tasks. The advantages of using appropriate software in support of your research are now outweigh the added complexity and time need to learn to use the software (Silver and Lewins, 2014). Nowadays a great deal of secondary and sometimes primary data comes from online sources and so it is a good idea to think about how you can manage these (Richards, 2009).

Software for fieldwork

Some kinds of narrative research will involve your gathering material in the field through interview and observation. The minimal suite of software that I would recommend for a fieldworker would comprise a wordprocessor and some kind of digital notebook such as Evernote or Onenote. With these you can enter and pre-code all of your narrative data as well as manage any kind of audiovisual material that you might collect. And with web access you can have synchronisation and the security of having an offsite back-up. This is not to say that traditional methods of pencil and paper cannot be recommended, in fact I still do a fair amount of work by hand and then scan my handwritten notes and sketches into a computer database program (Onenote in my case). This is a very effective workflow and it means that you don't have to be encumbered with a laptop or tablet, which might be inappropriate or unworkable in some fieldwork situations.

For most fieldworkers a digital voice recorder is an essential item, which carries the advantage that the recordings are already in digital form and that means you can take advantage of modern kinds of transcription software, even though these do not allow the fully automatic transcription of field recordings (an unfulfilled promise, as such software tends to be trained and tuned to just one user and such software would have great difficulty in getting any kind of reliable automatic transcription of the ebb and flow of conversation in a group of different people). A digitised interview recording already takes you some way towards analysis, in that many computer-assisted qualitative data analysis packages will allow you to store and annotate these recordings, and indeed many of these packages will also allow you to prepare and store full transcripts of a recording in the database along with the recording itself.

Coding

We discussed coding in Chapter 2, but here I want to address a practical matter of coding in the sense of flagging up passages or concepts in a way that will make it easy for you to access these text passages later, as a task to be carried out throughout your research project, irrespective of whether you are working in a mode inspired by grounded theory or any other established approach that relies upon the use of codes. Coding is essential in narrative research whether the approach is categorising or connecting. Conventions have emerged around coding. Open coding involves reading through the materials and tagging/highlighting anything of significance in terms of any prior conceptual framework (deductive coding) and in terms of anything your encounter that is of significance (inductive coding).

If you're working with material in narrative form then obviously you are going to be thinking about cases and concepts, and at the very least you should have some simple coding system to mark these. As you read through your materials you should tag anything of interest for further consideration and analysis. This tagging can be a formal assignment of codes as in grounded theory, or a theory or concept-first type of coding system where you begin with a set of concepts that are assigned codes which you then use to work further on the material; or it can be as simple as highlighting blocks of text and making a simple note to yourself as to the significance of each block of text. By tagging and annotating both your research materials *and* your journal entries as you proceed through your project, you will in essence be creating a coding system which you can later decide to formalise using some of the techniques discussed by Bazeley (2013: chapters 5 and 6) and Layder (1998: chapter 3). Even if you do nothing else, your tags, highlights and annotations will aid your ongoing reflection and analysis. The point here is to use the facilities of the software to tag and highlight as you go along.

Journaling software

Following are some of the software tools that might prove useful for journaling. These are all software applications I myself have used.

Writer's Cafe

Writer's Cafe (www.writerscafe.co.uk) has a built-in journaling tool that offers all the features you might need for keeping a research journal. It is a simple matter to search through the journal and export selected or all entries to a standard word processing format text. The software runs on PCs and Macs.

LifeJournal

The same holds true for LifeJournal (www.lifejournal.com), which runs natively on PCs and is also available as a web application. LifeJournal offers the standard entry, search and other features one would expect of journaling software. In addition, this package offers a full set of keyword tagging of entries: you can assign a tag or code to a word, any block of text or a whole entry, and you can make your own tagging system, which can be hierarchical. In effect, LifeJournal offers you the kind of categorising capability for text entries that you would normally find in specialist qualitative analysis software like NVivo (www.qsrinternatinal.com). When combined with the capability to organise entries on a timeline, LifeJournal, like Writer's Cafe, is in fact a versatile workstation for a narrative researcher, offering as it does tools to support both categorising (tagging features) and connecting (organising entries along a timeline, for plotting). Which of the two packages to use depends on personal preference.

Private blogs

The main advantage of a private blog is the ease of access from any internet-connected computer, and not needing to learn any Mac- or PC-specific modes of working with your journal data. The key point is to ensure that the blog really is private if that is what you intended. The responsibility to ensure the privacy of research data is yours, and whatever blog platform you choose to use as a private research blog it is entirely up to you to make sure that you have met the data protection requirements of your own discipline and institution. In my view a private blog is well-suited to keeping your own research journal, but is not as well adapted as either LifeJournal or Writer's Cafe for organising event data from which you intend to build a narrative research report.

Mindmapping software

The idea behind mind mapping as developed by Tony Buzan (2006) is that capturing thoughts through a combination of words and images, and using line, colour, and space on the page to indicate the relationship between

concepts, can facilitate a comprehensive use of cognitive abilities by drawing upon both left and right brain cognitive capabilities. In my own work
I use a combination of rough sketches by hand (which I scan and incorporate into my digital journal) and mindmapping software.

Here I want to direct you to some available software tools that will support these processes. Before doing so I must reiterate that mind and concept
mapping, and indeed general diagramming, can quite properly be carried
out with pencil and paper. Having said that, performing these tasks on a
computer will facilitate ease of creation and modification as well as integrating mind and concept maps into your research journal, your drafts, and
perhaps even the final research report.

There are many mindmapping software packages available; the ones I
have used are Inspiration (www.inspiration.com), Mindjet Mindmanager
(www.mindjet.com); Novamind (www.novamind.com), and Scapple
(www.literatureandlatte.com/scapple.php), all of which work on both the
Mac and PC, as well as tablets and the Web. On this book's website you will
find walkthroughs that demonstrate how to use these software packages for
brainstorming a narrative research project. I prepared the mind maps that
appear at the start of each chapter in this book using Novamind, and all of
the other diagrams using Inspiration.

Freemind (http://freemind.sourceforge.net) is free software and can be
obtained and used at no cost. It offers all of the features of a basic mindmapping package: maps can have links to other files and to web pages attached
to any of their branches; each branch can have notes attached; branches can
have keyword tags; and most importantly, the map and any notes can be
exported as a web page or as a rich text document, which facilitates incor-
poration into your drafts and final report. Freemind is available for Windows,
Mac and Linux.

Mindmanager and Novamind offer more advanced features than
Freemind, and especially more powerful diagramming tools, and the maps
they produce offer a wider range of designs and templates. Both have a tight
integration with Microsoft Word, and both make it easy to incorporate web
pages and RSS feeds into the map. In addition, both tools allow you to construct your map as a hierarchical text outline, which can be an effective way
to structure your final report. Both also run on Mac and Windows, but must
be purchased. There are educational discounts available. Both have 30-day
trial periods which will allow you to determine if either meets your needs.
Both come with built-in templates that can help you get started in mind
mapping, and both have substantial tutorial material and documentation.

Inspiration and its web-based version, Webspiration, both combine the
features of an outliner, a general diagramming tool, and mind mapping in
one. It is the easiest to use of these mapping tools, though its mind mapping
does not have the range of graphic styles found in Mindmanager or
Novamind. On the other hand, it can be used to produce a far wider range

of diagrams, and has some simple templates for story plotting and making timelines that, while intended for high school students, can be useful for the narrative researcher. Inspiration runs on Mac and Windows, while Webspiration is a web app and works on any computer with a web browser and Flash plugin installed. There is also an ipad version of Inspiration available. Like Mindjet and Novamind, it is easy to export your work to any standard word processor, or to PowerPoint for that matter. Webspiration is a subscription app while Inspiration has a purchase price. Educational discounts are available. Some scenarios in which these packages would be useful are:

- laying out your key concepts and themes;
- mapping the event data in graphical form, which is helpful for getting at the bigger picture of the story you aim to analyse or construct;
- making a graphical timeline of the key events in a narrative;
- conveying a plot in graphical form;
- building a 'character tree', in which each individual has a main branch, and with sub-branches for characteristics.

Box 6.3   Using journaling software for the entire project

The general writing and journal tools I have so far discussed (Writer's Cafe, or LifeJournal) can be used in any project based around a connecting strategy, where the aim is to present findings in narrative form, or for a project in which you are analysing already reacted narratives in text form, though it is not the most powerful tool for this second kind of project. LifeJournal, with its focus on journaling and autobiographical writing, is especially well-suited to life history, biographical and autobiographical work, and its facility for grouping entries on a graphical timeline, with time periods fully under your control, makes it an excellent tool for many kinds of narrative work. In addition to its journaling and timeline facilities this package offers tagging and keyword facilities, which mean that it can be used from the very start of a narrative project for the initial coding of materials.

For a small-scale narrative research project, involving up to ten cases and with all the source documents being less than a hundred, it may not be worth the effort to use a high-end package such as NVivo, and it is for this reason that you may want to consider a journaling package. If you have over a hundred source documents, materials in audio-visual format, or are using mixed methods or working in a team, then you will want to invest your time in learning how to use a specialist data analysis package such as NVivo, and setting it up as you need for your project. The following advice is for those working on a small-scale, one-person project, who are comfortable with journaling or blogging applications and do not wish to learn how to use specialist and highly complex software such as NVivo.

In using LifeJournal for a generic categorising analysis in which you are working with a set of materials in text and audiovisual form, you would do the following (the procedures for MacJournal and WinJournal are very similar):

1. *Prepare your materials.*

   If you want to import text then all of your text or transcripts should be in a rich text format (if you have web material that is not more than a few dozen pages or so, then you can copy and paste the text into a LifeJournal entry, or you can prepare your text documents in a word processor and save these as individual RTF or .doc files). Otherwise you can enter material by typing.

   Any graphics or pictures that can be copied into a word processor file, can be imported into LifeJournal.

   You cannot manage video files directly in this software, so you will need to make transcripts or summaries and annotations of the video material in text form and import these (if you need to handle video files directly, then you should look at NVivo or a similar package).

2. *Start a new journal with the project name* (you should password protect this journal).

   If you want to use a blog as a supplement to your journal software then set it up with proper privacy settings, and enter those settings into LifeJournal.

3. *Set up a keyword/tag system as appropriate for your project.*

   One top level tag for 'Research journal' with appropriate lower level keywords.

   One top level tag for 'Personal Journal' (optional but highly recommended).

   Depending on how you have designed your project, you could then create a top level entry for each case, person or event, for example, with subcategories for the characteristics of the

(Continued)

(Continued)

case that you want to track. You can add more tags as you go along, and change existing ones without affecting already tagged text.

If you are doing thematic analysis, then create a tag for each theme.

If doing structuralist analysis, then you can adapt the analytical scheme to a system of codes (I have several examples on the book's website).

4. Immediately you will begin to see the value of using journal software: every entry you make will have a date (and time stamp, if you need to have multiple entries on the same date).

5. You will then be able to use the basic yet powerful analysis tools in LifeJournal: you can search on tags, date, or the content of text; you can create new entries based on the result of a search (very useful for creating summary entries); and you will have an automatically updated timeline that you can collapse or expand as needed to show time periods from days to decades.

For a small-scale narrative project using mainly text-based materials, LifeJournal, and similar software such as MacJournal or WinJournal, can offer most of what you need to manage and analyse your materials. When you are ready to prepare your final report, you simply export what you need from the package in a universally readable .doc or rtf format. You can then finish the report with your word processor, adding any special formatting, citations and graphics that you need.

Writer's Cafe offers similar facilities to LifeJournal but is targetted specifically at fiction writers, which can be an advantage for a researcher creating a narrative report where they want to pay particular attention to adapting techniques from creative non-fiction. Writer's Cafe has tools for plotting that work at several levels, from chapters down to individual scenes, and for managing places and characters. It has a powerful plotting tool called Storylines, which is a sophisticated and excellent means of organising textual material along one or more plotlines. Given that the storied elements of novels and of many types of non-fiction narrative are structurally similar, Writer's Cafe turns out to be an effective tool for planning and writing a work of narrative analysis. While this software can in principle be adapted for a small-scale project of either deductive or inductive analysis of narrative, it does not have the tagging facilities of LifeJournal, and so I would advise using Writer's Cafe for journaling and narrative analysis, but not for analysis of narrative materials.

Scrivener is a powerful general purpose writer's tool that runs on Windows, Mac and Linux (I used Scrivener to compose the text for this book and it is my basic writing tool for any text beyond a few pages). It has powerful editing tools and is excellent for managing different versions of the same text. It offers, as does Writer's Cafe, tools for the graphical organisation of your material in an outline form or on virtual index cards. It does however not have any built-in timeline tool. Scrivener has powerful outlining tools that exceed those of Writer's Cafe, but the latter has better graphical tools for planning and exploring the sequencing of material in narrative text. Scrivener does not have a built-in journaling tool, but you can use it to keep a project journal if you are disciplined in heading up every journal entry in a YYYY-MM-DD format, which will yield a properly sorted journal.

In summary, any of these software packages would serve as a general purpose tool for a narrative analyst, allowing the keeping of a project journal, notes and memos, storing narrative texts, tagging text, and organising the final report. Scrivener has strong organisational tools, but will need to be used in conjunction with other software for timeline management. Scrivener is in my view best suited for preparing the final report for publication, and while some people use it to keep a journal and fieldnotes, doing so requires some more work than with the other two. I would suggest that either LifeJournal or Writer's Cafe should be used for keeping a research journal, which is essential. If needed, then either of these can be used to organise materials on a timeline, and both offer tagging and output tools. LifeJournal is stronger on a journal-based approach, while Writer's Cafe is more of an all-rounder. I use all three because I am a bit of software geek and like to try new things. For several years I kept my journals in Writer's Cafe, then moved to LifeJournal because of its stronger tagging tools. I now use Writer's Cafe for planning and organising narrative reports.

NVivo: A Complex Tool

NVivo, as with other specialist qualitative data analysis tools such as MaxQDA, is of most use with a project in which there is a large body of textual or audiovisual material to be analysed, and/or when several researchers are involved. While many of its text analysis and organisational tools are of value to a narrative researcher, you will need to think through your analytic strategy before creating an NVivo project (Bazeley & Jackson, 2013). Of the many features of NVivo, I will highlight those that are most useful to the narrative researcher (the other major software tools for qualitative data

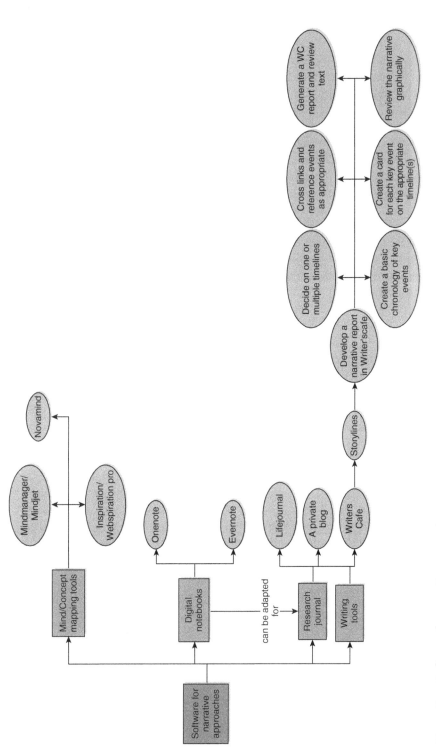

Figure 6.2   Software for narrative research

analysis have similar features; for a comparative treatment of these tools, see Silver and Lewins, 2014).

Managing data: NVivo can import and handle material in a text, audio and visual format; it can capture webpages from any website; it can import social media data from Facebook, Twitter and LinkedIn. It can also import data from Evernote and Onenote. It has tools for transcribing any imported audio or video material; it can help with your literature review as well if you import and code pdfs of journal articles; and it can synchronise with your reference manager software.

Analysis: NVivo is highly capable for carrying out analysis of narrative, whether inductively or theory-driven; it was designed for managing multiple texts and comparing these across categories and codes, so it is well suited to any form of structuralist analysis (note that you will have to implement your analytical framework as a coding system). It is also useful for thematic analysis in that themes can be assigned to codes, and texts once imported can be easily coded for analysis. NVivo can be used for close work on a single text, but may be overkill in such a scenario; it is most useful for work on multiple texts. It can handle any kind of discourse analysis and it has many built-in tools for qualitative and quantitative text analysis. It has visual modelling tools, and can link the graphic items in the model to underlying text or audiovisual materials. NVivo does not have a dedicated timeline organisation tool, but with some imagination, its graphical modeller can be adapted for the visualisation of plot elements. You can create any of the analytical templates I discussed in this book in NVivo, and I have included some examples of these on the book's website.

Reporting: you can generate various kinds of reports from your project file, but NVivo does not offer direct help in structuring a narrative research report.

Some ideas for using NVivo for narrative research:

- Creating a code structure:
  - Assign codes to key elements of any structural model you might be using (e.g. Labov)
  - Assign codes to any major themes, whether arrived at deductively or inductively
  - Assign codes to any elements of discourse analysis you use
- Use codes and memos to keep track of significant people, places, events and objects
- Use the model builder to create a graphical timeline and plot line for your narrative(s);
  - Coded passages of text can be linked to this graphical model
- Use the text search facilities to explore the textual features of the text(s)

See the template NVivo project on this book's website.

How I Work

As should be clear to you by now I am a geek, i.e. a technology enthusiast, and I do all of my work in a digital environment. I either gather data in digital form, or invest the time in digitising research materials. This is increasingly easy nowadays in fieldwork as the creation of digital recordings for audio and video is trivial and a matter of selecting and learning to use the right equipment. With regard to text most of what I use for analysis was originally in digital form or I invested the time in digitising. For work with archival material in physical forms I make summaries and detailed notes which I manage in software, going back to the physical source as necessary.

I plan all of my writing and teaching using a graphical/text outliner, either Inspiration or Novamind. Each project that I'm currently working on has an entry in my Onenote digital notebook. (Onenote is my own preference but Evernote on the Mac works just as well. I use both PCs and Macs. I did say I was geek.) Entering everything into a digital notebook greatly eases the searching and indexing of data and my own fieldnotes and drafts, and the online synchronisation gives me both secure and automatic back-up, as well as access to all of my project data from any web-connected computer.

For short individual narrative texts or for a project in which I have fewer than 20 or so texts to work with, I find it convenient to do the annotation and mark-up within my digital notebook itself. Once my texts exceed 50 in number then I will invest the time in setting up a new project in NVIVO (my preferred qualitative data analysis software package) and importing copies of the material from my digital notebook. I make a habit of writing up journal entries and memos at least twice a week, and I keep my personal and project journals separate, even though there is often some overlap of entries between the two. For organising narrative research reports I would give consideration to whether I want to adapt one of the tools intended for use by fiction writers, which are especially useful in writing up personal narratives. I use Writer's Cafe to organise materials for an ongoing biographical study. There is of course an investment of time entailed in learning to use all of these tools. But time invested in the right tools will yield dividends in data management and flexibility of analysis.

Summary

The design of narrative research projects entails careful planning. The design of the project will depend on the extent to which the research will be engaged in analysing narratives and/or in writing up their research in the form of a narrative report, or perhaps combining both. We discussed techniques for outlining and brainstorming, as well as journaling and memo writing, all of which are essential tasks at the conception and throughout the life of any kind of narrative research project. I introduced some basic concepts in data and information management, as an understanding of these will help the researcher to efficiently and effectively gather, manage and analyse data in digital form.

Software tools can help with project planning, data management, analysis, and reporting and presentation of findings. We then looked at a range of software tools that can be of use to the narrative researcher. As a minimum I would advise that you should have some form of web-connected digital notebook and several suggestions were made in this regard. I think that much more use could be made by social researchers of software tools that were designed for the creation of fictional narrative: I discussed some tools that can help in managing event timelines, in plotting and in keeping track of scenes and characters, all of which are especially useful for narrative analysis and for the production of narrative research reports. I gave a brief overview of NVivo, a very powerful but also highly complex software tool for qualitative data analysis; I also offered advice on when it might be appropriate to use software of that kind. Many of the analytical templates discussed in this book are available on the accompanying website as NVivo templates and as templates or skeleton projects for many of the other software applications that were discussed in the chapter.

Questions to consider

1. For a narrative research project you wish to carry out, identify the core set of software tools that would support your work.
2. Investigate different mindmapping and journaling software tools. Write a three to five page report on what you find.
3. Try to implement some of the suggestions for project design that were given in this chapter, either for a real project of your own or for an imagined one. See the book's website for sample narrative project designs.

Further reading

Bazeley, P. (2013) *Qualitative Data Analysis: Practical Strategies.* London: Sage.
Becker, H.S. (1998) *Tricks of the Trade: How To Think About Your Research While You're Doing It.* Chicago: University of Chicago Press.
Becker, H.S. (2007) *Telling About Society.* Chicago: University of Chicago Press.

Buzan, T. (2006) *The Ultimate Book of Mind Maps: Unlock Your Creativity, Boost Your Memory, Change Your Life*. London: Harper Thorsons.

Creswell, J.W. (2012) *Qualitative Inquiry and Research Design: Choosing Among Five Approaches* (3rd edn). Thousand Oaks, CA: Sage.

Fielding, N., Lee, R.M. and Blank, G. (eds) (2008) *The SAGE Handbook of Online Research Methods*. Los Angeles, [Calif.]; London: SAGE, Available from: http://SRMO.sagepub.com/view/the-sage-handbook-of-online-research-methods/SAGE.xml.

Maxwell, J.A. (2012) *Qualitative Research Design: An Interactive Approach: 41* (3rd edn). Thousand Oaks, CA: Sage.

Richards, L. (2009) *Handling Qualitative Data: A Practical Guide*. Second Edition edition. London: SAGE Publications Ltd.

Silver, C. and Lewins, A. (2014) *Using Software in Qualitative Research: A Step-by-Step Guide*. Second Edition. SAGE Publications Ltd.

CODA

What I sought to do in this book was to present some fundamental ideas from narrative theory and show how social researchers can apply these in designing, carrying out and assessing narrative research.

A narrative researcher must begin with Bruner's ideas on the two fundamental modes of cognition – the paradigmatic and the narrative. Our ability to take ourselves out of the present, reflect on the past and project our hopes into the future is what makes us fundamentally human. Storytelling is as basic a human competence as the ability to communicate through language; indeed the two competencies are closely interrelated.

After the various narrative twists and turns of the past fifty years, sociologists and anthropologists are more than ever comfortable with storytelling as a method and source of data. In fact the pendulum has swung very much in our favour. Scientists are embracing narratives as well. They always used narrative, but few admitted it, being concerned to remain in the lofty heights of objectivity.

We live in a rapidly expanding narrative economy. People everywhere are recording life events on an unprecedented scale. Blogging and the ubiquitous mobile phone connected to the Web mean that there is now an ease of capturing our life events that is new. In all of this there is some connection to the long-established diaristic tradition, but now far more people are using microblogging and social networking than ever kept personal journals. Even the journaling tradition has had a new lease of life.

I aimed to set my book apart by focusing on narrative use in and research on areas of life that have been impacted on by digital technology. Social networking, digital media and video gaming are ubiquitous elements of contemporary life. I hope this book has encouraged you to seek out and explore narrative texts in these and other areas.

We are human. We are networks. And we narrate.

REFERENCES

Abbott, H.P. (2008) *The Cambridge Introduction to Narrative* (2nd edn). Cambridge: Cambridge University Press.

Agar, J. (1995) 'Literary journalism as ethnography: exploring the excluded middle'. In J. Van Maanen (ed.), *Representation in Ethnography*. Thousand Oaks, CA: Sage. pp. 112–29.

Alleyne, B.W. (2002) *Radicals Against Race: Black Activism and Cultural Politics.* Oxford: Berg.

Anderson, L. (2006) 'Analytic autoethnography', *Journal of Contemporary Ethnography*, 35(4): 373–95. doi:10.1177/0891241605280449

Andrews, M. (1991) *Lifetimes of Commitment: Aging, Politics, Psychology.* Cambridge: Cambridge University Press.

Andrews, M. (2007) *Shaping History: Narratives of Political Change.* Cambridge: Cambridge University Press.

Angrosino, M.V. (1989) *Documents of Interaction: Biography, Autobiography and Life History in Social Science Perspective.* Gainsville: University of Florida Press.

Aronowitz, S. (2012) *Taking It Big: C. Wright Mills and the Making of Political Intellectuals.* New York: Columbia University Press.

Atkinson, P. (1990) *The Ethnographic Imagination: Textual Constructions of Reality.* London: Routledge.

Atkinson, P. (2006) 'Rescuing autoethnography', *Journal of Contemporary Ethnography*, 35(4): 400–4. doi:10.1177/0891241606286980

Atkinson, P., Delamont, S., Lofland, J., Lofland, L. and Coffey, A. (eds) (2007) *Handbook of Ethnography.* London: Sage.

Bal, M. (2009) *Narratology: Introduction to the Theory of Narrative* (3rd edn). Toronto: University of Toronto Press.

Banks, A. and Banks, S.P. (1998) *Fiction and Social Research: By Ice or Fire.* Walnut Creek, CA: AltaMira.

Barthes, R. (1993) 'Introduction to the structural analysis of narrative'. In S. Sontag (ed.), *A Roland Barthes Reader.* London: Vintage. pp. 351–295.

Bax, D.S. (2011) *Discourse and Genre: Using Language in Context* (1st edn). Basingstoke: Palgrave Macmillan.

Bazeley, P. (2013) *Qualitative Data Analysis: Practical Strategies.* London: Sage.

Bazeley, P. and Jackson, K. (2013) *Qualitative Data Analysis with NVivo* (2nd edn). London: Sage. Available at www.uk.sagepub.com/bazeleynvivo/ (last accessed 15 June 2014).

Becker, H.S. (2007) *Writing for Social Scientists: How to Start and Finish Your Thesis, Book, or Article* (2nd edn). Chicago: University of Chicago Press.

Becker, H.S. (1998) *Tricks of the Trade: How to Think about Your Research While You're Doing It.* Chicago: University of Chicago Press.

Becker, H.S. (2007) *Telling about Society.* Chicago: University of Chicago Press.

Berger, A.A. (1997) *Narratives in Popular Culture, Media, and Everyday Life.* Thousand Oaks, CA: Sage.

Berger, M. (1977) *Real and Imagined Worlds: The Novel and Social Science.* Cambridge, MA: Harvard University Press.

Berger, P. and Luckmann, T. (1967) *The Social Construction of Reality: A Treatise in the Sociology of Knowledge.* Harmondsworth: Penguin.

Berger, R.J. and Quinney, R. (2005) *Storytelling Sociology: Narrative as Social Inquiry.* Boulder, CO: Lynne Rienner.

Blaikie, N. (2007) *Approaches to Social Enquiry: Advancing Knowledge* (2nd edn). Cambridge: Polity.

Blaikie, N. (2009) *Designing Social Research: The Logic of Anticipation.* 2nd ed. Cambridge, UK; Malden, MA: Polity.

Blommaert, J. and Bulcaen, C. (2000) 'Critical discourse analysis', *Annual Review of Anthropology, 29:* 447–66.

Bold, C. (2011) *Using Narrative in Research.* London: Sage.

Booth, W. C. (2008) *The Craft of Research, Third Edition.* 3rd revised edition. Chicago: University of Chicago Press.

Boyd, D. (2011) 'Social network sites as network publics'. In Z. Papacharissi (ed.), *A Networked Self: Identity, Community and Culture on Social Network Sites.* New York: Routledge. pp. 39–58.

Boynton, R. (2005) *The New New Journalism: Conversations with America's Best Nonfiction Writers on Their Craft.* New York: Vintage.

Brown, P. (2014) *Through the Eye of a Needle: Wealth, the Fall of Rome, and the Making of Christianity in the West, 350–550 A.D. .* Princeton University Press.

Bruner, J.S. (1986) *Actual Minds, Possible Worlds.* Cambridge, MA: Harvard University Press.

Bruner, J.S. (1991) 'The narrative construction of reality', *Critical Inquiry, 18*(1): 1–21. doi:10.2307/1343711

Bulmer, M. (1986) *The Chicago School of Sociology: Institutionalization, Diversity and the Rise of Sociological Research* (new edn). Chicago: University of Chicago Press.

Buzan, T. (2006) *The Ultimate Book of Mind Maps: Unlock Your Creativity, Boost Your Memory, Change Your Life.* London: HarperThorsons.

Campbell, J. (1993) *The Hero with a Thousand Faces.* London: Fontana.

Campbell-Kelly, M. (2004) *From Airline Reservations to Sonic the Hedgehog: A History of the Software Industry* (new edn). Cambridge, MA: MIT Press.

Carrithers, M. (1985) 'An alternative social history of the self'. In M. Carrithers, S. Collins and S. Lukes (eds), *The Category of the Person: Anthropology, Philosophy, History.* Cambridge: Cambridge University Press. pp. 234–56.

Cassar, R. (2013) 'Gramsci and games', *Games and Culture, 8*(5): 330–53. doi:10.1177/1555412013493499

Castro, E.V. de (1998) 'Cosmological deixis and Amerindian perspectivism', *Journal of the Royal Anthropological Institute, 4*(3): 469–88. doi:10.2307/3034157

Chang, H.V. (2008) *Autoethnography as Method* (illustrated edn). San Francisco, CA: Left Coast.

Chatman, S. (1978) *Story and Discourse: Narrative Structure in Fiction and Film.* Ithaca: Cornell University Press.

Cheongbi, S. (2009) *The Bill Gates Story: The Computer Genius Who Changed the World* (3rd edn). Englewood Cliffs, NJ: DASANBOOKS.

Chicago Commission on Race Relations (1922) *The Negro in Chicago: A Study of Race Relations and a Race Riot [with plates]*. Chicago: Chicago Commission on Race Relations. p. 672.

Clandinin, D.J. and Connelly, F.M. (2000) *Narrative Inquiry: Experience and Story in Qualitative Research*. 1st edn. San Francisco, Calif: Jossey-Bass.

Claybaugh, A. (2007) *The Novel of Purpose: Literature and Social Reform in the Anglo-American World*. Ithaca: Cornell University Press.

Clifford, J. and Marcus, G.E. (eds) (1986) *Writing Culture: The Poetics and Politics of Ethnography*. Berkeley: University of California Press.

Coffey, A. and Atkinson, P. (1996) *Making Sense of Qualitative Data: Complementary Research Strategies*. Thousand Oaks, CA: Sage.

Coleman, E.G. (2012) *Coding Freedom: The Ethics and Aesthetics of Hacking*. Princeton: Princeton University Press.

Collier, A. (1994) *Critical Realism: An Introduction to Roy Bhaskar's Philosophy*. London: Verso.

Collins, H. (2010) *Tacit and Explicit Knowledge*. Chicago: University Of Chicago Press.

Conover, T. (1988) *Coyotes: A Journey through the Secret World of America's Illegal Aliens*. 1st edition in this form. New York: Random House USA Inc.

Conover, T. (2001) *Rolling Nowhere: Riding the Rails with America's Hoboes*. Reprint edition. New York: Vintage Books.

Conover, T. (2011) *Newjack: A Year as a Prison Guard in New York's Most Infamous Maximum Security Jail*. London: Ebury Press.

Corbin, J.M. (2008) *Basics of Qualitative Research Techniques and Procedures for Developing Grounded Theory* (3rd edn). London: SAGE. Available at http://srmo.sagepub.com/view/basics-of-qualitative-research/SAGE.xml (last accessed 15 June 2014).

Coupland, D. (1995) *Microserfs*. London: Flamingo.

Craib, I. (1997) *Classical Social Theory*. Oxford: Oxford University Press.

Crawford, C. (2003) *Chris Crawford on Game Design*. Indianapolis: New Riders.

Creswell, J.W. (2012) *Qualitative Inquiry and Research Design: Choosing Among Five Approaches* (3rd edn). Thousand Oaks, CA: Sage.

Crookall, D. (2010) 'Serious games, debriefing, and simulation/gaming as a discipline', *Simulation & Gaming*, 41(6): 898–920. doi:10.1177/1046878110390784

Crystal, D. (2005) *How Language Works*. London: Penguin.

David, M. and Sutton, C. (2011) *Social Research: An Introduction*. 2nd edn. London: Sage.

Deegan, M.J. (2010) 'Jane Addams on citizenship in a democracy', *Journal of Classical Sociology*, 10(3): 217–38. doi:10.1177/1468795X10371714

Denzin, N. (1989) *Interpretive Biography*. Newbury Park, CA: Sage.

Denzin, N. (2001) *Interpretive Interactionism*. Newbury Park, CA: Sage. Available at www.srmo.sagepub.com.libprox.gold.ac.uk:2048/view/interpretive-interactionism/n1.xml

Denzin, N. (2006) 'Analytic autoethnography, or déjà vu all over again', *Journal of Contemporary Ethnography*, 35(4): 419–28. doi:10.1177/0891241606286985

Dey, I. (1993) *Qualitative Data Analysis: A User-friendly Guide for Social Scientists* (1st edn). London: Routledge.

Dicks, B. (ed.)(2005) *Qualitative Research and Hypermedia Ethnography for the Digital Age*. London: SAGE. Available at http://SRMO.sagepub.com/view/qualitative-research-and-hypermedia/SAGE.xml

Dicks, B., Mason, B., Coffey, A.J. and Atkinson, P.A. (2005) *Qualitative Research and Hypermedia: Ethnography for the Digital Age*. London: Sage.

Dicks, B. and Mason, B. (2011) 'Clickable data: hypermedia and social research'. In: Hesse-Biber SN (ed.), *The Handbook of Emergent Technologies in Social Research*, Oxford: Oxford University Press, pp. 133–157.

Dijck, J. van (2012) 'Facebook as a tool for producing sociality and connectivity', *Television & New Media*, 13(2): 160–76. doi:10.1177/1527476411415291

Dijk, T.A. van (ed.)(2011) *Discourse Studies: A Multidisciplinary Introduction* (2nd edn). London: Sage. Available at www.uk.sagepub.com/books/Book233751?siteId=sage-uk&prodTypes=any&q=van+dijk#tabview=samples (last accessed 15 June 2014).

Dollard, J. and Yale University (1935) *Criteria for the Life History*. New Haven, CT: Institute of Human Relations/Yale University Press.

Dovey, J. (2006) *Game Cultures: Computer Games as New Media*. Maidenhead: Open University Press.

Du Bois, W.E. (1968) *The Autobiography of W.E.B. Du Bois: A Soliloquy on Viewing My Life from the Last Decade of its First Century*. New York: International Publishers.

Du Bois, W.E. (1994) *The Souls of Black Folk* (edited by S. Appelbaum). New York: Dover.

Du Bois, W.E.B. (1996) *The Philadelphia Negro: A Social Study*. Philadelphia: University of Pennsylvania Press.

Durkheim, E. (1966) *The Rules of Sociological Method* (8th edn). New York: Free. Available at www.aspresolver.com/aspresolver.asp?SOTH;S10021370

Dyer-Witheford, N. and Peuter, G. de (2009) *Games of Empire: Global Capitalism and Video Games*. Minneapolis: University of Minnesota Press.

Eco, U. (1976) *A Theory of Semiotics*. Bloomington: Indiana University Press.

Elliott, J. (2005) *Using Narrative in Social Research: Qualitative and Quantitative Approaches*. London: Sage.

Ellis, C. (2004) *The Ethnographic I: A Methodological Novel About Autoethnography*. Lanham, MD: Rowman & Littlefield.

Ellis, C., Adams, T.E. and Bochner, A.P. (2011) 'Autoethnography: an overview', *Historical Social Research/Historische Sozialforschung*: 273–290.

Emerson, R, Fretz, R. and Shaw, L. (2011) *Writing Ethnographic Fieldnotes, Second Edition*. 2nd revised edition. Chicago: University of Chicago Press.

Engels, F. (1993) *The Condition of the Working Class in England*. Oxford: Oxford University Press.

Eriksen T.H. (1995) *Small Places, Large Issues*. London: Pluto.

Fairclough, N. (2010) *Critical Discourse Analysis: The Critical Study of Language* (2nd edn). Harlow: Longman.

Fay, B. (1996) *Contemporary Philosophy of Social Science: A Multicultural Approach*. Cambridge, MA: Blackwell.

Fielding, N. and Lee, R.M. (1998) *Computer Analysis and Qualitative Research*. New Technologies for Social Research, London: SAGE.

Flick, U. (2009) *An Introduction to Qualitative Research*. London: Sage.

Foucault, M. (1977) *Discipline and Punish: The Birth of the Prison*. London: Penguin.

Foucault, M. (1979) 'What is an author?'. In: Harari JV (ed.), *Textual Strategies: Perspectives in Post-Structuralist Criticism,* Ithaca: Cornell University Press, pp. 141–60.

Franzosi, R. (1998) 'Narrative analysis – or why (and how) sociologists should be interested in narrative', *Annual Review of Sociology:* 517–54.

Galloway, A. (2004) 'Social realism in gaming', *Game Studies, 4*(4). Available at www.gamestudies.org/0401/galloway/

Garrand, T. (2006) *Writing for Multimedia and the Web, Third Edition: A Practical Guide to Content Development for Interactive Media.* 3rd edition. Focal Press, Available from: http://www.interwrite.com/book/.

Gee, J. P. (2005) *An Introduction to Discourse Analysis: Theory and Method* (2nd edn). New York: Routledge.

Geertz, C. (1988) *Works and Lives: The Anthropologist as Author.* Oxford: Polity.

Geertz, C. (1993) *The Interpretation of Cultures: Selected Essays.* London: Fontana.

Genette, G. (1983) *Narrative Discourse: An Essay in Method* (reprinted edn). Ithaca: Cornell University Press.

Genette, G. (1990) *Narrative Discourse Revisited* (trans. J.E. Lewin) (reprinted edn). Ithaca: Cornell University Press.

Gerring, J. (2004) 'What is a case study and what is it good for?', *The American Political Science Review, 98*(2): 341–54.

Giddens, A. (1991) *Modernity and Self-Identity: Self and Society in the Late Modern Age.* Cambridge: Polity.

Glaser, B.G. and Strauss, A.L. (1967) *The Discovery of Grounded Theory: Strategies for Qualitative Research.* Hawthorne, NY: Aldine de Gruyter.

Goffman, E. (1959) *The Presentation of Self in Everyday Life.* New York: Doubleday Anchor.

Good, K.D. (2012) 'From scrapbook to Facebook: a history of personal media assemblage and archives', *New Media & Society.* doi:10.1177/1461444812458432

Goody, J. (2006) *The Theft of History.* Cambridge: Cambridge University Press.

Green, B.S. (2002) 'Learning from Henry Mayhew: the role of the impartial spectator in Mayhew's London Labour and the London Poor', *Journal of Contemporary Ethnography, 31*(2):99–134.doi:10.1177/0891241602031002001

Grimshaw, A. and Hart, K. (1993) *Anthropology and the Crisis of the Intellectuals.* Cambridge: Prickly Pear Pamphlets.

Gubrium, A. and Nat Turner, K. (2011) 'Digital storytelling as an emergent method for social research and practice'. In: Hesse-Biber, S.N. (ed.), *The Handbook of Emergent Technologies in Social Research,* Oxford: Oxford University Press, pp. 469–4921.

Hacking, I. (1990) *The Taming of Chance.* Cambridge: Cambridge University Press.

Haggard, R.F. (2001) *The Persistence of Victorian Liberalism: The Politics of Social Reform in Britain, 1870–1900.* Westport, CT: Greenwood.

Halliday, M.A.K. (1973) *Explorations in the Functions of Language.* London: Edward Arnold.

Hammersley, M. (2012) *Ethics in Qualitative Research: Controversies and Contexts.* London: Sage Publications Ltd.

Hartley, J.R. and Hartley, R. and Rowley, J. (2008) *Organizing Knowledge: An Introduction to Managing Access to Information.* 4th revised edition. Aldershot, England; Burlington, VT: Ashgate.

Hegeman, S. (1989) 'History, ethnography, myth: some notes on the "Indian-centered" narrative', *Social Text* (23): 144–60. doi:10.2307/466425

Heider, D. and Massanari, A. (eds) (2012) *Digital Ethics: Research & Practice.* Digital Formations, New York: Peter Lang.

Herzfeld, M. (1997) *Portrait of a Greek Imagination: An Ethnographic Biography of Andreas Nenedakis.* Chicago: University of Chicago Press.

Hong, R. and Chen, V.H.-H. (2013) 'Becoming an ideal co-creator: web materiality and intensive laboring practices in game modding', *New Media & Society.* doi:10.1177/1461444813480095

hooks, b. (1994) *Teaching to Transgress: Education as the Practice of Freedom.* New York: Routledge.

Ip, B. (2010a) 'Narrative structures in computer and video games: Part 1: Context, definitions, and initial findings', *Games and Culture,* 6(2): 103–34. doi:10.1177/1555412010364982

Ip, B. (2010b) 'Narrative structures in computer and video games: Part 2: Emotions, structures, and archetypes', *Games and Culture,* 6(3): 203–44. doi:10.1177/1555412010364984

Jaworski, A. and Coupland, N. (eds)(2005) *The Discourse Reader* (2nd edn). London: Routledge.

Jordan, T. (2008) *Hacking: Digital Media and Technological Determinism.* Cambridge: Polity.

Josselson, R., Josselson, R. and Lieblich, A. (1995) 'Imagining the real: empathy, narrative, and the dialogic self'. In R. Josselon and A. Lieblich (eds), *The Narrative Study of Lives: Interpreting Experience.* Thousand Oaks, CA: Sage.

Juul, J. (2001) 'Games telling stories? A brief note on games and narratives', *Game Studies,* 1(1). Available at www.gamestudies.org/0101/juul-gts/

Juul, J. (2005) *Half-real: Video Games between Real Rules and Fictional Worlds.* Cambridge, MA: MIT Press.

Kelty, C.M. (2008) *Two Bits: The Cultural Significance of Free Software and the Internet.* Durham, NC: Duke University Press.

Kent, R.A. (1981) *A History of British Empirical Sociology.* Aldershot: Gower.

King, S. (2010) *How to Write Your Life Story in Ten Easy Steps.* Oxford: How To Books.

Kirkpatrick, D. (2010) *The Facebook Effect: The Inside Story of the Company that is Connecting the World.* London: Virgin Books.

Kluckhohn C. (1947) 'The personal document in anthropological science'. In: *The Use of Personal Documents in History, Anthropology and Sociology,* New York: Social Science Research Council, pp. 79–173.

Kozinets, R.V. (2009) *Netnography: Doing Ethnographic Research Online.* London: Sage.

Kuhn, T.S. (1970) *The Structure of Scientific Revolutions* (2nd edn, enlarged). Chicago: University of Chicago Press.

Labov, W. (2008) 'Oral narratives of personal experience,' *Cambridge Encyclopedia of the Language Sciences.* Available at www.ling.upenn.edu/~wlabov/Papers/FebOralNarPE.pdf

Langness, L.L. and Frank, G. (1981) *Lives: An Anthropological Approach to Biography.* Novato, California.

Lannoy, P. (2004) 'When Robert E. Park was (re) writing "the city": biography, the social survey, and the science of sociology', *The American Sociologist, 35*(1): 34–62.

Latour, B. (1993) *We Have Never Been Modern.* London: Harvester Wheatsheaf.

Law, J. (ed.) (1991) 'Techno-economic networks and irreversibility'. In *A Sociology of Monsters: Essays on Power, Technology, and Domination.* New York: Routledge. pp. 132–64.

Law, J. (2002) *Aircraft Stories: Decentering the Object in Technoscience.* Durham, NC: Duke University Press.

Layder, D. (1998) *Sociological Practice: Linking Theory and Social Research.* London: Sage.

Leonardi, M. (2010, February 9) 'Narrative as self performance: the rhetorical construction of identities on Facebook profiles'. Dissertation. Retrieved August 23, 2012, from http://repository.unm.edu/handle/1928/10316

Lévi-Strauss, C. (2001) *Myth and Meaning.* London: Routledge.

Lindner, R. (1996) *The Reportage of Urban Culture: Robert Park and the Chicago School* (trans. A. Morris). Cambridge: Cambridge University Press.

Marx, K. (1976) *Capital* (Vol. 1). London: Penguin.

Mason, J. (2002) *Qualitative Researching* (2nd edn). London: Sage.

Mauss, M. (1985) 'A category of the human mind: the notion of person; the notion of self'. In M. Carrithers, S. Collins and S. Lukes (eds), *The Category of the Person: Anthropology, Philosophy, History.* Cambridge: Cambridge University Press. pp. 1–25.

Maxwell, J.A. (2012a) *Qualitative Research Design: An Interactive Approach: 41* (3rd edn). Thousand Oaks, CA: Sage.

Maxwell, J.A. (2012b) *A Realist Approach for Qualitative Research.* Thousand Oaks, CA: Sage.

Mayhew, H. (2008) *London Labour and the London Poor.* Ware, Hertfordshire: Wordsworth Editions.

Maynes, M.J., Pierce, J.L. and Laslett, B. (2008) *Telling Stories: The Use of Personal Narratives in the Social Sciences and History.* Ithaca: Cornell University Press.

May, T. (1997) *Social Research: Issues, Methods and Process.* 2nd edn. Buckingham: Open University Press.

McClean, S. (2008) *Digital Storytelling: The Narrative Power of Visual Effects in Film.* Cambridge, MA: MIT Press.

McLean, K.C. and Fournier, M.A. (2008) 'The content and processes of autobiographical reasoning in narrative identity', *Journal of Research in Personality, 42*(3): 527–45. doi:10.1016/j.jrp.2007.08.003

McPherson, S.S. (2010) *Sergey Brin and Larry Page: Founders of Google.* Twenty-First Century Books (CT).

Mezrich, B. (2009) *The Accidental Billionaires: Sex, Money, Betrayal and the Founding of Facebook.* London: Heinemann.

Miles, M.B. and Huberman, A. (1994) *Qualitative Data Analysis: An Expanded Sourcebook* (2nd edn). Thousand Oaks, CA: Sage.

Miller, C. H. (2014) *Digital Storytelling: A Creator's Guide to Interactive Entertainment*. 3rd edition. Burlington, MA: Focal Press.

Miller, D. (1994) *Modernity: An Ethnographic Approach: Dualism and Mass Consumption in Trinidad* (edited by B. Bender, J. Gledhill, & B. Kapferer). Oxford: Berg.

Miller, D. (2011) *Tales from Facebook*. Cambridge: Polity.

Miller, N. and Morgan, D. (1993) 'Called to account: the CV as an autobiographical practice', *Sociology*, 27(1): 133–43. doi:10.1177/003803859302700113

Mills, C.W. (1959) *The Sociological Imagination*. Oxford: Oxford University Press.

Mills, S. (2004) *Discourse*. London: Routledge.

Mishler, E.G. (1991) *Research Interviewing: Context and Narrative* (new edn). Cambridge, MA: Harvard University Press.

Mitnick, K. (2011) *Ghost in the Wires: My Adventures As the World's Most Wanted Hacker*. New York: Little Brown & Co.

Morris, P. (2003) *Realism*. London: Routledge.

Mostern, K. (1999) *Autobiography and Black Identity Politics: Racialization in Twentieth-Century America*. Cambridge: Cambridge University Press.

Okely, J. and Callaway, H. (eds) (1992) *Anthropology and Autobiography*. London: Routledge.

Papacharissi, Z. (2009) 'The virtual geographies of social networks: a comparative analysis of Facebook, LinkedIn and ASmallWorld', *New Media & Society*, 11(1–2): 199–220. doi:10.1177/1461444808099577

Papacharissi, Z. (2011) 'Look at us: collective narcissim in college student Facebook photo galleries'. In Z. Papacharissi (ed.), *A Networked Self: Identity, Community and Culture on Social Network Sites*. New York: Routledge. pp. 251–73.

Park, R.E. (1915) 'The city: suggestions for the investigation of human behavior in the city environment', *American Journal of Sociology*, 20(5): 577–612.

Park, R.E. (1970) *Introduction to the Science of Sociology: Including an Index to Basic Sociological Concepts* (student edn). Chicago: University of Chicago Press.

Parks, M. (2011) 'Social network sites as virtual communities'. In Z. Papacharissi (ed.), *A Networked Self: Identity, Community and Culture on Social Network Sites*. New York: Routledge. pp. 105–23.

Patterson, W. (2008) 'Narratives of events: Labovian narrative analysis'. In M. Andrews, C. Squire and M. Tamboukou (eds), *Doing Narrative Research*. London: Sage. pp. 22–40.

Personal Narratives Group (ed.) (1989) *Interpreting Women's Lives: Feminist Theory and Personal Narratives*. Bloomington: Indiana University Press.

Plummer, K. (2001) *Documents of Life 2: An Invitation to a Critical Humanism*. rev. expanded edn. London: Sage.

Polkinghorne, D. (1988) *Narrative Knowing and the Human Sciences*. Langsdorf L (ed.), Albany: State University of New York Press.

Polkinghorne, D. (1995) 'Narrative configuration in qualitative analysis'. In J.A. Hatch and R. Wisniewski (eds), *Life History and Narrative.* London: Falmer. pp. 5–23.

Polletta, F. (2006) *It Was Like a Fever: Storytelling in Protest and Politics.* Chicago: University of Chicago Press.

Popper, K.R. (1972) *Conjectures and Refutations: The Growth of Scientific Knowledge* (4th edn, revised). London: Routledge & Kegan Paul.

Price, R. (1983) *First-Time: The Historical Vision of an Afro-American People.* Baltimore: Johns Hopkins University Press.

Price, R. (1990) *Alabi's World.* Baltimore: Johns Hopkins University Press.

Propp, V.A. (1968) *Morphology of the Folktale* (2nd edn). Austin: University of Texas Press.

Putnam, R.D. (2000) *Bowling Alone: The Collapse and Revival of American Community.* New York: Simon & Schuster.

Radin, P. (1925) *Crashing Thunder: The Autobiography of an American Indian.* New York: Appleton.

Rapport, N. (1994) *The Prose and the Passion: Anthropology, Literature and the Writing of E. M. Forster.* Manchester and New York: Manchester University Press.

Rapport, N. (1997) *Transcendent Individual: Towards a Literary and Liberal Anthropology.* London: Routledge.

Reed, A. (2005) '"My blog is me": texts and persons in UK online journal culture (and anthropology)', *Ethnos, 70*(2): 220–42. doi:10.1080/00141840500141311

Reed-Danahay, D. (ed.) (1997) *Auto/Ethnography: Rewriting the Self and the Social.* Berg Publishers.

Richards, L. (2009) *Handling Qualitative Data: A Practical Guide.* 2nd edition. London: Sage.

Richardson, J.E. (2007) *Analysing Newspapers: An Approach from Critical Discourse Analysis.* Basingstoke: Palgrave Macmillan.

Richardson, L. (1990) *Writing Strategies: Reaching Diverse Audiences.* Thousand Oaks, CA: Sage.

Ricoeur, P. (1984) *Time and Narrative* (Vol. 1). Chicago: University of Chicago Press.

Riessman, C.K. (2008) *Narrative Methods for the Human Sciences.* Thousand Oaks, CA: Sage.

Ritzer, G. (2007) *Contemporary Sociological Theory and its Classical Roots: The Basics* (2nd edn). Boston, MA: McGraw-Hill.

Roberts, B. (2002) *Biographical Research.* Understanding Social Research, Berkshire: Open University.

Rollings, A. and Adams, E. (2003) *Andrew Rollings and Ernest Adams on Game Design.* Indianapolis, IN: New Riders.

Roorbach, B. and Keckler, K. (2008) *Writing Life Stories: How to Make Memories into Memoirs, Ideas into Essays, and Life into Literature.* Cincinnati, OH: Writer's Digest.

Roos, J., Victor, B. and Statler, M. (2004) 'Playing seriously with strategy', *Long Range Planning, 37*(6): 549–68. doi:10.1016/j.lrp.2004.09.005

Rosaldo, R. (1993) *Culture & Truth: The Remaking of Social Analysis.* London: Routledge.

Rose, D. (1993) 'Ethnography as a form of life: the written word and the work of the world'. In P. Benson (ed.), *Anthropology and Literature*. Chicago: University of Illinois Press.

Ruggiero, V. (2003) *Crime in Literature: Sociology of Deviance and Fiction*. New York: Verso.

Ryan, M.-L. (2001) *Narrative as Virtual Reality: Immersion and Interactivity in Literature and Electronic Media*. Baltimore: Johns Hopkins University Press.

Said, E. (1985) *Orientalism*. London: Peregrine.

Salen, K. and Zimmerman, E. (2010) *Rules of Play: Game Design Fundamentals*. Cambridge, MA: MIT Press.

Sartre, J.-P. (1963) *The Problem of Method*. London: Methuen.

Saussure, F. de (1966) *Course in General Linguistics*. New York: McGraw-Hill.

Sayer, A. (1999) *Realism and Social Science* (illustrated edn). London: Sage.

Shippey, T. (2005) *The Road to Middle-earth: How J. R. R. Tolkien Created a New Mythology*. Revised, Enlarged third edition. London: HarperCollins.

Shapira, I. (2010, 09) 'A Facebook story | A mother's joy and a family's sorrow', *The Washington Post*. Available at www.washingtonpost.com/wp-srv/special/metro/facebook-story-mothers-joy-familys-sorrow.html?hpid=topnews (last accessed 27 January 2014).

Silverman, D. (1993) *Interpreting Qualitative Data: Methods for Analysing Talk, Text and Interaction*. London: Sage.

Silver, C. and Lewins, A. (2014) *Using Software in Qualitative Research: A Step-by-Step Guide*. Second Edition. SAGE Publications Ltd.

Sökefeld, M. (1999) 'Debating self, identity, and culture in anthropology', *Current Anthropology*, 40(4): 417–48. doi:10.1086/200042

Stanley, J. (1996) 'Including the feelings: personal political testimony and self-disclosure', *Oral History* (Spring): 60–67.

Stanley, L. (1995) *The Auto/biographical I: The Theory and Practice of Feminist Auto/biography*. Manchester: Manchester University Press.

Stewart, J. (1989) *Drinkers, Drummers and Decent Folk: Ethnographic Narratives of Village Trinidad*. Albany: State University of New York.

Stocking G.W. (1992) *The Ethnographer's Magic and Other Essays in the History of Anthropology*. Madison: University of Wisconsin Press.

Swingewood, A. (1975) *The Novel and Revolution*. London: Macmillan.

Sword, H. (2012) *Stylish Academic Writing*. Cambridge, MA: Harvard University Press.

Teddlie, C.B. and Tashakkori, A. (2008) *Foundations of Mixed Methods Research: Integrating Quantitative and Qualitative Approaches in the Social and Behavioral Sciences*. Thousand Oaks, CA: Sage.

Thompson, K. (2009) *Therapeutic Journal Writing: A Tool for Personal Development and Professional Practice*. London: Jessica Kingsley.

Thompson, P.R. (2000) *The Voice of the Past: Oral History*. 3rd edn. Oxford ; New York: Oxford University Press.

Thornton, R. (1983) 'Narrative ethnography in Africa, 1850–1920: the creation and capture of an appropriate domain for anthropology', *Man*, 18(3): 502–20. doi:10.2307/2801594

Todorov, T. and Weinstein, A. (1969) 'Structural analysis of narrative', *NOVEL: A Forum on Fiction*, 3(1): 70–6. doi:10.2307/1345003

Torvalds, L. and Diamond, D. (2002) *Just for Fun: The Story of an Accidental Revolutionary.* New York: HarperBusiness.

Turkle, S. (1985) *Second Self: Computers and the Human Spirit* (reprint). London: Pocket Books.

Turkle, S. (1995) *Life on the Screen: Identity in the Age of the Internet.* London: Phoenix.

Van Maanen, J. (2011) *Tales of the Field: On Writing Ethnography* (2nd revised edn). Chicago: University of Chicago Press.

Vogler, C. (2007) *The Writer's Journey: Mythic Structure for Writers.* Studio City, CA: Michael Wiese Productions.

Walder, D. (ed.) (1996) *The Realist Novel.* New York: Routledge, in association with the Open University.

Waletzky, J. and Labov, W. (1967) 'Narrative analysis: oral version of personal experience'. In J. Helm (ed.), *Essays on the Verbal and Visual Arts.* Seattle: University of Washington Press. pp. 12–44.

Wallace, J. and Erickson, J. (2005) *Hard Drive: Bill Gates and the Making of the Microsoft Empire* (1st HarperBusiness edn). New York: HarperBusiness.

Weber, M. (1930) *The Protestant Ethic and the Spirit of Capitalism.* London: Allen & Unwin.

Webster, L. and Mertova, P. (2007) *Using Narrative Inquiry as a Research Method: An Introduction to Using Critical Event Narrative Analysis in Research on Learning and Teaching* (new edn). New York: Routledge.

Wengraf, T. (2001) 'Qualitative research interviewing: biographic narrative and semi-structured, methods'. London; Thousand Oaks, Calif: SAGE.

White, H.V. (1987) *The Content of the Form: Narrative Discourse and Historical Representation.* Baltimore : London: John Hopkins University Press.

Wiggershaus, R. (1994) *The Frankfurt School: Its History, Theories and Political Significance.* Cambridge: Polity.

Williams, R. (1977) *Marxism and Literature.* Oxford: Oxford University Press.

Williams, S. (2002) *Free as in Freedom: Richard Stallman's Crusade for Free Software.* Sebastopol, CA: O'Reilly Media.

Winch, P. (2008) *The Idea of a Social Science and its Relation to Philosophy.* London: Routledge.

Wodak, R. and Meyer, M. (eds) (2009) *Methods of Critical Discourse Analysis* (2nd edn). Los Angeles, CA: Sage.

Wolfe, T. and Johnson, E.W. (1973) *The New Journalism.* New York: Harper & Row.

Wong, H.D. (1987) 'Pre-literate Native American autobiography: forms of personal narrative', *MELUS, 14*(1): 17–32. doi:10.2307/467470

Woolf, G. (2011) *Tales of the Barbarians: Ethnography and Empire in the Roman West.* Oxford: Wiley-Blackwell.

Yin, R.K. (2003) *Case Study Research: Design and Methods* (3rd edn). Thousand Oaks, CA: Sage.

Zeller, N. (1995) 'Narrative strategies for case reports'. In J.A. Hatch and R. Wisniewski (eds), *Life History and Narrative.* London: Falmer.

INDEX